Alexander Gordon

Historic Memorials of the First Presbyterian Church of Belfast

Prepared in Connection with the Centennial of its Present Meeting-House

Alexander Gordon

Historic Memorials of the First Presbyterian Church of Belfast
Prepared in Connection with the Centennial of its Present Meeting-House

ISBN/EAN: 9783337429522

Printed in Europe, USA, Canada, Australia, Japan

Cover: Foto ©Lupo / pixelio.de

More available books at **www.hansebooks.com**

WILLIAM BRUCE, D.D.

HISTORIC MEMORIALS

OF THE

FIRST PRESBYTERIAN CHURCH

OF

BELFAST.

PREPARED IN CONNECTION WITH THE CENTENNIAL

OF ITS PRESENT MEETING-HOUSE.

Porch
First Presbyterian Church

BELFAST
MARCUS WARD & CO: ROYAL ULSTER WORKS
LONDON AND NEW YORK
1887

PRINTED BY
Marcus Ward & Co., Limited
ROYAL ULSTER WORKS
Belfast

PREFACE

THE design of this work is to serve as the record of a congregational history which has extended over the space of two hundred and forty-five years.

During this period, events and changes of an interesting character, and some of public importance, have occurred. They will be found here narrated, it is believed, with accuracy; and, it is hoped, in that spirit of Christian liberality which is not the least valuable fruit of the study of the past.

The immediate occasion of the volume was the occurrence of the Centennial of the erection of the present meeting-house of the congregation—an event celebrated in the year 1883. The incidents of the celebration tended naturally to revive the memories of an ancient foundation, which, while it has ever held the warm love of those worshipping within its sanctuary, has always retained the respect of those outside.

In the publication of this book, not the least pleasing feature is the presence, upon the list of subscribers, of the names of a large number of honoured friends in no direct connection with the congregation, but willing to show an interest in its historic memorials.

To all who in this or in any other manner have aided the completion of the work, the thanks of the congregation are very heartily tendered.

Contents

List of Illustrations

[*] KEY:—F. D. Ward—J. W. Russell—Bowman Malcolm—John Rogers—W. T. Hamilton—J. R. Musgrave—H. F. Thomas
Nicholas Oakman
Jas. Carr—Geo. K. Smith—E. J. Harland, Bart.—Fredk. Little—Saml. Riddel—Wm. Spackman.

List of Subscribers

TO THE

"Historic Memorials of the First Presbyterian Church of Belfast"

	No. of Copies
Allen, George, J.P., Mountpanther, ...	1
Allen, William J. C., J.P. (*late*), Faunoran, Greenisland, ...	1
Allman, James Clugston, J.P., Park, Bandon, County Cork, ...	1
Andrews, Mrs., Comber, ...	1
Andrews, Hon. Mr. Justice, 51, Lower Leeson Street, Dublin, ...	2
Andrews, Mrs., Ardoyne, Belfast, ...	1
Andrews, Thomas, Ardara, Comber, ...	1
Andrews, George, Ardoyne, Belfast, ...	1
Andrews, Samuel, J.P., Sea View, Belfast, ...	2
Archer, Henry, J.P., Orlands, Carrickfergus,...	1
Armstrong, Major, Woking, Surrey, ...	1
Armstrong, Rev. George Allman, B.A., Dublin,	2
Armstrong, Henry Bruce, Union Club, Trafalgar Square, London, ...	1
Armstrong, Robert Bruce, Junior Carlton Club, Pall Mall, London, ...	1
Armstrong, Arthur, Glenavy, ...	1
Arthur, Miss, 64, Apsley Place, Belfast, ...	1
Bailie-Gage, Thomas R., General Post Office, Dublin, ...	1
Barbour, James, J.P., Ardville, Holywood, ...	2
Barbour, John D., J.P., Lisburn, ...	2
Barbour, John, Marlborough Park, Belfast, ...	1
Beale, Miss Catherine Hutton, Highfield, Chester, near Birmingham, ...	1
Bell, Mrs., Elmwood Terrace, Belfast, ...	1
Benn, Miss Harriet, Derryvolgie Avenue, Belfast,	1
Blackley, Mrs. Jane (*late*), Sandymount, Belfast,	1
Blackwood, James T., J.P., Ulster Bank, Belfast,	2
Boadle, John Ward, Birkenhead, Liverpool,	1
Bowles, Charles, J.P., Windsor Avenue, Belfast,	2
Boyd, Wm. Sinclair, Ravenscroft, Bloomfield,	1
Boyle, Wallace (*late*), Adelaide Terrace, Belfast,	1
Brigs, Henry, Surveyor of Customs, Dublin,	1
Broughton, Frederick, Chicago, ...	1
Brown, John Shaw, J.P., 12, Bedford Street, Belfast, ...	1
Bruce, Miss, The Farm, Belfast, ...	1

	No. of Copies
Bruce, Miss Charlotte, The Farm, Belfast, ...	2
Bruce, James, J.P., D.L., Thorndale, Belfast,	3
Bruce, Miss Jane E., The Farm, Belfast, ...	1
Bruce, Miss Eliza, The Farm, Belfast, ...	1
Bruce, William R., Master of Queen's Bench, Rockford, Blackrock, ...	1
Bruce, Samuel, Norton Hall, Campden, Gloucestershire, ...	1
Campbell, Miss, Windsor Avenue, Belfast, ...	1
Campbell, Rev. Robert, Wellington Park Terrace, Belfast, ...	1
Campbell, Nathaniel A., Lisburn Road, Belfast,	1
Campbell, John, Lennoxvale, Belfast, ...	4
Campbell, John, Rathfern, Whiteabbey, ...	2
Carey, Mrs., St. Leonards, Warrenpoint, ...	1
Carlisle, Mrs., Ashbourne, Strandtown, ...	1
Carr, James, Ulster Bank, Belfast, ...	5
Carroll, B. Hobson, Mus. Doc., T.C.D., West Elmwood, Belfast, ...	1
Carruthers, Miss, Belfast, ...	1
Chappell, Mrs., Newtownards, ...	1
Christie, John, Glenview, Crumlin, ...	1
Clarke, Edward Harris, Elmwood, Belfast, ...	1
Coey, Sir Edward, Kt., J.P., D.L., Merville, Whitehouse, ...	1
Collins, Robert, C.E., Fortwilliam Terrace, Belfast, ...	1
Combe, Abram, Arlington, Belfast, ...	2
Conkey, Joseph, Dunmurry, ...	1
Connor, Charles Cunningham, J.P., Linen Hall, Belfast, ...	2
Conrad, William, New York, ...	1
Corry, Sir James Porter, Bart., J.P., M.P., Belfast, ...	1
Cowan, Sir Edward Porter, Kt., J.P., H.M. Lieutenant, Craigavad, Co. Down,	2
Cronne, James, Posnett Street, Belfast, ...	1
Crooks, Rev. English, Ballyclare, ...	1
Dickson, John, Church Lane, Belfast, ...	1
Dobbin, Leonard, sen., 50, King Street, Cork,	1

	No. of Copies
Drennan, Lenox, Prospect Terrace, Belfast,...	1
Duffin, Adam, M.A., University Terrace, Belfast,	2
Duffin, Charles, jun., Danesfort, Belfast, ...	2
Dugan, John J., Claremont Street, Belfast, ...	1
Dunkerley, Rev. Thomas, The Manse, Comber, County Down, ...	1
Dunville, Mrs., London, ...	1
Dunville, Robert G., J.P., D.L., Redburn, Holywood, ...	2
Evans, Silas, 3, Upper Crescent, Belfast, ...	1
Ewart, William, M.P., Glenmachan, Strandtown, Belfast, ...	2
Ewart, Lavens M., Ballysillan, Belfast, ...	2
Fennell, William J., M.R.I.A., Chichester Street, Belfast, ...	1
Fenton, Samuel G., J.P., Edenbank, Windsor Avenue, Belfast, ...	2
Ferguson, Miss, Donegall Street, Belfast, ...	1
Ferguson, Henry, Belfast, ...	1
Ferguson, Henry S., M.D., Belfast, ...	1
Forsythe, Miss, Alfred Terrace, Mountpottinger,	1
Galt, James, Ballyclare, ...	1
Galt, John, Larne, ...	1
Galt, Robert, Doagh, ...	1
Gamble, James, 5, Royal Terrace, Belfast, ...	1
Garrett, E. W., The Temple, London, ...	1
Garrett, Mrs. Thomas, Scarsdale Villa, Kensington, London, W., ...	1
Gibson, William, Donegall Place, Belfast, ...	3
Girdwood, H. M., Manchester, ...	1
Glass, Hugh, Banbridge, ...	1
Gordon, Rev. Alexander, M.A., 9, Upper Crescent, Belfast, ...	2
Gordon, Alexander (Professor), M.D., Queen's College, Belfast, ...	1
Gordon, Mrs., Kenilworth, ...	1
Gordon, Mrs. Ellen W., Whiterock, Belfast,...	1
Gordon, Miss Alicia, Belfast, ...	1
Gordon, Rev. David, Downpatrick, ...	1
Gorman, Rev. T. Murray, M.A., Oxford, ...	1
Graham, James, Abbotscroft Terrace, Belfast,	1
Gray, Mrs. *(late)*, College Square North, Belfast,	1
Gregg, James, Ballyclare, ...	1
Greer, Edward, J.P., Moygannon, Rostrevor,	1
Grimshaw, Thomas W., Priorsland, Carrickmines,	1
Hall, William, Springfield Works, Belfast, ...	1
Hall, Rev. James, Glenarm, ...	1
Ham, Rev. J. Panton, 71, Parliament Hill Road, Hampstead, London, ...	1
Hamilton, William T., Wellington Park, Belfast,	1
Hancock, William, Stoke Bishop, Bristol, ...	1
Hannah, Miss, Wilmont Terrace, Belfast, ...	1
Harland, Sir Edward James, Bart., J.P., Ormiston, Strandtown, High Sheriff, Co. Down	5
Hartley, Mrs. William, University Crescent, Belfast, ...	1
Haughton, Thomas, J.P., Banford House, Gilford, ...	1
Heron, William C., J.P., Maryfield, Holywood,	1
Heyn, James A. M., Belfast, ...	1
Hill, Thomas, Ballyclare, ...	1
Hogg, John, Academy Street, Belfast, ...	2
Hollins, Mrs. W., Pleasley Vale, Mansfield, Notts, ...	1
Horner, George, J.P., The Lodge, Belfast, ...	1
Houston, John Blakiston, D.L., Orangefield, Belfast, ...	1
Hunter, Mrs. *(late)*, Lanneven, Knock, ...	1
Hunter, Miss Charlotte, Holywood, ...	1
Hunter, Miss, Ballycarry, ...	1
Hurst, Wm. J., J.P., Drumaness, Ballynahinch,	1
Hutton, Mrs. Lucius, 8, Fitzwilliam Place, Dublin, ...	2
Hutton, John, J.P., Legamaddy, Downpatrick,	1
Jardine, William, jun., Belfast, ...	1
Jellie, John, J.P., Carrickfergus, ...	1
Jeremy, Rev. Daniel Davies, M.A., 4, Appian Way, Dublin, ...	1
Johns, Alexander, J.P., Belfast Bank, Belfast,	1
Johnson, Sir William Gillilan, D.L. *(late)*, Belfast, ...	2
Johnston, William, York Street, Belfast, ...	1
Johnston, John, Richmond, Belfast, ...	1
Jones, Sir Thomas Alfred, President Royal Hibernian Academy, ...	1
Kedwards, Rev. J., Douglas, Isle of Man, ...	1
Kelly, Rev. John A., Rademon, Crossgar, ...	1
Kennedy, James, Richmond Lodge, Belfast,	1
Kennedy, Miss, 42, Fitzroy Avenue, Belfast,	1
Kennedy, Victor Coates, J.P., Clonard House, Belfast, ...	1
Kennedy, William H. *(late)*, May Street, Belfast,	1
Kennedy, Rev. James, Larne, ...	1
Kerr, J. King, M.D., Holmlands, Essex, ...	1
Kidd, George W., M.D., 58, Merrion Square, Dublin, ...	1
Kirker, Archibald M., Cultra, ...	1
Laird, Joseph, Ballyclare, ...	1
Laird, Marshall, Clifton Park, Belfast, ...	1
Lawrence, Sir James C., 75, Lancaster Gate, London, ...	1
Ledlie, Mrs. George, Allworthy Avenue, Belfast,	1
Ledlie, James C., Endsleigh, Cork, ...	1
Library, First Presbyterian Church, Belfast,...	1
Library, Dr. Williams's, Grafton Street, Gower Street, London, ...	1
Liddell, William, J.P., Donacloney, Lurgan,	1
Lincoln, Mrs., 91, South Circular Road, Dublin, ...	1

	No. of Copies.
Little, Frederick, West Elmwood, Belfast, ...	2
Lowry, Charles, Upper Frank Street, Mountpottinger, ...	1
Luke, William J., Ponsonby Avenue, Belfast,	1
Lynn, Mrs., Ballyclare, ...	1
Macartney, John Wm. Ellison, D.L., Clogher Park, Clogher, County Tyrone, ...	1
Macartney, William Ellison, M.P., Clogher Park, Clogher, ...	1
MacLaine, Alex., J.P., Queen's Elms, Belfast,	1
Macrory, Mrs., West Elmwood, Belfast, ...	1
Macrory, Miss, West Elmwood, Belfast, ...	1
Macrory, Robert A., Belfast, ...	2
Malcolm, William H., Holywood, ...	1
Malcolm, Mrs. Andrew G., 63, Atlantic Avenue, Belfast, ...	1
Malcolm, Bowman, Richmond, Belfast, ...	3
Malcolm, James, J.P., D.L., Lurgan, ...	1
Manley, Henry C., M.D., Whitehouse, ...	1
Manley, Hugh C., Belfast, ...	1
Masaroon, W. R., Junior Carlton Club, London, S.W., ...	2
Mercer, William S. (*late*), Linen Hall Street, Belfast, ...	1
Millar, Miss, Lisburn,...	1
Montgomery, John, Dunmurry, ...	1
Moore, Rev. Hugh, Yew Villa, Newtownards,	1
Moore, James, College Gardens, Belfast, ...	1
Morgan, John, 36, Lower Gardiner Street, Dublin, ...	1
Morrow, James, Ulster Bank, Larne,... ...	1
Murland, Clotworthy W., Annsborough, Castlewellan, ...	1
Murland, James Wm., J.P., Chairman G. N. R., Ireland, Nutley, Booterstown, Dublin, ...	1
Murland, Charles, J.P., Ardnabannon, Castlewellan, ...	1
Murland, James, Crown Solicitor, Downpatrick,	1
Murray, Henry, Albert Place, Belfast, ...	1
Murray, Robert, Albion Place, Belfast, ...	1
Musgrave, James, J.P., Drumglas, Belfast, ...	1
Musgrave, John R., D.L., J.P., Drumglas, Belfast, ...	5
M'Alester, Rev. Charles J., Beechcroft, Holywood, ...	2
M'Auliffe, George, J.P., Greenisland, ...	5
M'Calmont, Captain, M.P., Ulster Club, Belfast,	1
M'Cance, Finlay, J.P., Suffolk, Dunmurry, ...	2
M'Cance, Henry J., J.P., Larkfield, Dunmurry,	3
M'Cann, Alexander, Chichester Street, Belfast,	1
M'Caw, Rev. John (*late*), Lisbane, Lisburn, ...	1
M'Caw, Mrs., Elmwood Avenue, Belfast, ...	1
M'Caw, James Frazer, College Square North, Belfast, ...	2
M'Clelland, Andrew, J.P., Belmont, Banbridge,	1
M'Cloy, James, Kenbella Avenue, Belfast, ...	1
M'Clure, Sir Thomas, Bart., V.L. County Down, Belmont, Belfast, ...	1
M'Connell, John, J.P., Comber, ...	2
M'Crum, Robert, Pakenham Street, Belfast,	1
M'Crum, Robert, G., J.P., Milford, Armagh,...	1
M'Cully, Miss Frances Mary, Belfast, ...	1
M'Ervel, Edward J., 31, Rugby Road, Belfast,	5
M'Ervel, William, J.P., Castlederg, Co. Tyrone,	1
M'Ervel, Daniel, Crumlin, ...	1
M'Ervel, James, The Knock, Belfast, ...	1
M'Ervel, Thomas, Almeida House, Strandtown,	1
M'Fadden, William H., Wellington Park, Belfast, ...	2
M'Fadden, James, Portadown, ...	1
M'Giffen, R., Antrim Terrace, Belfast, ...	1
M'Gimpsey, Hugh, Belfast, ...	1
M'Kane, John, LL.D. (*late*), Dublin, ...	1
M'Keag, Miss, Frederick Street, Belfast, ...	1
M'Kinstry, Miss (*late*), Carrickfergus, ...	1
M'Kisack, James, Holywood, ...	1
M'Mordie, Hans, M.A., LL.D., 51, Blessington Street, Dublin, ...	1
M'Ninch, William, 29, Lonsdale Street, Belfast,	1
M'Tear, Miss, 3, Richmond, Cave Hill Road, Belfast, ...	1
M'Tear, John Smith, Solicitor, The Castle, Belfast, ...	1
M'Tear, Miss F. M., 3 Richmond, Cave Hill Road, Belfast, ...	1
M'Tear, George, Liverpool, ...	1
M'Tear, Thomas, Hughenden Terrace, Belfast,	1
M'Tear, Miss (*late*), Abbotscroft, Whiteabbey,	1
M'Tear, David, Mountcharles, Belfast, ...	1
Neill, Henry James, Rockport, Craigavad, ...	2
Neill, Sharman D., Donegall Place, Belfast,...	1
Nelson, William J., Academy Street, Belfast,	1
Nelson, Omar C., Craigavad, ...	1
Nelson, David, J.P., Larne, ...	1
Nelson, Rev. Samuel C., Downpatrick, ...	1
Nelson, Hon. Hugh, Ottawa,...	1
Oakman, Nicholas, Prospect Terrace, Belfast,	2
Orr, James P., Malone Park, Belfast, ...	1
Orr, Gawin, M.D., Ballylesson, Lisburn, ...	1
Palmer, Alexander (*late*), Little York Street, Belfast, ...	1
Patterson, William H., M.R.I.A., Garranard, Strandtown, ...	1
Patterson, Robt. Lloyd, J.P., F.L.S., Holywood,	2
Patterson, Mrs., sen., Holywood, ...	1
Patterson, Richard, Kilmore, Holywood, ...	1
Perry, Joseph, Downpatrick, ...	1
Pim, Joshua, Belfast, ...	1
Pim, Wakefield, High Street, Belfast, ...	1
Pollard, Rev. Joseph, London, ...	1
Porter, Miss, College Square East, Belfast, ...	1

	No. of Copies.
Porter, Drummond, College Sq. East, Belfast,	2
Porter, Right Hon. Andrew Marshall, Master of the Rolls, 8, Merrion Square, Dublin,	3
Porter, Rev. Classon (*late*), Ballygally Castle, Larne, ...	1
Preston, Sir John, Kt., J.P., Dunmore, Belfast,	2
Preston, George J., Whiteabbey, ...	1
Pring, Richard W., Firmount, Belfast, ...	1
Rafter, W. P., 22, Wellington Place, Belfast,	2
Rankin, Robert R., The Mount, Mountpottinger, ...	1
Reford, Robt., 23, St. Sacrament St., Montreal,	2
Rice, John, Belfast, ...	1
Rice, Mercer, Coningsby, Craigo Road, Belfast,	1
Rice, Richard, Lucyville, Whitehouse, ...	1
Richardson, Charles H., Shrub Hill, Newtownbreda, ...	1
Riddel, William, J.P., Beechmount, Belfast,	2
Riddel, Mrs. Edward, Hughenden Terrace, Belfast, ...	1
Riddel, Samuel, Beechmount, Belfast, ...	2
Ritchie, Thomas, Seaview, Belfast, ...	1
Robb, Alexander (*late*), Frederick Terrace, Belfast, ...	1
Roberts, William, Dunmurry,...	1
Roberts, James, 21, Vernon Street, Belfast, ...	1
Robertson, William, J.P., Netherleigh, Strandtown, ...	4
Robertson, William, jun., University Square, Belfast, ...	1
Robinson, William A., Culloden House, Cultra,	2
Roche, Mrs. William J., 66, Clifton Park Avenue, Belfast, ...	1
Roche, Edmund B., 66, Clifton Park Avenue, Belfast, ...	1
Rogers, John, Windsor Avenue, Belfast, ...	4
Rogers, Thomas, Belfast, ...	1
Russell, John W., Wilmont Terrace, Belfast,	1
Salvage, John S., Clifton, Bangor, ...	2
Scott, Miss, 4, The Mount, Mountpottinger, ..	1
Shattock, James May, Bristol, ...	1
Shillington, John J., J.P., Glenmachan Tower, County Down, ...	2
Simms, William, jun., Ballyclare, ...	1
Sinclair, George, 112, Wellwood Place, Mountpottinger, ...	1
Smith, George Kennedy (*late*), The Castle, Belfast, ...	5
Smith, John Galt, St. Leonard St., New York,	1
Smith, Samuel, Bank of Liverpool, Liverpool,	2
Smith, Robert, 7, Palmerston Street, Belfast,	1
Smith, Mrs. H. Southwood, Holmwood, Surrey,	3
Smyth, Miss, William's Place, University Road, Belfast, ...	1
Smyth, Brice, M.D., 13, College Square East, Belfast	3

	No. of Copies.
Smyth, John, M.A., Lenaderg, Banbridge, ...	1
Smyth, William, Banbridge, ...	1
Spackman, William, Wellington Park, Belfast,	4
Stevenson, George, Shankhill Road, Belfast,	1
Stevenson, Miss, Shankhill Road, Belfast, ...	1
Stevenson, H., 43, Moyola Street, Belfast, ...	1
Stevenson, Thomas, Ballyclare, ...	1
Stewart, Charles, Dunedin, Whiteabbey, ...	1
Taylor, Sir David, Kt., J.P., Bertha House, Belfast, ...	1
Taylor, John Arnott, J.P., Drum House, Dunmurry, ...	1
Tennent, Robert, J.P., Rushpark, Whitehouse,	2
Thom, Rev. J. Hamilton, Oakfield, Wavertree, Liverpool, ...	2
Thomas, Henry F., Lower Crescent, Belfast,	2
Thompson, Rev. David, Dromore, County Down, ...	1
Thompson, Mrs., Macedon, Belfast, ...	2
Todd, William B., 14, Arthur Street, Belfast,	1
Todd, Robert, Belfast, ...	1
Trail, Mrs., Antrim Road, Belfast, ...	1
Valentine, Thos., J.P., The Moat, Strandtown,	1
Valentine, William, J.P., Glenavna, Whiteabbey,	2
Vinycomb, John, Holywood, ...	1
Walker, William, J.P., Banbridge, ...	1
Walkington, Robert B., Craig Gorm, Helen's Bay, County Down, ...	1
Wallace, William Nevin, J.P., Downpatrick, ...	1
Ward, Francis D., J.P., M.R.I.A., Clonaver, Strandtown, ...	5
Ward, James, Albert Bridge Road, Mountpottinger, ...	1
Ward, Marcus J., Belview, Holywood, ...	1
Ward, George G., Eversleigh, Strandtown, ...	1
Ward, Mrs., Wilmont Terrace, Belfast, ...	1
Ward, M. J. Barrington, M.A., F.L.S., F.R.G.S., H.M. Inspector of Schools, Thorniloe Lodge, Worcester, ...	1
Ward, Miss Elizabeth H., Clonaver, Strandtown, ...	1
Ward, William Hardcastle, Coombe Mavis, Chislehurst, Kent, ...	1
Warnock, George, Ballyclare,...	1
Warnock, John, Downpatrick, ...	1
Watson, Wesley, Whiteabbey, ...	2
Whitelegge, Rev. W., M.A., Ballinlough House, Cork, ...	1
Wilson, Thomas, 38, Euston Street, Dublin,...	1
Wilson, Mrs. Alexander, 29, Oakley Square, London, N.W., ...	1
Woodside, Mrs., Ballyclare, ...	1
Young, Robert, C.E., Rathvarna, Antrim Road, Belfast, ...	1

CHAPTER I

WHAT OUR RELIGIOUS COMMUNITY HAS DONE FOR BELFAST.—Belfast in 1642. Features of the origina Presbyterianism of Ulster. Westminster Confession and Nonsubscription. Toleration and its results. Education of the Presbyterian clergy. Secession Church and its influence. New generation of Nonsubscribers. Remonstrants. Nonsubscribing Association. Footprints of our forefathers—industries—public philanthropy—literary culture—educational institutions—religious character.

CCORDING to a sententious writer, "Happy is the people that has no history." Happy, on this estimate, must have been the condition of Belfast for a series falling not far short of a thousand years, beginning in the dim twilight of that legendary age, when a battle of the Farsad (A.D. 666) mingled a Celtic prince's blood with the waters of the contested Ford, and closing our reckoning with the outbreak of hostilities between King and Parliament, in the full blaze of the most exciting period of British history. To animate the vast stretch of time which lies betwixt these extreme landmarks, we have only glimpses, here and there, of imperfectly recorded contentions, for which Belfast was the occasional theatre, but in which it cannot be said to have played any independent and active part.

Indeed, the Belfast of 1642 was an insignificant place, though its strategical position was destined soon to bring it into prominence. Unprotected as yet by any wall, it consisted of a few rows of mean houses, with a small Norman fortress at one end of the main street, and a small Norman church at the other extremity. The incidents which immediately preceded the great Civil War brought to Belfast importance and Presbyterianism; the two came together.

As early as 1613, Presbyterianism had gained a footing in Ulster, on an errand of religious duty to the Scottish colonists; but it had not found in Belfast material for its purpose. The Corporation of the little town passed, in 1617, a bye-law that every burgess should attend at the Sovereign's house every Sabbath-day, and whenever there was public prayer, in order to accompany their municipal head to the parish church.

Arms of Belfast.

To his visitation, held within the walls of

that old church, in August, 1636, Bishop Henry Leslie (1580–1661) cited the five principal Presbyterian divines of Ulster. Leslie was himself of Scottish birth, yet in his opening sermon (from the ominous text, Matt. xviii. 17) he describes Scotland as "the land of Noddies," and the Presbyterian position as "this dunghill." In a two days' conference he endeavoured, with the stout assistance of the famous John Bramhall (1594–1663), then Bishop of Derry, to reduce his Presbyterian neighbours to submission by force of argument. Failing in this, he adopted another system of reasoning, with the aid of the civil power.

Five years later came the fierce insurrection of the Irish Catholics, which struck terror to the heart of the nation. An army from Scotland was despatched, by successive instalments, to Ulster, in order to quell the insurgent hordes. Belfast was made secure by a wet ditch and earthen rampart (1642), and, with extreme reluctance, Colonel Chichester admitted a portion of the Scottish troops to share in the defence of the town with the English garrison. These Scottish soldiers needed the religious ministrations of a divine of their own faith. A Presbyterian chaplain, one John Baird, was appointed to come every third Sunday to our town, to conduct the simple worship of the Scottish people. The appointment was made by the army Presbytery, which first met at Carrickfergus on 10th June, 1642. Shortly after this, an eldership was erected at Belfast. So was our Church begun; this was the little seed out of which the whole Presbyterianism of Belfast has developed and grown.

Arms of Carrickfergus.

The religious system thus introduced was the Presbyterianism of Scotland of the older school, before its theology had been stiffened and dried up by the Westminster Confession of Faith. Its principles of faith and statement of public policy are admirably expressed in the Solemn League and Covenant (A.D. 1643), which pledged all who took it to endeavour the reformation of religion throughout the three kingdoms "in doctrine, worship, discipline, and government, according to the Word of God and the example of the best reformed churches." Copies of this noble document were brought to Ireland very soon after it was drawn up. Lying in a drawer at our Museum in College Square is one of these first copies, which somehow escaped the hangman's hand and the vengeful fire of 1661. It still bears its 67 original signatures, collected at Holywood on 8th and 9th April, 1644, by William Adair, who came from Scotland for the purpose. Among the names is a John M'Bryd, possibly the father of the outspoken John M'Bride who ministered here fifty years later.

It was this league of faith, with its stern opposition to Popery and Prelacy, its direct reliance upon the Bible as the Word of God, and its noble protest on behalf of "the common cause of religion, liberty, and peace,"—it was this, and not the Confession of the Westminster divines, which really formed the religious mind of the first Presbyterians of Ulster. This was what they subscribed, when they subscribed at all. At a later day (1705) they did indeed enact subscription to the Westminster Confession, in a panic raised by the daring heresies of Emlyn. Yet the enactment was not, and could not be, rigidly enforced. Throughout the last century, and indeed up to the year 1836, it was found impossible to secure in Ireland, even on the part of orthodox men, the subscription which was accepted in Scotland as a matter of course.

Many things contributed to this freer attitude of the Irish offshoot from the religion of Scotland. It never enjoyed the privileges or wore the fetters of an Establishment, and was free to develop in its own fashion. During the Commonwealth, it had to give way to Independency; and this broke, to some extent permanently, the hold of its ecclesiastical discipline. The depression of its power came about in this wise. On the execution of the King, the Presbytery at Belfast protested against the trial and its issue, in the strongest terms they could use, as "an act so horrible, as no history, divine or human, ever had a precedent to the like." Thereupon, Cromwell's Latin secretary, John Milton, assailed them with that vituperation of which, as well as of the divinest poetry, he was so great a master, calling them "blockish presbyters of Claneboye," "that un-Christian synagogue of Belfast," and "a generation of Highland thieves and redshanks." Cromwell's officer, Venables, expelled them, along with (it is said) 800 of their hearers; and William Dixe, a Baptist preacher, was set to minister to those inhabitants of the town who were not Episcopalians.

It must further be remembered that the Scottish type of Presbyterianism was not the only one which had found its way into Ireland. Scotland furnished, with few exceptions (*e.g.*, at Antrim), the Presbyterianism of Ulster; but in Dublin and the South of Ireland it was the English type of Presbyterianism, freer both in doctrine and discipline, which gained an entrance. Its existence there had an indirect influence on the severer views and ways of the North. Nay, in Belfast, the influence of English Presbyterianism was direct. Letitia Hickes, who became Countess of Donegal, was an English Presbyterian. William Keyes, who stands first in the uninterrupted succession of our own ministers, was an English divine under her patronage. Sore was her displeasure when his congregation and co-presbyters permitted him to leave for Dublin; many the obstacles placed in the way of the appointment of a Scottish divine as his successor, though that Scottish divine was no less distinguished a man than Patrick Adair. She would not attend his services. In the Hall of the Castle, Samuel Bryan (contemporary with Keyes) and Thomas Emlyn (contemporary with Adair) successively officiated as chaplains. Bryan had been Fellow of Peterhouse, and held a Warwickshire living until the Uniformity Act of 1662 compelled even moderate men, possessed of consciences, to quit the Establishment. Half-a-year's incarceration in Warwick gaol, for the crime of preaching the Gospel at Birmingham, had induced him to leave his native land. Emlyn was so far from ever sympathising with the Scottish peculiarities of Presbyterianism, that, while resident in Belfast, and still retaining intact the Puritan theology, he held no communion with Adair, but willingly preached by invitation in the parish church, the then Vicar, Claudius Gilbert, being an ex-Dissenter. Thus, in Belfast, there was present in very early times, side by side with the Scottish discipline, the mellowing influence of a type of Nonconformity less severe.

Nor must it be forgotten that the delay of legal Toleration to Irish dissent brought with it a compensating advantage of the highest moment. Toleration in England, granted in 1689, was made dependent on subscription to the doctrinal articles of the Established Church. Toleration in Ireland, not granted till 1719, was given at length to all Protestants without any doctrinal stipulations whatsoever, except the oath against transubstantiation, and a clause directed, not against those who abandoned, but against those who impugned, the doctrine of the Trinity. This was indeed a greater freedom than the Presbyterians had themselves asked for, or dreamed of. They had drawn up certain doctrinal clauses, milder than the English articles, to be inserted in the Bill. Tradition says that King George I., "upon receiving the proposals of the Irish ministers," struck out the doctrinal clauses with his own royal hand, saying, "They know not what they would be at; they shall have a toleration without a subscription."

In other respects, indeed, Presbyterians were not free. They could not celebrate marriages among themselves, at least not without incurring severe penalties in the ecclesiastical courts. They could hold no public office, except on the condition of communicating at the Established churches. But the law laid no pledges upon them as regards the doctrines they were to accept as their bond of union, or to teach in their meeting-houses.

Hence, in Ireland, the position of the Nonsubscribers was perfectly legal from the first, which it never was in England till the Relief Act of 1779. When Haliday, on being installed in 1720, the very year after the Irish Toleration Act, refused to subscribe, it was at once plain that a movement of far-reaching importance was begun. He set an example which was soon followed. Seven successive Synods took the matter up, being plainly at a loss what to do. At last the advocates of the Westminster standards hit upon the notable expedient of gathering all the Nonsubscribing men into one presbytery. It was easy to do this for they were men who had already set on foot a union among themselves, having been accustomed for twenty years to meet for purposes of Biblical study under the name of the Belfast Society (1705). The members of this society were formed into the Presbytery of Antrim (1725). Next year, this body was expelled from the Synod, neck and crop.

The deed was deftly done. But the members of the expelled Presbytery were the ablest men of the Presbyterian body. Their influence was perpetually being reinforced, and their example tacitly followed, by the more educated men in the Synod itself. In those days, and for long after, the great place of education for the Irish Presbyterian ministry was Glasgow College. And the leading professors of Glasgow were prevailingly New Light men. John Simson, Professor of Divinity, was censured for alleged Pelagianism (1717), and deprived of ecclesiastical recognition for alleged Arianism (1728), but was not removed from his chair. Francis Hutcheson (1694–1747) the philosopher, himself an Irish Nonsubscriber, and William Leechman (1706–1785) the divine, taught the Irish students to think for themselves on the highest subjects.

Until the Seceders came from Scotland, shortly before the middle of the last century (1742), the general spirit and tone of Irish Presbyterianism was moving in the line marked out by the Nonsubscribers. At the end of the century, out of fourteen Presbyteries, only five exacted subscription. The Seceders, however, began that reaction towards the doctrines of the Westminster Confession which it took almost a hundred years to accomplish, and which gained no very decided victory until the issue of the momentous conflict between Henry Cooke (1788–1868) and Henry Montgomery (1788–1865) was reached in the voluntary withdrawal of the Remonstrants (1829). Even Dr. Cooke did not succeed in carrying an unqualified subscription to the Confession of Faith till seven years after the Remonstrants had left the Synod. At five o'clock on the morning of Friday, 12th August, 1836, the wisdom of Westminster carried it by a large majority against the Word of God. Four years later was accomplished that union between the Synod and the Seceders which set the seal upon the reaction against the true genius of Irish Presbyterianism, and formed the present General Assembly (10th July, 1840).

The new generation of Nonsubscribers, the Remonstrants who withdrew from the Synod of Ulster, were influenced in their withdrawal by doctrinal considerations much more direct and radical than those which had produced the expulsion of the Antrim Presbytery over a century before. They did not amalgamate with the earlier body, preferring to constitute a separate Synod of their own in 1830; but in a few years they entered with the Antrim Presbytery into an Association for mutual protection and aid, which embraced also the Nonsubscribers of the South, known as the Synod of Munster. This Association of Irish Nonsubscribing Presbyterians (1835), which in the eye of the law, and according to ecclesiastical discipline, comprises four distinct, though cognate, Presbyterian bodies (besides two independent congregations, admitted in 1872 to share the elastic name "other Free Christians"), is the only organisation which has any claim to represent the whole community of Nonsubscribing Christians in this country.*

What, from first to last, has this body done for Belfast? We have seen that the rise of Belfast into significance was due to its becoming a stronghold of the Presbyterian army before the Civil War. Will anyone call this a simple coincidence? It is impossible so to dispose of the story of the subsequent growth and greatness of our town. The development of Belfast, material, intellectual, and moral, has been not merely coincident with, but dependent upon the enterprise, the public spirit, the culture and acquirement, the stable character of its Presbyterian inhabitants.

We, as a church, may not unfairly claim to hold a representative position in regard to the Presbyterianism of Belfast.

We may put forward this claim on historical grounds. Our congregation is the mother church of Belfast Presbyterianism; for two generations it was the one focus of Presbyterianism in the town. The older divines of our ministry, and the original leaders of our staunch laity, are owned and revered by the whole Presbyterian community around us, accepted as being their founders quite as much as they were ours. Patrick Adair (1625?–1694) and John M'Bride (1650–1718) and James Kirkpatrick (1674?–1744) belong to us; but they are the men who paved the way, not for us alone, but for Presbyterianism generally. On one of our alms-dishes is inscribed the sentence—

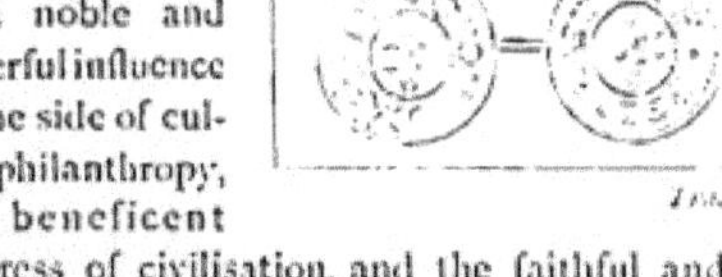

John Heseltons Gift to all the Meeting houses In Belfast 1721

Inscription on Old Plate.

We may say of the Presbyterian faith and strength that these also are the gift of our ancestors, under God, to "all the Meeting-houses in Belfast."

In another and a broader sense we may make this claim. The spirit which has made Presbyterianism valuable, not only as a protest against Popery and Prelacy, but as a noble and powerful influence on the side of culture, philanthropy, the beneficent progress of civilisation, and the faithful and charitable life of pure religion, is the spirit which has been persistently fostered by the ministry and exemplified by the laity of this church.

Look through the history of Belfast; watch the growth of its trades and manufactures. From the Presbyterian potters of 1698, the Presbyterian ship-carpenters of 1712, and the wealthy Presbyterian merchants a little later, down to the leaders of industrious enterprise at the present day, we trace one unbroken line of able and far-seeing men, the hand of whose diligence has made rich the town whose prosperity they have created. No inconsiderable proportion of these men, whether we speak of numbers or of leading power, has been contributed by the membership of our church. Study the lists of the founders of our successive linen-halls; the names of our bankers and merchants, since banking and merchandise

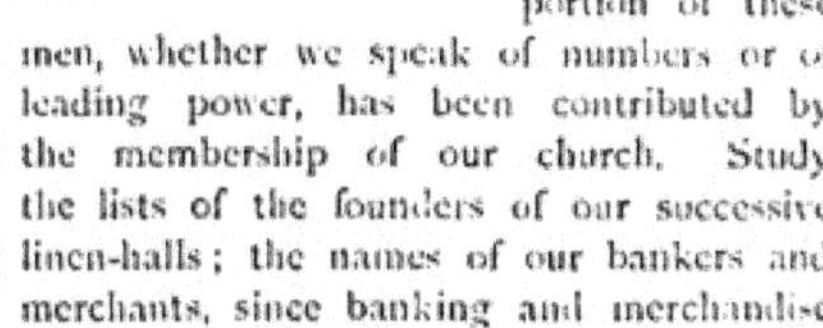

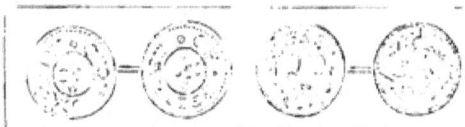

Trade Tokens.

* The representation is not quite complete, since there are one or two congregations not in the Association.

began in Belfast; of the originators of our Chamber of Commerce, established in the same year in which our meeting-house was rebuilt. Among the prominent names, not the least prominent are names which figure also in the roll of our own congregational constituency.

If we speak of philanthropy, and inquire for the originators of hospitals general and special, of charitable institutions old and new, for the good of the many without reservation to the disciples of a creed, the result of our investigations is to bring us again and again to Rosemary Street for the religious impulse which had inspired the deed of wise and unexclusive charity. In such operations of applied Christianity, individuals from among us have been ever ready to show the way. By the general contributions of our people, whether given privately or acting as a church, such projects and organisations of benevolence have always been generously supported. What is infinitely more, our people have never been slow to dedicate thought, care, time, zeal, energy, out of the abundance of an unselfish determination to promote, by every means in their power, the amelioration of the lives of the distressed.

THE
PSALMS
OF
DAVID
In MEETER.

Newly Translated, and diligently Compared with the Original Text, and former Translations: More plain, smooth, and agreeable to the Text, than any heretofore.

Allowed by the Authority of the General Assembly of the Kirk of *Scotland*, and appointed to be sung in Congregations and Families.

BELFAST,
Printed by *Patrick Neil* and Company, and sold at his Shop. 1700

Old Psalm Book.

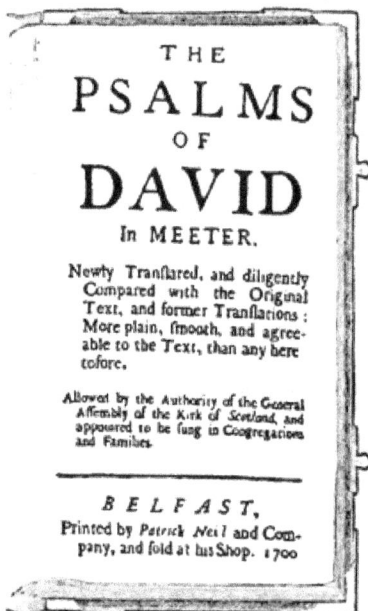

David Smith's Gift to Belfast Meeting house 1715

Fly-leaf Inscription in book figured above.

Turn we to the annals of our local literary renown. The leading printers and publishers of Belfast, from Neill and Blow down to Joy and Hodgson, and later but not less distinguished names, were Presbyterians of the Nonsubscribing freedom. Professor Witherow, of Derry, has published two most interesting volumes of "Historic and Literary Memorials of Presbyterianism in Ireland" (1879 and 1880). These were placed not long ago in the hands of a gentleman not of our body, and in returning them to the lender he remarked, "How is this? Nearly all these men, these writers and divines, were Presbyterians of your sort." "How is it?" was the reply. "Why, it is this way. If the book was to be written at all, it must be filled with our men and their works, for there are no other materials to make a book with." So of that later literary circle which gave to Belfast the name of the Athens of the North of Ireland. Its chief ornaments were men and women of genius and culture, bred in the bosom of our own religious community.

If we think of the educational institutions, large and small, which have fostered in Belfast and throughout Ulster the spirit of learning and of science, to whom must we ascribe their rise and their fame? The pioneers of educational advance, from David Manson onwards, the founders of the Academy, the professors and teachers who gave tone to the Academical Institution, the originators of Sunday and daily schools for the neglected classes; who were they? The roll of our membership will largely tell.

Could you tear from the history of Belfast the names and the influence of our forefathers, distinguished in commerce, learning, philanthropy, education, and genius, you would not only remove the pages inscribed with some of our most eminent and best citizens, but you would find that you had drawn out as well the inspiring examples which have been a source of power and of impression, extending far beyond the limits of the small community which they illustrated.

Yet it will perhaps be said, 'All this is not religion.' There are some people, it would appear, who think that effects may be produced without the existence of causes; that the highest results can come without the operation of the highest influences; that works may be originated and sustained and live, without faith as their basis; that you may have all the finest fruits of the activity of the human mind and spirit and life, and be entitled nevertheless to say, 'There is no religion, in it or under it.' The outcome of the practical life of a community discloses what the substance of its moral ideal, and what the nature of its religious faith and spirit, really are. We shall trace the inner history of the religion of our forefathers in subsequent chapters of this volume; at present we are contemplating it in its powerful and beneficent outer working. If, to-day, we are "citizens of no mean city," it is largely because we are inheritors of no mean traditions, fostered by the faithfulness of the founders and maintainers of this and kindred churches.

In the Belfast of to-day we are, in one sense, outnumbered and outweighted; the masses are not with us. Yet we occupy a unique position, neither unimportant nor inglorious, and we cannot help doing so. We are the heirs and administrators and assigns of the true original Presbyterianism; of its liberty, its learning, its broad and beneficent aims. God, not we, has placed us where we are. He who planted the heavens, He who laid the foundations of the earth, it is He, and He only, who hath put into our mouths His words; who hath kept us, throughout our course, in the shadow of His hand; and who saith to us now, by the voice of His Spirit, "Thou art my people" (Isa. li. 16).

DATES.—Introduction of Presbyterianism in Ulster, 1613; in Belfast, 1642. Westminster Confession published, 1648. Sacramental Test Act, 1704. Synod orders subscription to Westminster Confession, 1705. Belfast Society, 1705. Toleration Act, 1719. Haliday refuses to subscribe, 1720. Antrim Presbytery (Nonsubscribing) formed, 1725; excluded from General Synod, 1726. Dissenting Marriages allowed, 1738. Seceders came from Scotland, 1742. Test Act repealed, 1828. Remonstrant Synod, 1830. Association of Irish Nonsubscribing Presbyterians, 1835.

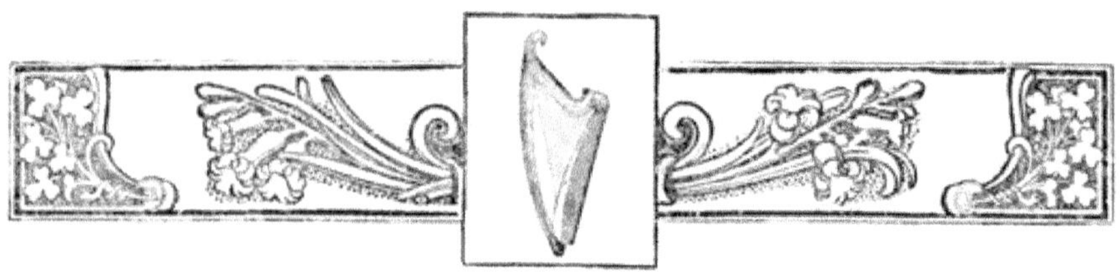

CHAPTER II

Historic landmarks in the career of our own Congregation. Our successive places of worship—North Street—Rosemary Lane; off shoots from us; public buildings of Belfast in 1783. Our trusts and title deeds; Dissenters' Chapels Act. Our Ecclesiastical Changes—General Synod—Antrim Presbytery—Northern Presbytery of Antrim. Personnel of our ministers and laity. Congregational resources—Regium Donum—disestablishment. Our position at the present day.

N the oldest authentic map of Belfast, a sketch-plan drawn by Thomas Phillips in 1685, there is figured at the north-west extremity of Hercules Street (removed in 1883 to form the Royal Avenue), in close proximity to the North Gate, a small building without chimneys, which, as some fancy, represents the original Presbyterian Meeting-house of Belfast. Tradition assigns to the first structure erected as a home for Belfast Presbyterianism a site near the gate just mentioned, but wavers between North Street and Hercules Street as the precise thoroughfare on which it stood. Inasmuch as these streets converged upon the North Gate, the building depicted on the map may be thought to answer, fairly well, to the conditions of locality implied in the floating tradition.

When was it erected? There is no trace of any meeting-house in Belfast prior to the Restoration of the monarchy. When the Presbyterian system was introduced, in the manner described in the previous chapter, we may take it for granted that, as was usual, its worship was held in the old Parish Church at the foot of the High Street. But now comes a curious episode in the religious history of our town. For seven years (1649–56) during the Cromwellian occupation, after the 800 Scots had been driven from the town, and the Independent *régime* was in power, there was no available house of prayer of any kind within this borough. The old church and its graveyard were converted into a citadel and fortification; and where the people worshipped we cannot tell. An Episcopalian preacher and a Baptist preacher were maintained at the public expense, and they must have conducted their ministrations in casual places, or in the open air. More than once the municipal authorities of the little town addressed the Council of State, begging for the restoration of their church; or, if not, requesting that public meeting-houses might be provided. The church was at length given back, in a ruinous condition, and appears to have been then treated as a "Publique Meeting Place" for the religious use of all sects. When the Restoration came (A.D. 1660), we find it in the hands of the Presbyterians, though apparently not devoted to their exclusive use. But, with the King, came back the Bishops.

Jeremy Taylor (1613–1667), the new Bishop of Down and Connor, was a startling illustration of the maxims that circumstances alter cases, and that preaching and practice are different things. Jeremy Taylor, dwelling in a Welsh exile, his living of Uppingham having been sequestered because he had joined the army against the Parliament, composed and printed his *Liberty of Prophesying* (1647), a classic defence of the rights of conscience. Jeremy Taylor, promoted to an Irish Bishopric, at once assumed to himself the liberty of putting down all prophets who did not happen to be in Episcopal orders. Three months after his consecration (1661) he, in one day's visitation, cleared the Presbyterians out of 36 churches in his diocese. We are told, in Jeremy Taylor's funeral sermon by George Rust, his friend and successor, that "this great prelate had the good humour of a gentleman, the eloquence of an orator, the fancy of a poet, the acuteness of a schoolman, the profoundness of a philosopher, the wisdom of a chancellor, the sagacity of a prophet, the reason of an angel, and the piety of a saint." It should have been added, to make the picture complete, that he had the bowels of a bumbailiff. In England, the Presbyterians were not ejected as such, until the State had passed the Act of Uniformity of 1662. In Ireland, the Bishops took time by the forelock, the legislature followed suit, and Taylor was the man who, by his prompt work in his diocese, and by his sermon before the two Houses of Parliament, both showed and led the way.

Old Silver Communion Cups.

Hence it was that, in 1661, the Presbyterian worshippers of Belfast found themselves homeless. Some time afterwards, we cannot tell exactly when, but it was probably in 1668 (so we gather from Adair's *Narrative*), they erected their first meeting-house, near the North Gate. In the manuscript Minutes of the "Antrim Meeting," under date 3rd March, 1674, John Adam, merchant, appears as a commissioner from the Belfast congregation (then without a minister), to petition the brethren to make interest with Lord and Lady Donegal on two points; and one is "anent the House of Worship," in regard to which the Meeting appointed two brethren humbly to represent to the peer and peeress "what weighty reasons make for the people having their liberty as other congregations have, without irritation so far as possible." The inference is that the Meeting-house was in being, but that the use of it was in some degree controlled by the great people at Belfast Castle.

But what has that long-perished building, on a forgotten site, to do with us to-day? Here are we in Rosemary Street, by help of our good M'Bride. On this pleasant spot of ground he planted us, when it was an open field, abutting upon a crooked lane, with the scent of rosemary still about it, and leading to the backs of the houses in another lane, which bore originally, it is believed, the name of Ardglass, later dignified into the mythological title of Hercules. M'Bride knew his way to the favour, if not to the sympathies of the Earl of Donegal, and secured for us this queer, triangular piece of land, which stands so invitingly vacant on the map of 1685. Here, on the green sward of the meadow, an oblong structure arose. An excrescence to the west gave it the shape of a T; but there were outside stairs to the three galleries, which varied the configuration of its exterior; and, at the north-east corner, there was a small session-house, stuck on to the main building. In the south-west angle of the field, a minister's

The Gift of James Stewart to the Meeting house of Belfast 1693

Inscription on Cup.

dwelling was put up for the worthy M'Bride; and there, except when his refusals to take the oath of abjuration forced him to flee to Scotland (a circumstance which took place no less than four times), he had his abode. His successors occupied the same premises until Crombie's time, in fact till the building of the Academy (1786).

The occupancy of the Rosemary Street property by the Presbyterian congregation may be dated from about 1695; but there is no trace of any lease or legal document giving a title to it, either then or for long after. In fact, it would have been impossible to have executed a legal conveyance for the benefit of Presbyterians, while they remained untolerated in the eye of the law, existing only upon sufferance, and much better protected in their position by the good-will and pleasure of a powerful Earl, than by a trust which the

Donum Tho: Craford Cœtui Presbyter: de Belfast 1698

Inscription on Cup.

courts would not recognise. But in 1767, when Toleration had been granted some forty-eight years, Arthur, Earl of Donegal, afterwards the first Marquis, gave us a lease. It begins by reciting that "the said Arthur, Earl of Donegal, is minded and desirous that the said first congregation of Protestant Dissenters shall and may, at all times hereafter, have and enjoy a certain place in his town of Belfast for the publick worship of Almighty God, and that the minister of the said congregation for the time being may be provided with and enjoy a messuage or tenement, near the same, for his better accommodation;" then, after describing the buildings, and appointing the trustees (Robert Gordon, Joseph Wallace, and John Galt Smith), it grants to them the same "for the uses, intents, and purposes hereinafter mentioned . . . and for no other intent and purpose whatsoever." These uses and intents, as relates to the Meeting-house, are simply as follows: "and that the said building, now used as a Meeting-house, . . . may continue and remain as

James Martin

Inscription on Cup.

and for a publick Meeting-house for the use of the said first congregation, and their successors, for ever."

This is what is called an "open trust:" a more open one is scarcely possible. But, prior to the Dissenters' Chapels Act of 1844, open as the trust is, the building would have been tied up in law to the precise opinions and modes of worship held and practised by its original founders; the silent voice of the men of 1767 (perhaps of 1695) would have been entitled to decide the faith and to rule the usages to which the building could be devoted to-day. Moreover, even if it could be proved that the founders of an old meeting-house were actually Anti-trinitarians in their faith, the lawyers would say: 'That was, at the time of the foundation, an illegal profession, prohibited by statute; and a trust for the maintenance of such an opinion is void in law.' The Irish Toleration Act (as we saw in the previous chapter) did not exclude Anti-trinitarians, but it forbade them to open their mouths against the doctrine of the Trinity. However, the Dissenters' Chapels Act swept away both classes of restriction. It provided that all opinions, which had since become legal, were to be regarded as legal from the first. It substituted for the opinions of the founders the unbroken usage of twenty-five years. Any opinion, which had held its ground in a Dissenting meeting-house for a quarter of a century, undisputed at law, was fully legitimised, unless there were any express provision in the trust deed which excluded it.

In the obtaining of this salutary measure of relief and freedom, services of the first rank were rendered by one who, we may be proud to think, was long a seatholder and always a warm friend of this house; the mighty, the eloquent, the indomitable advocate of truth and justice, Henry Montgomery, who sacrificed time, health, and overwhelming energy in the common cause. It was no unreal danger from which he and his able coadjutors delivered us. The placid pages of our congregational Minute-book, at the period of the passing of the Bill, quiver with the agitation of that momentous struggle. No wonder the leaders of the congregation were alarmed. Clough and Killinchy had trusts as open as our own; but the law was set in motion. "The enthusiasm of orthodox solicitors," as has been well said, was "associated with the rapacity of acquisitive divines;" and the Meeting-houses of Clough and Killinchy, ruthlessly taken from their owners, were given to the men who subscribed the Westminster Confession and forgot the eighth commandment. The enemies of our faith, nay of our very existence, were confident of expelling us also from the sanctuary of our fathers, and were filled with elation in the hope of humiliating and even of crushing us. They had already their plans devised, for the disposal to their own uses of our sacred property, as soon as they had wrested it from our hands. They did our Meeting-house the honour of thinking that (after being subjected, of course, to suitable lustration) it would serve exceedingly well as a hall of assembly for the General Synod. Well, peace be to the memory of those old strifes! Let us rather recollect the combination of noble minds, the ornaments of our supreme legislature, who, in no party spirit, and indeed acting together with a total disregard of the restraints of party, carried the measure of liberty and safety which secured us in the tranquil possession of our own. Peel and Lyndhurst, Russell and Gladstone, Macaulay and Shiel—never should we lose a grateful sense of what we owe to their disinterested and persevering support. There is perhaps no speech in the English language more withering in its sarcasm, more grand in its glow, than the speech of Shiel, the Roman Catholic, for justice to the Unitarians.

Ten years after the passing of the Act, our congregation acquired the fee-simple of the estate on which its buildings stand. The Meeting-house and the site of the old manse are thus absolutely our own; the area which surrounds both Meeting-houses we hold in common with our neighbours of the Second Congregation. The carrying out of this improved arrangement we principally owe to the foresight and the business power of our honorary secretary. Never was congregation better served, or with a warmer and stronger regard to all its best interests, than this congregation has been, for the past forty-six years, by George Kennedy Smith, the representative of the oldest of our families. His Minute-books are models of what such records should be, and will remain to future ages a permanent monument of well-directed zeal and scrupulous care; his administration of our affairs has proved him sound in judgment, firm yet patient of purpose, young in heart.

Our oldest existing record is the Funeral Register (1712-36); but its entries do not

Old Print of Meeting-house. (Engraved by J. Thomson.)

refer exclusively to our own congregation, or even to the Presbyterian burials of Belfast alone. The first volume of our Baptismal Register was lost before 1790; the second volume opens in 1757. Our Congregational Minutes begin in the year 1760, with the proceedings of a meeting which added to our constitution a Committee, as distinct from the Session. Twenty-one years later, the Minutes record the first steps taken with regard to the rebuilding of the Meeting-house. On Sunday, 1st April, 1781, the congregation resolved that the old building should be taken down. Its materials sold for £200 10s. 9d. On Friday, 1st June, the foundation stone of the present structure was laid. Exactly two years were occupied in its erection and completion. On Sunday, 1st June, 1783, it was opened for public worship. Our Minute-books are full of entries which prove how completely the superintendence of the work was a labour of love, and how minutely it was looked after, even to the tempering of the mortar. The treasurer of the Building Fund, Mr. John Galt Smith, was so deeply interested in the progress of the work, that he watched the laying of each successive course of the masonry.

Originally it had been intended that the new building should be somewhat of the old type, but without galleries, and with accommodation for 600 on the ground floor (the old building, with its three galleries, seated 723). On 12th May, 1781, the Building Committee decided on the elliptical figure, and new plans were accordingly prepared by the architect and contractor, Mr. Roger Mulholland. Francis Hiorn, the London architect of St. Anne's, took a great interest in the structure, and furnished valuable suggestions, especially as regards the pewing of the interior. With a view to improve the appearance, a gallery was decided upon, with some misgivings as to whether it would be required, and, by a sort of prophetic anticipation, a part of it was already called the "organ gallery," though no organ was erected in it till February, 1853.

Gallery, after renovation in [illegible], and Organ.

The total cost of the new structure was £1,923 7s. 9d., British currency. Towards this, Dr. Crombie gave a donation of 10 guineas, and lent a sum of £276 18s. 5½d. (£300 Irish), which is an indication that he had private means; his stipend was never more than £110 15s. 4½d. (£120 Irish), but then he had a Manse and *Regium Donum*, though *Regium Donum* in those days did not amount to £10 a-year. The Bishop of Derry (Earl of Bristol) sent a donation of 50 guineas, purely out of admiration of the beauty of a building which, as his letter to Mr. Rainey Maxwell expressed it, "does equal honour to the taste of the subscribers and the talent of the architect." Among other ways of raising the requisite funds, the Committee bought for £5 15s. 4¾d. a lottery ticket, "which was a blank." The pulpit, costing £27 18s. 4d., was presented by the ladies of Belfast, irrespective of creed. In this pulpit, in 1789, John Wesley preached. He minutely describes the building in his *Journal*, calling it "the completest place of worship I have ever seen." He would have preached a second time, but on the first occasion the crowd swarmed all over the building, and in the commotion some unconverted hearer managed to abstract the silver rim and clasp from the pulpit Bible, so the Trustees declined to grant their Meeting-house again to the great evangelist.

To Crombie we largely owe it that we continue to exist at all as a separate congregation. For there were those who thought, until his courage and determination reassured them, that it was needless for the First Congregation to have a Meeting-house of its own, and that it might fitly be wiped out of existence by reamalgamation with its eldest offshoot in the Second House.

That first swarming off from the old hive

took place in 1708, and simply meant that at that date, with 3,000 Presbyterians in Belfast, one Meeting-house was not big enough to accommodate them. The two congregations were, for a time, practically one. Even when they agreed to be distinct, the stipend, £146 13s. 4d., continued to be collected in common, and was equally divided. They still share the property of the ground above referred to,

Pulpit, after renovation, and Table made from Sounding Board, removed 18[illegible]

and the use of the same cups* for the administration of the communion.

The second offshoot from us was of a different and less harmonious character, due to the disputes upon ecclesiastical freedom, which soon produced their usual result in doctrinal differences; and these, as is too often the case, led to an almost complete estrangement and alienation. This double series of divergences between our point of view and that consistently maintained by the Third Congregation, since its origin in 1721, will be considered in the next chapter.

Let us, before we pass from the subject of the successive religious edifices which have arisen on or near this spot, recall the interesting fact that 1783 was not far from the culmination of an important building period in Belfast. The oldest public building still remaining in this town is the Old Poor House, crowned by the most elegant of our spires; its foundation stone was laid in 1771. Next came the Brown Linen Hall, in 1773; then the Parish Church (St. Anne's), begun in 1774; and just on the very day (28th April) in 1783 when this Meeting-house was so far finished that the congregation were invited to fix upon their sittings, the first stone of the White Linen Hall was laid with much ceremony. In 1784 Donegal Place was projected, as a grand new quarter for the residences of the rich, cutting through the Castle Gardens, in which King William delighted during his short visit to Belfast. It took almost a hundred years to bring our citizens to the point of extending this handsome thoroughfare on the other side of Castle Place, for purely business purposes.

But we must not bury the larger interests of our subject beneath questions of architecture or heaps of bricks and mortar. This congregation has passed through changes more important than those involved in the transference from the North Gate to Rosemary Lane, or from edifice to edifice. Briefly let us review our ecclesiastical changes. Our first home was in the Antrim Meeting, and when this expanded into the General Synod (A.D. 1690), we were connected with its Belfast Presbytery. We did not leave the General Synod; it drove us out. It treated us very much as Jeremy Taylor had treated us two generations before. He had said, 'Conform, or quit.' The Synod said, 'Sign,

* Figured page 17.

or be off.' To Jeremy Taylor we had replied, 'We shall not conform, and we shall not go. You may put us out of the Parish Church; but you can neither exclude us from the Church of Christ, nor from the town of Belfast. We are Christians, we are citizens, and we mean to live.' Precisely the same answer did we render to the General Synod: 'We shall neither sign nor decamp. Once more you may cause us to suffer expulsion from church courts; we can bear it. It is in your power to gather up your skirts and renounce connection with us. You cannot cut us off

Jeremy Taylor. (From an Old Portrait.)

from that which alone makes church courts desirable. We stay here, in the name of God and in the strength of Christ, a witness for faith in freedom.'

Thus did we take our stand, cheerfully, with our brethren of the Antrim Presbytery, who preferred the simple dignity of serious conviction to the orthodox repute of a religious bondage. If any one ask why, twenty-three years ago, this congregation severed the long-standing tie which had united it in happy union with the Antrim Presbytery, and entered a second time, after 136 years, into a new ecclesiastical connection, the answer is, that this step was only taken as the issue of a deep and deliberate assurance that it was necessary again to bear testimony to the vitality of the religious convictions which underlie our freedom. The Northern Presbytery of Antrim, to which we now belong, is the child of controversies of which the immediate soreness has passed away. On either side men were in earnest, and had the courage of their conclusions; and, where men are in earnest, they will respect each other sooner or later. We have no quarrel with our old friends of the Antrim Presbytery, though in our new ecclesiastical relation we put prominently forward, as we think to be right and demanded by the times, a principle which they deem it unnecessary to embody in the terms of their corporate union, viz., that without faith in Christ and in Revelation, our ministry would be a mockery, our position a snare.

It remains to say a few words respecting the distinguished line of ministers who have been the pastors and teachers of this church. Advance, then, from your dim and distant shades, ye fearless leaders of our people through dark and perilous hours. John Baird, Anthony Shaw, and Read, what know we of you but your names? Your gifts and talents, your deeds and hopes, are covered o'er with the impenetrable shroud of time. But ye were the first in this cause. Others have tended and spread the flame; yours were the hands which lighted the lamp. Come, William Keyes, from thy southern retreat, and tell us whether Dublin to which thou didst betake thee, or Belfast which thou didst leave, now pleases thee best. We have learned some freedom since thy days. The old Covenanting spirit, perchance too stern for thee, is in us still. As in our first youth as a people, so to-day, we shall not yield or flinch, falter or give way, where truth or duty calls. But there is a leaven among us, so we trust, of patience and of charity, which has worked some changes in our temper, without impairing the force and fulness of our spirit. Rise, Patrick Adair, pillar of our ancient strength; historian, diplomatist, trusted of Kings and beloved of thy people; shrewd and strong at the council board, and most melting preacher. Read in the fortunes of thine old flock some further pages of the *Narrative* thou didst begin; and say, Wilt thou reject us, who have followed thine instructions in their power and spirit, rather than copied the fashion and the mould in which thy living thought ran freely in its day? Once more let us look upon thee, honest John M'Bride, tart of tongue, tender of conscience, with the work of God in thy heart, and with no fear of man before thine eyes.

James Crombie, D.D.

Thy jolly visage on our Vestry wall tells us more of thee than all thy sermons and thy books. Apt were thou to contend for thy "true-bleu" Presbyterianism, with the "jet-black" Prelacy, as thou quaintly calledst it. What wouldst thou do in these more tranquil days? Where find antagonists worthy thy doughty spear? We thank thee for our hold upon this soil where now we worship, none daring to make us afraid; far more do we thank thee for the bold uncompromising frankness to which thou didst incite and train the men whom God gave to thee as a charge for thy keeping, for out of their solid strength the sinews of our freedom came. And thou, John Kirkpatrick, physician, author, and divine, not long we had thee as our own; but when we remember thee, we will not forget the old remembrances of brotherhood, brotherhood in the privations of dissenting citizens and in the triumphs of broadening toleration, brotherhood in the excommunications of Synods and in the joy of new fellowships, wherewith we and our neighbours of another House, though twain, were one. How shall I speak of thee, faithful vindicator of our ancient liberties, Samuel Haliday, dauntless and dignified, who first didst teach us to use the Nonsubscribing name? With thee our direct perceptions of the pure Gospel simplicity, derived from Scripture immediately and alone, first began to tremble into life. Then began men to call us heretics, Arians, infidels. "They say," so runs the famous inscription on the wall of the Marischal College in Aberdeen, "They say—What say they?—Let them say." But thou didst trust, with one of fearless speech and boundless charity, that even as they are of Christ, so also we.

With rapid step we pass along this gallery of spiritual portraits. The gentle and pathetic scholar from whom the poet-patriots of the Drennan line descend; Mackay, the uncle and foster-father of Elizabeth Hamilton; Crombie, of whom in vain we seek some monument, either in the Church which he built, or in the town to which he gave the Academy; the descendant of Scottish Kings, and, prouder distinction yet, heir of a line unbroken since the Reformation, of Gospel ministers of the King of kings, William Bruce, teacher, theologian, pastor, public man, who first proclaimed, with no uncertain sound, the Unitarian conclusions to which our theology had long been tending. Further we need not go. The marble slabs on either side our pulpit speak the love of this congregation for the imperishable memory of two scholars, thinkers, divines, whose various gifts and special qualities, contrasted in themselves, were united in the edification of the Church they served.

From the time when the *Regium Donum* began to play a regular part in the State provision for the religious wants of Ireland, Presbyterianism was in a sort of way, and to a minor and strictly subordinate extent, an established form of worship and discipline in this country. Of this quasi-establishment, such as it was, and whatever its advantages and disadvantages, our congregation partook, until the whole system of State aid to religion in Ireland was dissolved in 1869. Henceforth we depend mainly upon our own efforts. We

Mural Tablets.

have few endowments: the site of our old manse; a property in Waring Street, of which a share was left to us by the late William Tennent in 1832; the proceeds of the commutation of the *Regium Donum;* these are the chief of our extraneous resources. Our strength must always lie more in the men and women whom we can interest, secure, and educate in our principles, than in any outward props to our cause. Our wise and thoughtful laity are the real hope and stability of our movement. That movement was not hasty in its origin, its spirit has not been flighty in its direction. Firm, steady, persistent, hopeful has been its course. God has gone before it; will He not be its rearward?

DATES.—Succession of our regular ministry begins, 1660. Regium Donum first granted, 1690; enlarged, 1784, 1792, 1803. Removal to Rosemary Lane, about 1695. Second Congregation founded, 1708. Third Congregation founded, 1722. Our Baptismal Register begins, 1757. Our oldest title and trust deed, 31st August, 1767. Congregational Minute-book begins, 1760. Meeting-house rebuilt, 1783. Skipper Street property, 1833. Dissenters' Chapels Act, 1844. Meeting-House registered for Marriages, 1845. Fee-simple of Meeting-House, &c., acquired, 1855. Northern Presbytery of Antrim, 1862. Disestablishment Act, 1869; came into effect, 1871.

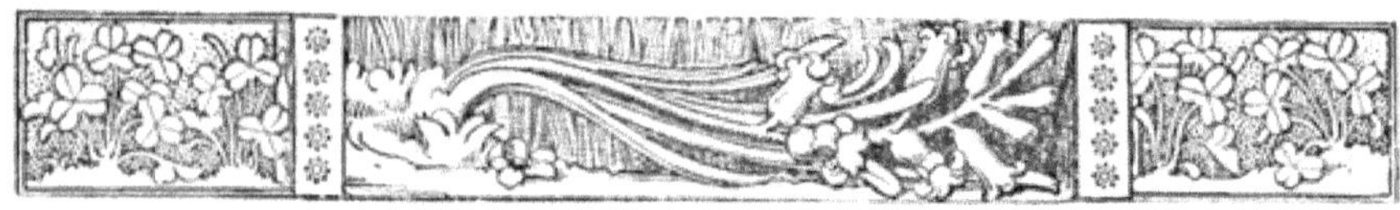

CHAPTER III

How the Doctrines we hold have grown out of the Principles which hold us. The "Six Propositions," or Charter of Nonsubscription; preamble of Nonsubscribing Association. Essence of the Nonsubscribing position. New lights from England—Scotland—America. Doctrinal developments: Calvinism—Arminianism—Arianism—modern Unitarianism. The Divine Character—Holy Scripture—authority of Jesus Christ—meaning of Salvation—the Life beyond this. Prospects of our doctrinal views.

NEVER, in all probability, was there a more disgraceful prosecution, for a matter of Christian opinion, than that which was inflicted upon Thomas Emlyn (1663-1741). The indictment was for a "blasphemous libel"; and these were the words specially incriminated as blasphemy: "I see no reason," Emlyn had written, "there will be to oppose those Unitarians who think him (Jesus Christ) to be a sufficient Saviour and Prince, tho he be not the only supreme God; nor can any, with reason, attempt to prove him to be such, from his works and office as king of his church, since 'tis implied, that as such he must do homage to God the Father, in delivering up his kingdom to him. And this very expression, to God the Father, makes it plain, that there is no God the Son in the same sense, or in the same supreme essence with the Father. . . . So then, Jesus Christ, in his highest capacity, being inferior to the Father, how can he be the same God, to which he is subject, or of the same rank and dignity. . . . So that . . . I may . . . safely say thus much, that the blessed Jesus has declared himself not to be the supreme God, or equal to the Father, as plainly as words could speak, or in brief express." This was the blasphemy.

Emlyn was a Unitarian: the first and the last minister in Ireland who distinctly avowed himself to be such, until within living memory. His expression of Unitarianism was studiously temperate and moderate, as may be judged from the specimens just given; the only ones produced as the foundation of the odious and atrocious charge of blasphemy. But on the strength of these words, after a most iniquitous mockery of a trial, the Chief Justice of Ireland (Richard Pyne), having two Archbishops sitting beside him on the bench, and four or five others present in court, sentenced (16th June, 1703) a Presbyterian minister to be led round the Four Courts, with a paper of accusation on his breast; to be incarcerated

THOMAS EMLYN. V.D.M.
Nat. 27. Maij. 1663. Obiit. 30. Iulij 1741.

for a year, certain; then to pay £1,000, and continue to be in prison till the money was handed in; lastly, to find security for good behaviour during life. Nice men those bishops were, nor even content with overawing the jury by their presence. One of them, and he the Primate of all Ireland, had a statutory claim, it seems, as Queen's Almoner, to a shilling in the pound, on the fine. After two years' imprisonment, Emlyn was allowed by the Lord Lieutenant (James, second Duke of Ormond) to go free, on payment of £70, instead of £1,000. But this did not suit His Grace my Lord Archbishop Narcissus Marsh of Armagh. "Give me my full poundage," said that Most Reverend man; and he got it, too, in hard cash, before the Presbyterian heretic was permitted to avail himself of the more Christian mercies of the State.

So conspicuous a display of theological ferocity excited throughout Ireland, and extended to England, a tumult of various feeling. What the unprejudiced thought about it, may be learned from a caustic review of the case, published by Sir Richard Steele, but in reality written by the great Whig Bishop, Benjamin Hoadly (1676-1761). "To bring down the Father to a level with his own Son, is a commendable work, and the applauded labour of many learned men of leisure; but to place the Son below his own Father in any degree of real perfection, this is an unpardonable error; so unpardonable, that all hands were united against that unhappy man; and he found at length that he had much better have violated all God's commandments, than have interpreted some passages of Scripture differently from his brethren. The Nonconformists accused him, the Conformists condemned him, the secular power was called in, and the cause ended in an imprisonment and a very great fine; two methods of conviction about which the Gospel is silent."

In Ulster, the effect of the trial of Emlyn was distinctly felt in two opposite directions. The moderate were saddened, and set a thinking; those who stood upon the old paths were alarmed amid their rejoicing. Before the trial, the General Synod, in an address to Queen Anne, had taken credit to the Presbyterians for having cast off Emlyn, and forbidden him to preach. While he yet languished in prison, they took no steps for his release. But when the news came that Ormond had ordered the reduction of the fine, and that the dreadful heretic might shortly be expected at large, then the General Synod evidently thought that the time had arrived for precautionary action. Accordingly they enacted (5th June, 1705) that all candidates for licence and ordination should subscribe the Westminster Confession. Observe, that they did not venture to impose the test upon those already in orders.

The resolution of Synod was unanimously carried. Having concurred in passing it, some of the wiser heads appear to have bethought them of a duty even more pressing and imperative than that of securing an enforced allegiance to the doctrines which Emlyn had impugned; namely, of enquiring at the fountain-head into the teachings of the Christian oracles themselves, on the momentous topics which had begun to agitate the public mind. Thus, in the same year in which the Westminster Confession became the authoritative document of the Irish Presbyterian Church, the ministerial club, known as the Belfast Society, was formed.

This was a society of ministers from various Presbyteries, men of open mind, of great intelligence, and of competent learning, who began to meet periodically, for a free and prayerful examination into the contents of the Scriptures in their original tongues. Needless to say what this always leads to, when men are not bound beforehand by the fetters of a system. It led, in the case of these candid and scholarly divines, to the determination that, for their parts, they would never set their hands, in slavish subscription, either to the Westminster system of doctrine, or to any other product of human wisdom.

Haliday's gallant refusal (when called to the ministry of this Church, at the beginning of 1720) to renew, in any way, his subscription, brought matters to a crisis. Haliday's appearance as a recruit in the ranks of the liberal party was a fact of the first importance. He had been a member of the Belfast Society, and, though of Irish birth, had never yet been settled in Ireland. But he had done good service in London, on behalf of the liberties of Irish Presbyterians, and had earned the grateful vote of the Synod, in reward of his exertions. In London, also, he had learned the principle of Nonsubscription, during the debates at Salter's Hall, in 1719, when "the Bible carried it by four." On his refusal to subscribe, the Synod was in a fix. An accusation of Arianism and anti-Presbyterianism raised against Haliday had utterly broken down. What was called a Pacific Act had been passed, in June, 1720. Its name was as delusive as that of the Pacific Ocean. The Pacific Act provided that in future "all intrants into the ministry," even if already ordained out of Ireland, must subscribe the Westminster Confession; but that if they should scruple "any phrase or phrases," they might substitute for such phrases their own expressions, and the Presbyteries were to judge whether such substituted expressions were sound or not. 'But,' said Haliday, when called upon to subscribe, on 28th July, 'I scruple at every phrase; not that I disbelieve the truths which the Confession contains; but I say, "Scripture is a sufficient test of orthodoxy, and the only legitimate test."' The Belfast Presbytery installed Haliday on this footing. The Synod, appealed to in the following year (1721), decided at length to let the matter drop; but, to ease their consciences, a large proportion of the members availed themselves of a permission to attach their signatures voluntarily to the Confession, as a public sign of adhesion to it. Those who did not do this were henceforth called Nonsubscribers.

Among these Nonsubscribers was Thomas Nevin (d. 1744), of Downpatrick. The talk ran one day, in Captain Hannyngton's parlour at Moneyrea, on the subject of blasphemy; a crime which, according to the Confession, the magistrate is bound to punish. Nevin, who was present, called attention to the case of the Jews, who, he said, could not be fairly condemned for blasphemy, though they conscientiously denied Christ to be God. 'What,' said Hannyngton, 'is it no blasphemy to call Christ a creature?' 'How can it be,' retorted Nevin, 'when we all own Christ to be man as well as God?' Gossip flew from mouth to mouth, asseverating that Nevin had nakedly avowed "it is no blasphemy to say Christ is not God." The inference was obvious; Emlyn, that blaspheming Unitarian, must have a warm sympathiser at Downpatrick. Nevin was arraigned before the Synod (1724). Ten days were spent, without success, in endeavouring to bring him to book. At length a resolution was carried, requiring him, in obedience to the Synod, then and there, to make a declaration of his belief in the supreme Deity of Christ. Nevin very properly declined to obey this peremptory mandate. He said it was the duty of his accusers to prove their charge; and the Synod had no right to take this way of disposing of it. He would make no declaration; but he bade them observe that his refusal proceeded from no disbelief of the doctrine. The Synod at once declined all further ministerial communion with him, and decided to proceed no further with the trial. Evidently the temper of the body was huffed. The spirit of angry disputation was roused. Nonsubscribers could expect no quarter.

Haliday, to prove the reasonableness of their objections, published an attack on the theological language of the Confession, in a "Letter" (1725) to Gilbert Kennedy, of Tullylish. The point he selects is one which will strike a modern reader as rather a small one. It is the phrase in which the Confession speaks of the two natures of Christ as joined "without composition." The notable thing, however, is that Haliday takes exception to the Confession, not on the ground that it excludes or condemns heresy, but because it opens the door for theological inaccuracy.

Let this distinction be observed very closely. The whole religious meaning and drift of Nonsubscription will be missed, unless there be a firm grasp and full mastery of this strong position, which it took at the outset. Nonsubscription does not mean, and never did mean, a plea for mere liberty; it rests on a plea for truth, for honest and conscientious exactitude in the momentous matters of Christian doctrine. Nonsubscribers rejected the clauses of the Confession as fetters; but how did they experience them to be shackles? Not because they had embarked in a quixotic pursuit of religion without definite opinions; but because, comparing the creed with the New Testament, and studying carefully among themselves the language of Christ and his Apostles, they had discovered that, though in the main the doctrines of the Confession were such as their education and training had taught them to approve, yet they could not conscientiously say that all its particular statements were true in fact. Truth was the watchword of these men. They found that the simple truth of Jesus Christ was one thing; the Westminster Confession, however admirable from some points of view, was another thing. Hence they said: 'We will be judged by the truth of Christ; we will not be judged by the Confession. Examine us, as much as you will, by the standard of the Master's own teaching; the Westminster Confession was not spoken on the Mount; the Westminster Confession has no claim to be an arbitrary rule of faith.'

This was the gist of the famous Six Propositions, offered as an Expedient for Peace, to the General Synod of 1726, and erected into the very Magna Charta of Nonsubscription, when, in that memorable year, the main body of the Presbyterians of Ulster drove from their midst the principles and the persons of their Nonsubscribing brethren. Beneath some antique verbiage, the meaning they embody is full of fresh and wholesome life, needed, and soon to be demanded, by the Ulster of to-day. The General Assembly, though it has rejoiced the shade of Jubal by its debates tending to show the need of a little liberty to such as handle the organ, would reject the Six Propositions to-day, as its ancestors rejected them more than a century and a-half ago. But when the gathering of the clans of Presbyterianism, from all parts of the world, took place in Belfast recently (1884), a body (the Cumberland Presbyterian Church of America) was admitted into the Presbyterian Alliance, which had formally superseded the Westminster Confession, in accordance with the demands of a fuller experience of God's truth. Nor will this question be finally settled, until the principles of Nonsubscription have received, in the light of the nineteenth century, a consideration which was denied to them in the twilight of the eighteenth.

The first of the Six Propositions contains the pith of the whole. It is, that Christ himself has sufficiently laid down the terms of communion and conditions of office in his Church; and that no body of men has a right to add to what is "settled in the Gospel." This means, in short, that our Lord, when he planted his religion among men, knew his own business, and asks no assistance from a conclave of Commonwealth divines, in laying the foundations of his Church. Accordingly, the second Proposition maintains that, without recourse to subscription, it is easy to ascertain whether persons have, or have not, the faith of Christ. The third and fourth affirm that, to impose subscription on ministers, or on "parents, as the condition of the baptism of their children," is to go beyond the precept and the warrant of Christ. The fifth and sixth deal with recent cases of soreness: the one condemns the exaction of a declaration of faith from a person who could not be fairly convicted of false doctrine on evidence (referring to Nevin's excommuniaction); the other very properly declares (with a reference to the action of the Synod after excusing Haliday) that to call that a voluntary subscription into which men were urged through fear of "a popular odium," was to shelter an act of injustice under an abuse of language.

The substance of this historic manifesto is here given, partly in more modern words, partly in its original terms. Even at the risk of some tedium, it is desirable that its standpoint should be fully understood; for it is the very ground on which we have rested secure and strong, from the days of Haliday until now. Precisely the same, in its force and bearing, is the preamble of the representative Association of Irish Nonsubscribing Presbyterians, founded in 1835. "Allegiance to the Lord Jesus Christ, as the only King and Head of the Church," and "the maintenance of the great principles of the Reformation, viz., the sufficiency of the Scripture, the right of Private Judgment, and the rejection of human authority in matters of faith," these are the solid planks of our Nonsubscribing platform.

Our Nonsubscribing fathers were, in one sense, as orthodox as our neighbours of the General Assembly. In another sense they were as unorthodox as ourselves. If orthodoxy means the holding of Trinitarian opinions, then they were genuinely orthodox. But if orthodoxy means that questions of theology were settled, once and for ever, by a committee of experts, sitting in the Jerusalem Chamber, to do what Christ left undone, then they would have repudiated the notion of orthodoxy, root and branch. And unfortunately this is what orthodoxy is commonly taken to imply, when the word is used by Presbyterians. It ought to mean upright opinion; well formed, intelligible, honest opinion; just as orthography means well formed, intelligible, honest writing, not the cramped and clerkly hand of ages past. But it has come to mean sixteenth century opinion in the Episcopal Church, and has not yet got beyond seventeenth century opinion in the majority of the Presbyterian Churches. Our forefathers said: 'We belong to the eighteenth century; and we have just as good a right as any people had, seventy or eighty years before us, to learn the meaning of the New Testament for ourselves.' This was horribly unorthodox; even though, with their previous training and associations, they actually aimed at conclusions very little different from those of their contemporaries. And when we, their children, say: 'We also have a right, nay it is our Christian duty, to learn, in like manner, for ourselves, what is the truth of Christ,' we are following their example and their instructions. To Christ they led us, to Christ this day we go, resolved, with our own living hearts and open minds, to reach a present and personal interpretation of the message of our Divine Master, even as did those heroes of conscience and of hope, who reared by their sacrifices a shrine of God, devout and free, where, through coming ages, men might enter into the salvation of Christ, live the life of purity and charity, and worship the Father in spirit and in truth.

No sudden leap of doctrinal aberration transferred our theology from the Calvinistic restraints of Scotland or of Westminster to the Unitarian discipleship in which we now rejoice. The steps were deliberate, slow, and sure. Our body, though strangers coming among us often mistake its temper, is essentially conservative in its instincts; cautious in its movements; changing, not for change's sake, but under pressure of recognised truth; ready, nay eager, to accord an unprejudiced hearing to what any honest mind may offer, but quite unwilling to part with any principle which time and experience have approved as sound, for any novelty of the passing hour. Influences from other countries aided the gradual development of our doctrinal changes. England, whose discarded Confession our divines had adopted, now furnished us with literature that counteracted the effect of the Westminster theology. From the Establishment came, very early in the century, Dr. Samuel Clarke's famous book on the Trinity (1712), the fountain-head of the so-called Arian views; a book, the influence of which, after forty-four years, led Bishop Robert Clayton, of Clogher, to move in the Irish House of Lords (1756), that the Athanasian and Nicene Creeds be expunged from the Prayer Book. From the Dissenters came, near the middle of the century, Dr. John Taylor's book on Original Sin (1740), which, more perhaps than any other work, contributed to the liberalising of the theological intelligence of the age; it was reprinted in Belfast in 1746, and the list of subscribers, and catalogue of theological works sold by the publishers, should be carefully studied by all who are interested in the mental history of the Province. Scotland continued to educate our Irish Presbyterian clergy in liberal ideas, as has already been remarked and illustrated in our first chapter. Scotland, that had given us the stalwart, fervid Calvinism of Patrick Adair, gave us also the calm, enlightened wisdom of James Crombie. Lastly, America sent us across the sea the quickening word of the most exquisite of writers and most elevating of reformers, the pure and sweet genius of William Ellery Channing. We had, indeed, some right to avail ourselves of the light of Channing's lamp, for throughout his ministerial life it burned in a house of worship founded by John Morehead of Newtownards, and long known as the "Irish Church"; and we may add that, though native hands had prepared the soil, the first seed of the spreading tree of American Unitarianism was sown in 1783, by William Hazlitt, of Shronehill, Tipperary.

William Ellery Channing.

The first great stride in our development was that which drew us from Calvinism, the Gospel of the love of God for the elect, to Arminianism, the Gospel of the love of God for the world. Many of the original Non-subscribers ultimately took this step; few, or probably none, got any further. The next decisive move was that which conducted us from Trinitarianism with its mysteriously three-fold God, to Arianism with its clear presentation of the Eternal Father, whose attributes are visibly mirrored in the spotless brightness of His only Son. Silently this move was made. We cannot say precisely when, or by whom, the transition to the Arian view was first accomplished. For, in spite of the largeness of the Toleration Act, the statute book still (and up to so recently as 1817) laid pains and penalties upon all who should speak or write against the received doctrine of the Trinity; and the fate of Emlyn warned men that open speech might be a dangerous experiment. The change, accordingly, was effected in comparative silence, but it was a silence that might be felt. Trinitarianism is, for the most part, an excrescence upon Christianity; the excrescence was quietly laid aside, without direct attack or public proclamation. Trinitarian ideas and expressions, borrowed from the Creeds, were calmly dropped; the language of the New Testament was reinstated in their place. This we may safely say, that since the appointment of Thomas Drennan (1736), the doctrine of the Trinity has never been preached or owned by any minister of this Church.

Now these two great changes, from Calvinism to Arminianism, and from the Trinitarian to the Arian position, really, and in substance, involve all the rest. That God loves man, not merely some men; that Christ is the Son, not the identical Self, of God; these axioms comprise the whole story of our theological advance. Whatever else there may be to tell, is included within the full meaning of these two propositions. Modern Unitarianism is their outcome.

The Unitarian name was introduced to the North of Ireland in a publication which has escaped the notice of our historians, a *Gospel Defence of the Unitarian Doctrine*, printed in Belfast, in 1774. Its unknown author, who took the name of Epaphras, was a layman in sympathy with the views of Priestley. The opinions of that great writer never made much way in this part of the world, and it is probable that Epaphras' publication found few readers. Certainly it did not succeed, either in recommending the particular standpoint of Priestley, or in naturalising among us the Unitarian name. So long as that name was identified with Humanitarianism, it was rejected (and this is not surprising) by the Arians of Ulster. In 1821, the managers of the Unitarian Fund in London, who had long meditated a movement in Ireland, despatched a missionary to Ulster, John Smethurst (1793-1859). He was an amiable and a scholarly man, but his mission was a dead failure; one may even say, deservedly so. For its object was, not so much to win new ground for Unitarianism, as to convert the Ulster Arians into Humanitarians of the then prevalent English type. The Ulster Arians thought themselves fully competent to manage their own theological affairs, and very generally turned the cold shoulder upon John Smethurst. He was not allowed to preach in any Meeting-house in Belfast, but he lectured in the Lancasterian Schoolroom.

But though this mission fell signally flat, it was productive, both directly and indirectly, of very important results. It summoned forth, for the first time, the tremendous theological energies of Henry Cooke, who went from place to place after Smethurst, literally annihilating his chances of influence, and who, from that time forward, embarked on his life-long career of animosity to Unitarianism in every shape and form. It brought out, also, the great Dr. Bruce as a controversial theologian, not in defence of Smethurst, but in opposition to his tenets, from another point of view. Dr. Bruce was the first minister in the North of Ireland who took the Unitarian name; and he was encouraged to do so by the new currency which had been given to it by the Baltimore Sermon (1819) of Dr. Channing, which electrified America, and taught the world that there was a broader, a more comprehensive, and a more spiritual type of Unitarianism in being than that presented for the moment by the insular English school.

Dr. Bruce's theology is on lines coincident with those which formed the doctrinal aspect of Channing's mind, with more of systematic nicety, based on a much closer and more connected study of scripture; at the same time, with far less ardour of spiritual appeal. The weak places in Dr. Bruce's armour were searched out with keen acumen by Dr. John Paul, in his *Refutation of Arianism* (1825). But neither this powerful criticism, nor the mass of subsequent publications, has rendered Dr. Bruce's *Sermons on the study of the Bible, and of the Doctrines of Christianity* (1824, improved edition, 1826) out of date; though,

Mural Monument.

of course, there are points on which sixty years have tended to revise our conclusions. Less suasive, perhaps, than the sermons of John Mitchel of Newry, on *The Scripture Doctrine of the Divinity of our Lord Jesus Christ*, which appeared four years later (1828, second edition, 1830), they are strong, manly, ably argued, and admirably written; right worthy of their historic place, as constituting the first elucidation of Unitarian Christianity committed to the press by any Ulster Presbyterian clergyman.

Following the same lines, is the better known and more accessible defence of Unitarianism by John Scott Porter, in the discussion with Dean Bagot, in 1834. This controversy is unique among expositions of Unitarianism, in that it inseparably joins together both sides of the argument; so that no one can procure the work of the Trinitarian advocate, without procuring also the work of his Unitarian opponent, or consult the argument for the Divine Unipersonality, without having the counter-argument before his eyes. To studious and candid minds, to whichever side disposed, this is a great gain. Our more recent literature is now pretty abundant in statements and defences of our faith; and for facilitating its circulation, we have two voluntary institutions, the Unitarian Society (1832) and the Ulster Unitarian Christian Association (1875), maintained respectively by those who take opposite views of some modern controversies.

Device of Ulster Unitarian Christian Association.

Unitarianism, which takes its name from its vindication of the doctrine of One God in One Person, is even more conclusively distinguished by its view of the Divine Character than by its account of the Divine Personality. That God is One, we receive as the central truth of the Old Testament; that God is Love, we take to be the essence of the New Testament. It is this persuasion which has practically reconstructed the whole scheme and spirit of our theology; making it impossible for us to believe the Almighty Father a Being implacable towards any who truly repent and turn to Him; and causing us to see in the mission and the work of Christ, not the antithesis to the sterner mind of God, not the deprecation of the Creator's wrath, not the arbitrary satisfaction of an otherwise inexorable severity in the Most High, but the manifestation and the fulfilment of the Father's love.

The same principle has guided us in our estimation of the place, purpose, and meaning of the Holy Scriptures of our faith, which we read in the constant light of the Fatherhood and lovingkindness of God, perusing and interpreting them as divinely adapted for the gradual unfolding of His spiritual truth to the minds of men in successive ages, till at length the full blaze of the sun of heavenly knowledge shone in the revelation of Jesus Christ. We do not go to the Scriptures to teach us the lower sciences, which God has given us faculties to acquire in other ways. We do not open the volumes of revelation as though they were text-books of history, of chronology, of physics, of astronomy. We search them for richer results; we approach and revere them as the great treasury of the records of God's dealing with the human soul. We experience in them the touch of the Spirit of God; we feel the inspiration which they communicate to mind and heart, to conscience and character; and therefore we say that they are inspired, because we know that they inspire.

Even above the New Testament we place him whose picture there is faithfully and sublimely drawn, and whose authority we hold ourselves, as Christians, bound at all hazards to abide by and to maintain. Though we do not deify him, we cannot separate Christ from God. His image is the one perfect likeness of the Divine Love; it is through him—and this not by help merely of the words which he spake, nor only through the awe of his wonderful deeds, but through his overcoming presentation of a perfect goodness, a holiness unflawed, and yet in living sympathy with men—it is through him that we understand the very heart of God, and have access to the Father. Therefore Christ is the highest authority in religion that we can approach or imagine; the one true way to God, because the one true expression of the life of God, sent from the bosom of the Father to be the light of men below.

We mean by Salvation a deliverance from something more than punishment, with its apprehensions and terrors; namely, from that which is its justification and its cause, the evil and misery of sin. The Christian religion makes men safe by making them honest, true, upright, and good. It effects its appointed end by bringing into sinful man a new spirit from above, a spirit which regenerates his heart, refines his temper, purifies his dispositions, regulates his conduct, subdues his passions, and reforms his life. The salutary office of Christ is accomplished in the human soul; where at length he reigns as conqueror, not by pacifying God, but by gaining supremacy over the rebellious will, as the fruit of his love, his labours, and his sacrifice.

To the Life beyond this we look forward with hope, because there is that within us which says "We shall not die;" with faith, because God is good; with certainty, because Christ our Lord lives, and we shall also live. In the eternal world, we believe there shall be for every sinner, and for every sin, "tribulation and anguish," according to the righteous judgment of God, who will render to every man according to his deeds. Yet we believe not that sin can, in the realm of God, maintain against His love and power an everlasting abode in any heart. We look forward to the fulfilment of the promise that "there shall be no curse any more" (Rev. xxii. 3), but God at length be "all in all."

If the enquiry arise as to the prospects of the spread and acceptance of the views of Christian doctrine outlined in the preceding sentences, the reply is, that already the vital substance of these views, welcomed or dreaded, acknowledged or disowned, dominates the thinking mind of the Christian world. The Unitarian name is shunned; the Unitarian spirit has proved too powerful for its opponents. It has invaded their own strongholds, it dictates the tone of their most

JOHN SCOTT PORTER.

popular sermons, it presides over the developments of their Biblical criticism, its gladdening light shines with emancipating ray into the heart and intelligence of the young; the ominous shadow of its growing power falls heavily upon the breast of the anxious maintainer of old traditions. It is not within the walls of Unitarian Meeting-houses alone that our essential principles find voice and acceptance. Pass by our doors with averted eye, and the library, the newspaper, the countless influences daily operating, which go to form the temper of the modern mind, will insensibly impel you in our direction. Send the text and the translation of the New Testament to the most trusted of scholars for revision, the Unitarians are the only theologians who are gainers by the results. Let history, science, scholarship, philosophy, conduct you to the most certain issues of their advancing knowledge, and there is a Unitarian argument in every position thus wrested from the ignorance of the past. The reception won by our actual teachings is considerable; the permanence of our principles is even more signally apparent. Our way of looking at Scripture, our sense of the brotherhood of man, our proclamation of the Redeemer's humanity, our confidence in Almighty love; all these have told, are telling, and will yet tell, upon the religious mind of the age. If the victory is not with us, at any rate the victory is ours.

And still the Unitarian name is shunned. Perhaps this is not altogether wonderful. Indeed it is something to our credit that it is so. For, in an age of pious inconsistencies and halting betwixt the old and the new, an age of see-saw and zig-zag, we are an uncompromising people. We must have the naked truth, and nothing less divine will satisfy us. We have passed the stage of half measures, of religious reticence, of endeavouring to fill old bottles with new wine, or to patch fresh cloth on tattered vestures of decay. All this is matter of history with us; we have done with it. The period of temporary expedients is over in our case. Our forerunners felt their way through it; our grandfathers came clean out of it. Amid the wild experiments and alarmed reactions and hesitating liberalisms of our day, we stand secure in the possession of tried and verified truth.

We need not expect an immediate recognition. In whose footsteps do we follow? "A disciple is not above his Master, nor a servant above his Lord." Children of a rejected Christ, what more dare we ask, than to have present fellowship with him who saw of the travail of his soul, and was satisfied? But we have an unfailing promise: "Because thou didst keep the word of my patience, I also will keep thee from the hour of trial, that hour which is to come upon the whole world, to try them that dwell upon the earth. I come quickly: hold fast that which thou hast, that no one take thy crown" (Rev. iii. 10, 11).

DATES.—Emlyn's Trial, 1703. Clarke's "Scripture Doctrine of the Holy Trinity," 1712. Nevin's Trial, 1724. Haliday's Letter to Kennedy, 1725. "Six Propositions" published, 1726. Professor Simson, of Glasgow, suspended, 1728. Taylor's "Scripture Doctrine of Original Sin," 1740. Bishop Clayton's "Essay on Spirit," 1751; motion in Irish House of Lords to expunge Athanasian and Nicene Creeds from the Prayer book, 1756. "Gospel Defence of Unitarian Doctrine," 1774. Trinity Act, 1817. Channing's Baltimore Sermon, 1819. Smethurst's Mission, 1821. Dr. Bruce's doctrinal Sermons, 1824. Unitarian Society, 1831. Porter and Bagot Discussion, 1834. Ulster Unitarian Christian Association, 1875.

CHAPTER IV

WHAT OUR RELIGIOUS LIFE HAS BEEN AND OUGHT TO BE. A Christian Church. Variations in our public services—prayer—praise—preaching. Religion in common life. Spiritual culture of young and old. Mission work. Propagandism. Our relation to other religious bodies. Personal religion.

THE Centennial which has called forth the preparation of this volume is not the centennial of our origination as the First Presbyterian Church in Belfast; for this dates back above 240 years. It is not the centennial of our tenure of a religious home in Rosemary Street. We have been on this hospitable ground for nearer two centuries than one, and may hold our Rosemary Street bi-centennial in 1895, if God spares us. It is not the centennial of our Nonsubscription; brave Haliday won the battle of our Christian liberty 165 years back. It is not the centennial of our Arianism, or of our Unitarianism, for, as we said in our last chapter, the doctrine of the Trinity has never been preached among us since Drennan lifted up his gentle voice in 1736. What, then, did we commemorate in 1883? The re-erection of a building, and therewith the revival, the re-organisation, and practically the re-establishment of our congregational cause.

We were in such low water in 1781, that the dilapidated structure was looked upon as a fit emblem of a falling interest, and if timorous counsels had been attended to, we

William Bruce, A.B.

might have commemorated in 1883, not the new birth of a Meeting-house, but its destruction; not the rejuvenescence of a religious society, but its evaporation or absorption. The courage of our forefathers, under their calm and intelligent leader, James Crombie, was rewarded by the rise of this beautiful House of Prayer, and by the beginning of a new period of religious prosperity for the Church which reassembled within its walls. Fresh heart, quickened energy, an invigorated life had been gained in the experiences of the common work, into which all had thrown themselves with cordial zeal and activity, during the two years of rebuilding.

When the welcome day arrived, and the Church took possession of its finished sanctuary, it was with increased adherents and brightened hopes. Friends and neighbours in all ranks and denominations had given their sympathy and their encouragement. The lord of the soil, a prelate of the Establishment, the gentry round, the citizens within Belfast, old friends in distant quarters, all had recognised the honourable position, the ancient services, the prospects of further usefulness, the gathered warmth of commendable enterprise, which belonged to the mother church of Presbyterianism, freedom, philanthropy, in Belfast. A spirit ripe and ready for the times animated the congregation, and flinging wide its reconstructed doors with songs of gratitude and praise, it opened on Sunday, 1st June, 1783, a new era of its vitality and its fame.

More than once since that memorable day there has come a period of depression, of anxiety, of searching of heart, in view of the affairs and the apparent prospects of this congregation. More than once have the thoughts of the elders been grave, in the presence of a spirit of listlessness or of timidity. It has never been proposed to pull down this building and do away with it; but there was a passing suggestion, many years ago, to curtail its proportions. Since then it has been necessary, more than once, to amplify its accommodation. Once for all we may learn, as we look reverently back upon what our fathers feared and what they did a hundred years ago, that the right remedy, in every time of apprehension and drawback and inclination to feel uneasy, is to be found in new engagements, fresh enterprise, a bold seizure of opportunity by hearty co-operation with united mind and will. It is not a history only that we recall, as we go back to the memories of 1781–3; it is a promise we touch, a prophecy that speaks to us. Both God and man help those who have faith and spirit to help themselves.

Monument to William Tennent, benefactor to the Congregation.

Hence the value and preciousness of the occasion commemorated by our Centennial lay emphatically in this. It was far more than the successful issue of a building scheme. Under the divine blessing it inaugurated an important revival in our general church life. It is an interesting fact that the first publication by Dr. James Crombie, our second founder, as he may be called, was an *Essay on Church Consecration* (1777), in which he vigorously repudiates the idea of any spiritual virtue or hallowing grace, as residing in any fabric which the hand of man's diligence may raise, or the breath of man's words may set apart. The sanctity of a Christian church, he tells us, is not to be discovered in its habitation, but in its members; consisting, as it does, in "just sentiments of God, impressed upon the soul," in the temper of the worshipping mind, and in the righteous practice which "makes us happy here, and constitutes our bliss hereafter."

The requisites of a Christian church are three; a Creed, a Worship, an organised and beneficent Life.

A Creed we have. But so much has the word been abused, that it is indispensable to explain that when we say *Sic credo*, "Thus I

First Presbyterian Meeting-house, 1886.

believe," we do not immediately proceed to crush a personal conviction into an instrument of exclusive privilege. We do not say *Sic credendum est*, 'So you must believe, or you are outside the pale of the church and of salvation.' Our creed is the flower of our history, that history which has been already sketched in its salient features. We are Unitarians, believing in the Unipersonality of God and in the universal benevolence of the Divine Character, believing in the manifestation of the Eternal Father, through the Perfect Son, whose manhood came from heaven to make God's goodness known. We are Unitarians in our conclusions, yet we do not thereby cease to be Nonsubscribers. We are Unitarians on conviction; Unitarians who rejoice to spread those principles which we have formed, proved, and found to be the strength and blessing of our lives. We are not Unitarians on compulsion, nor would we wear again, or impose on any, the kind of servile yoke from which our fathers were happily delivered. No Unitarian formulary have we signed. Our creed is in our hearts, engraven on our minds. It is inseparable from ourselves. Intelligently we hold it; gladly we proclaim it. We do not enact it into an iron rule by which the faith or the fellowship of future ages is to be restricted and determined.

A Worship we have; and in this most sacred attitude of our minds, this most spiritual purpose of our public association together, we rejoice to know that we are in entire harmony, both of thought and word, with our predecessors, notwithstanding the various phases of theological opinion through which our congregation has passed. Amid all these changes, our worship has uniformly been characterised by its direct address to the Father of all. To forget this, would be to miss the explanation of what puzzles and perplexes those who wonder at us from the outside. How have you kept together, they ask, amazed, during these intellectual revolutions, which have led you from Calvinism to Arminianism, from Arminianism to Unitarianism? What has been your bond, your stay, your common base of religious identity? Why, it has been simply this, that we have always prayed together; offering, with all our differences, a united and continuous worship to Him to whom our Saviour prayed; feeling that though in other matters we might not think alike, in this, the expression of our highest homage, we were truly one, in aspiration, in spirit, in aim. In the matter of religious emotion, no feeling heart will lay down laws in the temper of a martinet. If we have strong feelings towards Christ, we should not hesitate to give them voice, in the invocation of a hymn, or in the frank warmth of a devotional utterance. But that the supreme object of all prayer, all praise, all adoration of the soul, is found in God the Father only, this has been, all along, the one guiding thought of our religion, and this the regulating fact of our sacred and solemn exercises.

Till the first year of this century, we employed no other hymnal than that sometimes quaint, but often sweet and powerful version of the Psalms, by the Cornish statesman, Sir Francis Rous (1579-1659), which our Scottish ancestors accepted, with some

Memorial to John H. Houston.

revision (in 1650), as their own; supplemented at a later date by the Scripture Paraphrases (1781). Thus was our book of praise, throughout our earlier history, completely in unison with the theological convictions of our latest growth, presenting no word or hint of the unscriptural doctrines which we came in course of time to discard. The first edition (1801) of our Psalms and Hymns was a tiny collection of 246 pieces. Since the preparation of the existing edition (1818) containing 300, the stores of modern hymnology have been marvellously enriched in beauty, life, and fulness, and a new book is in progress. But we owe much to the collection which we have so long employed, especially to its marked devotional quality, and would not willingly lose the treasures, dear to many a religious association, which its familiar pages enshrine. The introduction of an organ among us was strongly resisted for a long period; and though the architect who designed our galleries, himself a churchman, intended from the first that the organ gallery should serve its present use, it was seventy years before an instrument was placed there. What was feared by Dr. Bruce, was, that the mechanical aid might prove the destruction of congregational psalmody, a danger, perhaps, not wholly unreal. No litany, and no responsive prayer have we. But in sonorous hymn and simple chant, all may join, and be the better of it. The most impressive song of worship is that in which the chorus of the congregation rises, in honest, not self-conscious notes, with melody, perhaps unskilled, but from the heart. For music more elaborate, the anthem, which forms a part of all our regular services, gives scope. Our present collection of Chants and Anthems, edited under the superintendence of our accomplished organist, Dr. Carroll, dates from 1866.

Preaching, with us, as with all Presbyterians, has been viewed far more as an integral part of worship than as an extraneous addition to it. Listening to sermons constitutes one of our best recognised religious engagements. Mindful of this, successive preachers here have directed their efforts mainly to practical points of religious edification; not inculcating theological niceties, but endeavouring to reach the conscience, to elevate the moral tone, and to deepen the spiritual life. It has been an interesting task to read and compare, for the purposes of this historical survey, a large number of specimens of the pulpit work of this church, some in print, some in manuscript, from Patrick Adair downwards through all the variations of theological change. Very remarkable is the great similarity of spirit, even when controversy is in question; very marked is the essential harmony of the prevailing tone of the general teaching, which is decidedly not controversial. The strain has been didactic, rather than emotional; but

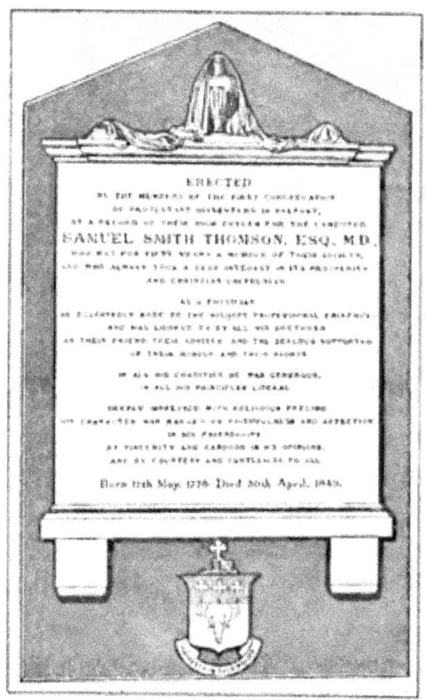

Memorial Tablet to Samuel Thomson, M.D., to whose musical taste and direction the congregational psalmody was long indebted.

the main business and substance of the preacher's discourse has not been to give lectures in theology, but lessons of life, aids to the perfecting of the moral ideal, encouragements to the waiting upon the power of God in the soul. When Patrick Adair says, "on a sacrament day," in 1672: "Whatever way people do seek Christ, they do find him. Those that seek no more than Christ's outward presence, he will consent to give them that; but those that seek his spiritual presence, he will hear them also in that," he exhibits a power of generous appreciation of different stages of religious experience, and points, at the same time, to the true line of religious advance. Or when John M'Bride, also at a sacramental season, preaches, as his manner was, four successive sermons on the

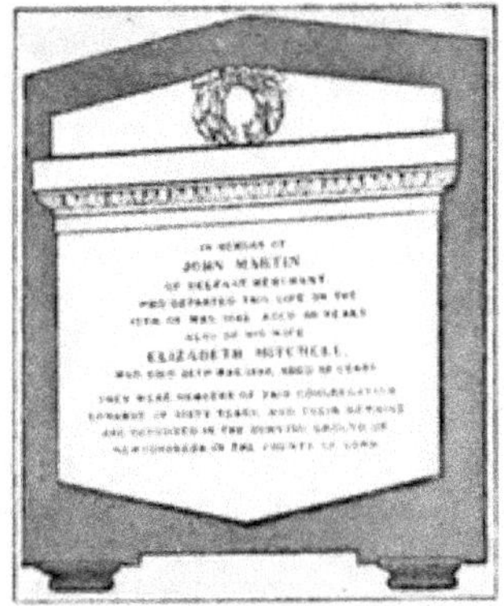

Memorial Tablet to John Martin, father of the founder of the Throne Hospital.

same text, and that the text which speaks of a good conscience, enforcing this as the test of spiritual health and vigour, we feel that, though the doctrines on which his eye was fixed were different from ours, his point of view was essentially one with our own.

If resort to preaching be the most prominent and comprehensive of our religious observances, attendance on communions is the most significant. Our ancestors regarded this rite with an awe and reverence approaching the confines of superstitious dread. Hence the infrequency of their celebrations (originally but once a-year in each congregation), the sedulous and searching care of their preparations, and their public thanksgiving days after participation. Early in the last century, the communion was celebrated among us in February and August, but the change to April and October preceded the erection of our present Meeting-house. Our conservative ways are still apparent in our traditional use of unleavened bread, though we have discarded the qualifying tokens, and have recently abandoned the ancient custom of sitting around the Lord's table in successive relays. But the communion is still to us the binding ordinance of our public religion. The symbol and the pledge of our Christian fellowship and profession has a hold upon our affection, stronger than that of our ordinary worship. A minister accustomed to English usages, who was present at one of our recent communions, declared it to be a wonder and a joy to him, to see a whole congregation of Unitarians staying to participate in this beautiful and solemnising rite, which is at once the crown of our devotion to the Giver of all spiritual food, and the seal of our adherence to the cause of Christ.

Vestry.

An organised Church Life we have. Inheritors of the free traditions of a popular Presbyterianism, we have found its machinery elastic enough to provide for the expansion of our ideas, and the altering conditions of our various work. In 1760, was added to a lifelong eldership, a congregational committee, forming a sessional body, periodically renewed.

The Presbyterian system may legitimately be regarded as that of which the outline is foreshadowed in the New Testament. But it would neither be just nor wise to stickle for it as constituting a part of the substance of revelation. Forms of church government are matters of constitutional expedience, rather than of divine right, in an exclusive sense. Presbyterianism, fairly administered, has proved itself a most valuable and sufficient instrument for training the mind, disciplining the energies, eliciting and giving effect to the

Memorial Tablet to Alithea Ferguson.

real convictions of a religious body. Besides this, it has rendered important services in directing the aid of strong congregations to the conservation of weak ones, both by moral support, and by material aid. No system, however, can do more for congregations than they are willing to do for themselves. Nor can any reliance upon religious ordinances supply the lack of the personal life of religion; nor any creed suffice to make men good.

Great store is set, by people of our creed, upon the religion of common life, and rightly so. A good home religion, a good Monday religion, a good business and market religion, a religion of week-day duties and veracities and generosities and charities, a religion that follows men behind the counter, and is not left in the pew, a religion that is not stifled in the hour of pleasure, to be roused again in the hour of prayer, a religion that keeps the heart clean, and the conduct straight; this is the religion which commands our suffrages, holds our esteem, and animates our ideal of the life that best serves God. But it would be a fatal mistake to suppose this religion, the religion of life and conduct, the practical religion of character, attainable in any high degree, without spiritual culture. You cannot regulate the actions of the outward man, without educating the motives of the inward man. As our Saviour says, "Make the tree good," if you want the fruit to be wholesome and sound.

This work of spiritual culture is our great business with the young. This is the object of our Sunday Schools, our classes, our children's services. We have to train young minds in our ideas, not simply because they are ours, but because we believe them to be the best. We have to awaken in young hearts a glad response to the verities of our pure and holy faith, that their lives may be biassed in the right direction from the first. We have to encourage them to think for themselves, and spur them to act for themselves; but we are bound to give them, at the beginning, the best materials for thinking, and best guidance for action. If we neglect this, we neglect their future, we surrender the prospects of our cause, we destroy our best hope. Not one of us would wish to see our young people converted into Unitarian bigots; but we do all of us desire to see them grow up intelligent Unitarians, knowing something of the historic past from which we spring, and understanding how to value it and to apply its lessons, having our principles at heart and ready to stand by them, permeated with our faith in God, actuated by what we have learned of Christ, at home in the sacred Scriptures, and prizing them with an appreciative and grateful love. This we do earnestly desire, and this we must all aim at, and determine to bring about. This if we cannot do, we can do nothing. A hundred years have passed since our forefathers, with Christian manliness, resolved not to accept a verdict of unsuccess, but reared our Meeting-house, in confident and courageous faith. We have learned to speak out our thoughts more boldly since then, to call things by their right names, to define our position, to own and to defend our theology. What were all this, if we cared not to provide for our own household? Better, according to the Apostle, to deny the faith at once; the worst species of infidelity to our sacred cause is to believe that it is not worth while to secure its influence over the rising life of our own immediate flock. Nothing which we have devised to celebrate this Centennial of ours, gives promise of so much permanent advantage as this, that we have seized the golden opportunity of making new provision for the housing of our Sunday School, our Libraries, our gatherings for religious and intellectual improvement, under the auspices of such fraternities as our Institute of Faith and Science.

That we have a mission to the world outside is most true. But practical men to whom we may address ourselves, will measure our movement by measuring us; will estimate it not by the abstract beauty of our tenets, but by the degree and quality of the results which they perceive to be registered in our individual characters, and in our church life. A prosperous, animated, energetic, and united church is always a missionary church. It always exercises a demonstrable influence on behalf of the principles it espouses. It earns the right to some attention; it conciliates respect; it creates a presumption in its own favour. People say, 'There is power in it; there is an example about it; we must look at it; we may learn from it.'

Memorial Tablet to Ellen Mercer.

Upon this church of ours, two classes of eyes are steadily fixed. Turning towards us in warm sympathy and cordial hope, the sister churches of our communion throughout the North of Ireland await our movements, and scan our course. Naturally they expect it of us to set a tone, to keep a lead in good works, to encourage others, to present, not merely a fair Meeting-house, as our inheritance from the past, but an earnest, living church, thoroughly abreast of the times, as our pledge of the future.

Again, we are exposed to a tolerably shrewd and searching scrutiny, cast upon our doings and not-doings, by the great mass of religionists who refuse to admit us within the pale of their brotherhood. Criticism from the outside, however unsympathetic, never does much harm to a resolute cause. It acts as a tonic; bitter, but bracing. We have long been made conscious that whatever we do for our religion, we must do in a sort of ostracised isolation. None but weak minds will waste time in complaining of this. We must accept it as a part of the conditions of the situation, a factor in our particular problem, and determine not to be rendered idle by lack of hearty co-operation and friendly fellowship, in quarters where our principles are painted black. We must show what these dreadful Unitarians are capable of.

And further, we must take into account that there is very much latent and covert sympathy, both with our persons, as men of honour and principle, as citizens who have won respect, and with our views, as giving decided expression to tendencies powerfully felt in all denominations. There are those who are looking at us, not inimically, but

Memorial Tablet to John and Annabella Riddel.

wistfully, acknowledging our constancy, envying our freedom, in much accord with many or most of our conclusions, finding in us much to admire; conscious that they would gain in consistency, thoroughness, mental purity, if they came over to our position, yet wondering whether, on the whole, they would not lose something which is spiritually precious to them, by a clear identification with us; and finally kept aloof from us, because they are told (and find some colour for the calumny) that we are cold in our own despite, indifferent to our own interests; our principles firm, our energies slow; our wealth rarely applicable to our own objects; great opportunities before us, the pulse of our zeal somewhat slack to embrace them. We shall not admit the justice of this feeling, but we must all have observed its existence. Every one of us must do what in us lies to remove it, not for our own sakes only, but for the sake also of those to whom it will prove the greatest of religious blessings to learn that Unitarianism can be compatible with ardour, enterprise, endeavour, the mainspring, the influential creative force of a strong and flourishing cause.

The mission beyond our own borders, in which we take the keenest interest, and to which we render our most active aid, is a service of Christian benevolence, a work not of propagandism, but of moral elevation and wise charity. Here we feel deeply in earnest, and here, accordingly, we succeed. This mission has taken many forms in our past history. The Domestic Mission (1853) which we largely support, and which owes its inception to the awakening word of one of our excellent ladies, is but one phase of the various schemes and unselfish agencies, from time to time originated and sustained by the members of our communion, in fulfilment of a recognised duty towards souls and bodies languishing around us.

Scarcely, as yet, is our conscience profoundly stirred by the obligation "to do good and to communicate," as respects our positive tenets and principles as a denomination. Hence the personal energy which we throw into this work is very slight, and does not at all represent the value we really set upon our express doctrinal beliefs. Lukewarm we are not, as is proved when we are roused to the defence of what we hold dear, by the assaults of the supposed "orthodox," or the attempts of those who do not understand that we cherish a distinctive Christian creed, and have no notion of surrendering it. But at ordinary times, and when not specially put upon our mettle, we are very placid in our contentment with the possession of the truth, and exceedingly calm in our contemplation of the world's neglect of it. Offering in a quiet way the stores of our literature to the

passer by, we say, in effect, 'Take it, or leave it.' There is something of mental dignity in this self-contained and uneager attitude. But is it really all we are capable of?—all that we find in our heart of hearts? Are we quite satisfied with it? Is it not fair to interpret the needs of our time by urging the imperative and present claims of a Unitarian enthusiasm, a Unitarian activity, yes, of a Unitarian propagandism? Let none start at the term. It is a wise husbandman's word. We must plant out bravely and boldly to-day, if we are to have a growth that is to flower and thrive in future years.

Our relation to other religious bodies is, as has been already said, one of isolation; a feeling of suspicion on their part, a sense of ostracism on ours. Old memories tell us it was not always so. But let us look back a little, beyond the memory of the oldest. In the early days of the settlement of our cause, things were far more severe and trying in this respect than they are now. Think of the times when Church and State combined against us, times of penal Acts and vindictive prosecutions, when our ancestors and our spiritual harbingers were ejected, exiled, incarcerated. Some of the dread experiences of those times have been recounted in the preceding chapters. Our forerunners endured the worst that men could do to shake and bend them. Men saw that they meant to live, and learned to respect them accordingly. A Bishop drove us from the "publique meeting place," and compelled us to seek and make a habitation of our own. Another Bishop, after 120 years of our independent persistency, sent his donation to the building of the house in which we meet. A clergyman (William Bristow) fulminated against us for what he was pleased to term our "schism," though, as colonists from Scotland, we had never owned or owed allegiance to the Episcopal Establishment; later on, that same clergyman, in spite of Crombie's bold reply, came hither on a Sunday evening, and held the collecting plate, after a sermon for one of our charities. That was in the halcyon days, when religious animosities slept, and good men of all creeds felt the harmony of their work, in presence of common dangers. Then came the terrible outspokenness of this Unitarianism. Neighbours fell back; members deserted us; the timid and careless sought a shelter from odium in the safe places of the Establishment. Some, doubtless, were drawn from us by an awakened conviction that we were wrong. For there had been much indifference in those happy days; other things slept besides religious animosity; and the Unitarian avowal forced men to have real opinions on one side or the other.

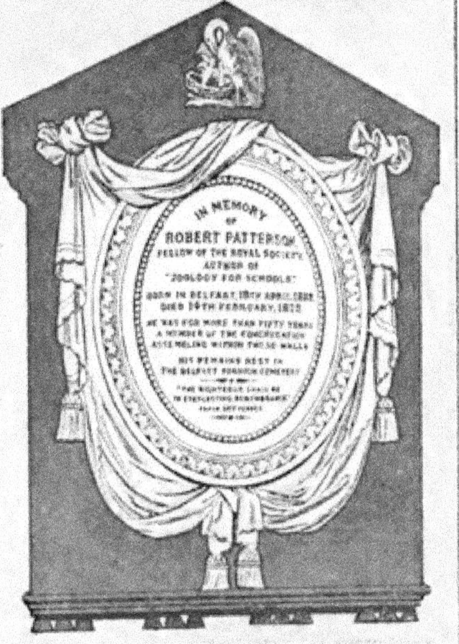

Memorial Tablet to Robert Patterson, F.R.S.

What was the meaning of this outspokenness which severed so many ties? It meant that we could no longer keep to ourselves, or restrain the inward pressure of imperative truth. We knew that to be serious, frank, and genuine, was better than being petted. Our avowed Unitarianism has not yet held its own for the period which intervened between the Bishop who persecuted, and the Bishop who patronised us. Yet, even now, people are beginning to appreciate, better than they once did, the true significance of our position, to recognise that we take our stand, not for a whim of being singular, nor because we have no religion, but because we set the Christ of God above the creeds of men, and conscience above conformity. Keep true to your own principles; let men see that they make you earnest, united, thorough, energetic, benevolent; and they will hold out the hand by-and-by.

The root of all success lies in personal qualities, and in their persistent application to some definite end. Our end and aim, as a congregation, is to spread the Kingdom of God, to diffuse the spirit of Christ, to deepen the power of religion. We cannot do this, unless first we have that Kingdom in our hearts, obey that spirit in our lives, feel that power in our own souls. Personal religion is, beyond all things else, the one great need. Our ancestors were men of courage, for they were men of faith, men of power inasmuch as they were men of prayer. In deep distresses their hearts were full of joy; the praises of God were on their lips, because the sense of His mercies filled their souls. They followed the simple word of Christ, through difficulty and danger and temptation, through good report and ill, because they knew in whom they believed. There is no other way for us than their way. We have outgrown the measure of their thoughts; but their spirit, their example, their devoutness, their sincerity, the enthusiasm of their allegiance to truth and goodness, their self-surrender to God, in the love of Christ, these are their imperishable bequests. Taught of the Lord through them, we have to transmit the lesson to those that shall come after us, that great may be the peace of our children; that so, in days to come, they who shall worship in our places when we are gathered to our fathers, may forget our mistakes, and take no pattern by our shortcomings, but sometimes remember our aspirations and our hopes, and, cleaving fast to whatsoever things are true, honourable, just, and pure, may still, when we are dust, "offer up spiritual sacrifices, acceptable to God, through Jesus Christ."

Alexander Gordon, M.A.

DATES.—Crombie's Essay on Church Consecration, 1777. Our Hymn-book, first edition, 1801; second edition, 1818. Congregational Library founded, 1838. Sunday School begun, 1838. Day School established, 1838. Organ introduced, 1853; new Organ, 1856. Domestic Mission, 1853. Minister's Library, 1868. Mission Fund of Nonsubscribing Association, 1881. Centennial celebration, 1883.

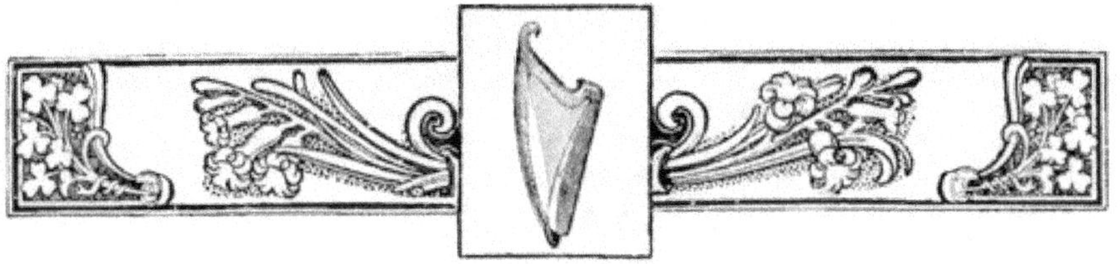

LIST OF MINISTERS

1. JOHN BAIRD ... ... 1642—1646.

[Came to Ireland as chaplain to the Earl of Argyle's regiment. Reid thinks that in 1646 he was installed to the charge of the congregation of Dervock, in the Route.]

2. ANTHONY SHAW ... ... 1646—1649.

[A Scotch divine. Graduated at Edinburgh, 17th April, 1639. Licensed by Stranraer Presbytery, 12th March, 1645. Ordained at Belfast, Sept., 1646. Became minister of Colmonell, Scotland, in 1649, and was deprived for nonconformity, 1st Oct., 1662. He was indulged in 1672, and preached in the Abbey Church, Paisley. On 2nd Aug., 1683, and again on 10th Jan., 1684, he was imprisoned, and his indulgence declared void; he was soon released, on finding caution, but bound to exercise no ministry. He died before 20th September, 1687, aged about 68.

3. —— READ ... ... about 1650.

[Nothing is definitely known of this minister. During the Commonwealth, the Presbyterian divines were superseded in Belfast by Independent and Baptist preachers. The regular succession of ministers begins with the next name.]

4. WILLIAM KEYES ... ... 1660—1673.

[A native of England. During the Commonwealth he held the rectory of Heswall, Cheshire. He is said to have removed to Dublin, and to have become minister at Glaslough, Co. Monaghan, before 1660. At the Restoration, he was one of the Presbyterian deputation sent with an Address to Charles II. Removed to Carrickfergus, and ministered there and at Belfast. Soon after this he was banished to Galway, but returned in 1664. The original meeting-house is believed to have been erected in his time (about 1668) in North Street, near the North Gate. On 19th February, 1672, he was ordered by the Antrim Meeting to fix his residence in Belfast. From July to December, 1673, he was sent to supply at Bull Alley, Dublin, and had a call to that congregation. His removal from Belfast was opposed by commissioners of our congregation—viz., William Muir, Michael Briggart, and John Briggart. On 8th April, 1673, he was called to Plunket Street, Dublin, and this removal was confirmed by the Antrim Meeting, in spite of the opposition of the Belfast commissioners, Anderson and Chalmers. He died in Dublin about 1693. His son Jonathan was educated for the ministry.]

5. PATRICK ADAIR ... ... 1674—1694.

[Third son of Rev. John Adair, of Genoch, Galloway. An eye-witness of the scene in the Edinburgh High Church, 23rd July, 1637, when stools were flung at the Dean and Bishop, on the introduction of the Service-book. Ordained minister of Cairncastle, 7th May, 1646, and demitted thence to Belfast, 13th Oct., 1647. Died 1694. Author of *True Narrative of the Rise and Progress of the Presbyterian Government in the North of Ireland.* He married, first, his cousin Jean (d. 1675), second daughter of Sir Robert Adair, of Ballymena; second, Elizabeth Anderson (née Martin). He left four sons—William (ordained at Ballyeaston 1681, removed to Antrim 1690, and died 1698), Archibald, Alexander, and Patrick (minister at Carrickfergus, died June, 1717), and a daughter Helen. For further particulars of Adair, see *Dictionary of National Biography*, edited by Leslie Stephen, vol. i., 1885, and references there.]

N.B.—At the time of Adair's appointment, SAMUEL BRYAN preached in Belfast as Presbyterian chaplain to the Donegal family. Bryan had been Fellow of Peterhouse, and Vicar of Allesley, Warwickshire; he was ejected in 1662, and had been imprisoned six months in Warwick gaol for preaching at Birmingham, before he obtained the post of household chaplain to Arthur, first Earl of Donegal, who, in his will (dated 17th March, 1674), left him £50 a year for four years, besides his salary. From 1684 to 1688, THOMAS EMLYN, the English Presbyterian chaplain of the Countess of Donegal, preached on Sunday evenings in the Hall of the Castle, Belfast, and occasionally at other times in the Parish Church. Emlyn was not in communion with Adair; his patroness had been attached to Rev. W. Keyes, and was displeased at his removal.

6. JOHN M'BRIDE ... ... 1694—1718.

[A native of Ireland, born probably in 1651, and educated at Glasgow, where he entered in 1666 as "Johannes M'Bryd, Hybernus," and graduated, 15th July, 1673. Ordained, in 1680, minister of Clare, County Armagh. Having left Ireland, he became minister of Borgue, near Kirkcudbright, in 1688. He was called to Ayr in 1691, but the Presbytery would not translate him. In 1692, he was a member of the General Assembly of the Scottish Church. He was installed at Belfast, 3rd Oct., 1694. His influence obtained from the Donegal family the lease of the site in Rosemary Lane, on which the Meeting-house was built in the early part of his ministry. Moderator of Synod, 1697. Though no Jacobite, became a Nonabjuror in 1703, *i.e.*, refused to make oath that the Pretender was not the son of James II. In 1704 he gifted some books to the Library of Glasgow College. Fled to Scotland in the winter of 1705-6, and preached in Glasgow. Returned to Belfast 1708, but was again obliged to fly in 1711, returning in 1714. Died 21st July (buried 23rd July), 1718. Author of a synodical Sermon, and three anonymous works in vindication of Presbyterians, including *A Sample of jet-black Pr——tic Calumny*, 1713. Prepared students for the ministry. Many stories of his caustic humour are current. His son, Robert M'Bride, was minister of Ballymoney. His grandson, Admiral John M'Bride, brought over Princess Charlotte in 1760, to marry George III. His great-grandson, John David M'Bride, D.C.L., Principal of Magdalen Hall, Oxford, died 21st January, 1868, aet. ninety. The ill-starred genius, Edgar Allan Poe, was a descendant of M'Bride.

From a private manuscript, written early in this century, the following curious particulars of M'Bride's second flight (wrongly dated, however, in 1709) are extracted. "Being a Non-juror, an order was issued to seize his person. Of this he had private information, and made his escape in the night, disguised. The guard who was placed on the Long Bridge, being one of his parishioners, though he knew him, permitted him to pass. This was in the winter. The night being dark, and the weather tempestuous, he was obliged to shelter himself in a field in Ballymacarret, not far from the bridge. On account of frequent watchings for many nights previous to this, he was overcome with fatigue; and, happy to escape from the grip of those who wished to imprison him, he went into an adjoining field, where he fell asleep. On awaking, he found himself benumbed with cold, and, rubbing his hands to promote circulation, he rubbed off his finger a valuable gold ring, which he never recovered. Next morning he proceeded to Donaghadee, and from thence to Glasgow, where he remained three years, and was offered the professorship of Divinity, which he refused, as he hoped and wished to return to his congregation in Belfast, which he did, immediately after the death of Queen Anne." "The morning after his escape, Mr. Warring, the Sovereign of the town [incorrect; William Warring was Sovereign in 1669 and 1670; the Sovereign in 1710 and 1711 was Roger Haddock], having received an order to apprehend him, came to his house, and after a very strict search, not finding him, was so zealous in the cause in which he was engaged, that from disappointment in not having it in his power to render the state a singular service, and to have his name recorded to posterity, on finding his picture *only*, hanging against a wall in his bedchamber, he thrust his rapier through the cambric band. N.B.—At the time of Mr. M'Bride's residence in Glasgow, he gave orders for his furniture [in Belfast] to be sold by auction, and by mistake his picture [portrait] was sold, and purchased by one of his parishioners. Some years afterwards, it was exposed to sale at an auction of this parishioner, when, by accident, Mr. John Rainey, of Greenville, Co. Down, seeing and knowing it, purchased it, and presented it to Mrs. Dyatt, of Belfast, daughter to Mr. M'Bride." [This portrait is now the property of the congregation, and bears still the marks of the Sovereign's rapier.]

The manuscript further says: "The first account of the death of Queen Anne was brought to Belfast by express, on the morning when the doors of the meeting-houses were to be nayled up [Anne died on Sunday, 1st August, 1714, the very day on which the Schism Act was to come into effect; in Ireland, where there was no Toleration Act, the passing of the Schism Act led to fresh outrages on Presbyterian liberties; the Meeting-houses at Antrim, Downpatrick, and Rathfriland were actually nailed up], to Isaac M'Cartney, merchant, who came to communicate it to Mr. Lenox, merchant, at a very early hour, daybreak. On hearing this news some hours after, Robert M'Bride, a youth living in Belfast, and son of the Rev. John [Robert] M'Bride, afterwards pastor in Ballymoney, and father of the late Admiral M'Bride, wishing to inform some of his friends of the pleasing news, mounted an old sorry-looking jade of his father's, and on his journey was met and accosted by a high churchman, thus, 'Hey, youngster, I suppose you and your mare are Presbyterians: she is so lean and meagre, and her ears hanging down, and you much in the same puritanical plight. Though I pity you, you deserve what you have got.' 'I thank you, sir,' replied the boy; 'but my mare will prick up her ears anon, and fling at all rough riders, since we know that Queen Anne is dead.' 'From whence have you the news?' asked the other, aghast. 'Go,' said he, 'to Mr. M'Cartney and Mr. Lenox, and they can inform you.'"

The manuscript also states that John M'Bride's "remains are interred in the old churchyard of Belfast [? St. George's], under a red marble tombstone, whereon are his coat of arms [motto: "Scopus vita Christus"], and the following inscription [not now to be seen either at Shankill or St. George's]:—

Reverendi admodum Dni Johannis M'Bride, V.D.M., ossa suscipit hoc marmor; viri omnigena eruditione eximii. Anno 1680, Claræ sacris initiatus est; ecclesiam Christi tam Borgæ quam Glasguæ in Scotia, diligenter instituit. A° 1694, ecclesiæ presbyterali in hac urbe designatus est. Summa fidelitate ac utilitate pastorale officium peragens, pastorem evangelii omnibus exoptatissimum se præbuit. Lugente ecclesia tanti viri obitum, in Christo requievit Julii 21 A° 1718, ætatis suæ 68."

Perhaps "pastorem" is a mistranscription for "præconem."]

7. JAMES KIRKPATRICK, D.D., 1706—1708.

[A native of Scotland. Son of Rev. Hugh Kirkpatrick, minister of Lurgan and Ballymoney. Educated at Glasgow. Ordained, 7th August, 1699, minister of Templepatrick; demitted thence to Belfast, 24th Sept., 1706, as colleague to the absent M'Bride, and with a view to form a new congregation. On 18th June, 1706, M'Bride had written from Stranraer that if there were 3,000 persons in the congregation, there must be two Meeting-houses, and two distinct congregations. The second Meeting-house was built 1708, and Kirkpatrick became its first minister. Kirkpatrick was the first Belfast minister who upheld the principle of Nonsubscription. In later life, he successfully combined a physician's practice with his pastoral duties, being M.D. as well as D.D. Died 1744. Author of three Sermons, and six anonymous works, including *An Historical Essay upon the Loyalty of Presbyterians*, 1713.]

8. THOMAS MILLING ...1714—1719 (?)

[Assistant to M'Bride.]

9. SAMUEL HALIDAY, M.A. ... 1720—1739.

[Son of Rev. Samuel Haliday of Raphoe and Ardstraw. Educated in Scotland and at Leyden. Licensed, after subscribing the Westminster Confession, 1706, at Rotterdam, and ordained 1708, without subscription, at Geneva. Present at Salters' Hall Conferences, 1719. Called to Belfast, 1719, and installed 28th July, 1720. The opposition to his installation, without subscription, led to the erection of the Third Congregation, Belfast, 1722; and to the formation of the Antrim Presbytery, 1725, which was excluded from the General Synod, 1726. Died 5th March, 1739. Author of a Sermon and four other works. His son Alexander became the most eminent physician in Ulster.]

10. THOMAS DRENNAN, M.A. 1736—1768.

[Born in Belfast, 25th Dec., 1696. Graduated at Glasgow, 1715. Licensed in Belfast, 1726. Ordained at Holywood, where he had pupils, June, 1731. Installed at Belfast, 1736. Died 14th February, 1768.]

11. ANDREW MILLAR, M.A....1745 (?)—1749.

[Assistant to Drennan; removed to Summerhill, Co. Meath, where he was ordained, 1749.]

12. CLOTWORTHY BROWN ...1749—1756 (?)

[Ordained minister of Ballinderry, Feb., 1746. Removed to Ballymore, 1747, where he was installed by the Antrim Presbytery. Assistant to Drennan.]

13. JAMES MACKAY ... ... 1756—1781.

[Ordained minister of Bangor, 15th Nov., 1732. Removed to Clonmel, 1740. Installed at Belfast, 1756. Died 22nd Jan., 1781. Author of Funeral Sermons for Drennan and for Gilbert Kennedy, minister of the Second Congregation.]

14. JOHN BEATTY ... ... 1768—1770.

[Minister of Holywood, but acted also as Mackay's assistant.]

15. JAMES CROMBIE, D.D., ... 1770—1790.

[Son of James Crombie, mason, of Perth, where he was born, 6th December, 1730. Educated at St. Andrews and Glasgow. Licensed by Strathbogie Presbytery, 8th June, 1757. Schoolmaster at Rothiemay. Ordained minister of Llanbryd, Co. Elgin, 11th Sept., 1760. Demitted thence to Belfast, 4th Dec., 1770. Made D.D. of St. Andrews, Sept., 1783. Founded the Belfast Academy, 1786. Died 1st March, 1790. He was married, 23rd July, 1774, to Elizabeth Simpson, who survived till 1824. See further particulars in *Disciple*, April, 1883.]

16. WILLIAM BRUCE, D.D. ... 1790—1841.

[Born 30th July, 1757. Educated at Trinity College, Dublin, Glasgow, and Warrington. Ordained minister of Lisburn, 1775. Called to Strand Street, Dublin, 24th March,

1782. Called to Belfast, 11th March, 1790, where he succeeded Crombie as Principal of the Belfast Academy, 1st May, 1790. Retired from active duty, 21st Jan., 1831. Died 27th Feb., 1841. Author of five works, including *Sermons on the Study of the Bible and the doctrines of Christianity*, 1824. See further in *Dict. of Nat. Biog.* and Rev. Classon Porter's *Seven Bruces.*]

17. WILLIAM BRUCE, A.B. ... 1812—1868.

[Son of the preceding. Born 16th Nov., 1790. Educated at Trinity College, Dublin, and Edinburgh. Ordained at Belfast, 3rd March, 1812, as colleague to his father. Professor of Greek and Latin in the Belfast Academical Institution, 1822. Retired from active duty 21st April, 1867. Died 25th Oct., 1868. See further in *Dict. of Nat. Biog.* and Rev. Classon Porter's *Seven Bruces.*]

18. JOHN SCOTT PORTER ... 1832—1880.

[Son of Rev. William Porter, A.M., of Newtownlimavady, where he was born, 31st Dec., 1801. Educated in Belfast. Licensed October, 1825, by the Bangor Presbytery. Ordained minister of Carter Lane, London, 2nd March, 1826. Called to Belfast, 11th Sept., 1831, as assistant and successor to Dr. Bruce, and installed 2nd February, 1832. Professor of Theology, 1838; also of Hebrew, 1851. Died 5th July, 1880. Author of publications, including the *Discussion* with Dean Bagot, 1834, and the *Principles of Textual Criticism*, 1848. He was married, 8th Oct., 1833, to Margaret, eldest daughter of Andrew Marshall, M.D. His eldest son is the Right Hon. Andrew Marshall Porter, Master of the Rolls. For further particulars of Mr. Porter, see *Memorial Addresses and Sermons*, 1880.]

19. ALEXANDER GORDON, M.A. 1877—

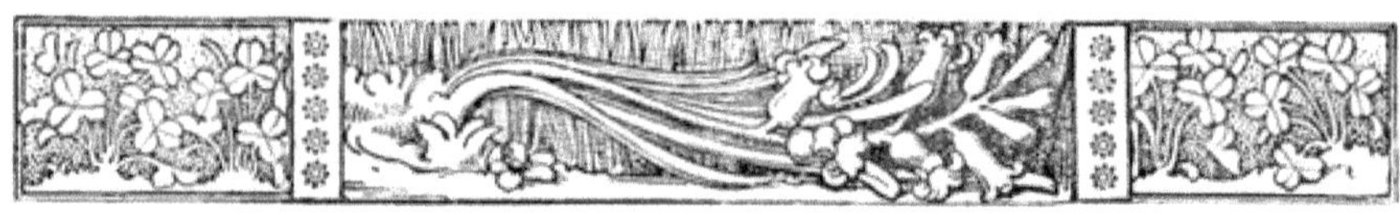

BAPTISMAL REGISTER

[The first volume of the Baptismal Register was missing as far back as the year 1790, and has been several times inquired after by advertisement and otherwise, without result. The existing book, still in use, bears the following title: "Register of Births in the old congregation of Protestant Dissenters in Belfast commencing April the first 1756 Vol IId" A few leaves are lost from the beginning; and the first three surviving leaves have been cut or torn. Up to the year 1790, the entries were made, after the baptism, either by the sexton or by the parent, and are often exceedingly illiterate. From 6th May, 1790, the entries were made by the minister. What follows is a literal copy of the earliest remaining portion of the Register.]

1757

Blow (Arthur) of Daniel Blow, born friday the 22d July 1757 and baptized by the Revd Mr Thomas Drenan on Monday following.

Wallace (Robert) of Joseph Wallace Born on Thursday 21st July 1757 & baptized by the Reverend Thos Drenan On the Sunday following

Mussenden (Francis Thomas) of Wm Mussenden born the 24th August 1757

Geattey (James) of Mr Geattey of peters Hill marchent was Born the 26 Junry 1757

Halledey (Alexander) of Haledey Sandleen born the 28 of Julcy, 1757

Knard Sarey of Andrew Knard from the whit hous born Julcy 30

Starlen (Richeart) of Willean Starlen from the falls born the 1 octebr 1757

megines (Ketren) of Laglean megines labrear from Stranmiles was born the 17 of Sebtembr 1757

willeams (James) of Ries willeams born the 2 of octr 1757

Ros (griseal) of James Ros born the 29 of octbr 1757

Magee (Thomas) of James Magee Printer, born Thursday ye 27th of October, 1757.

. . . .

........Doleway born the 23 of febry 1758

Sinclaire . William Fredk of Thoms Sinclaire born Fryday 24th June 1758. & baptizd by Mr Drenan same day

Douglass Anne born July the 24th 1758 of Willm Douglass—Baptized by Mr Drennon Wednesday 26th 1758

Doaren John of Thomeas Doaren of mellon was born the 26 of Jun 1758

Logean / Isbell of Jeames Logean of blleygomerten born July the 2 1758

Litell / John of Robt Litell of Carmoney born novr the 5 1758

Dllape / Ann of Sanders Dllape of the falles born Sept the 15 1758

Kalwall Willeam of Robt Kalwall merchent born Sept the 1 1758

Dasion / Hweu of Jeames Dasion of Carmoney born nofmbr 23 1758

Dasion thomeas of James Dason born April 5 1760

Hamltion / mearey of James Hamltion brekliear born Nofr 23 1758

Blear / Bricas of James Blear Shou mekaer born Decmr 8

Caroline of Will Mussenden born the 23d day of Decemr 1758

Blow (Mary) of Daniel Blow, born friday the 22d of Decemr 1758 and baptised by the Revd Mr Thomas Drennan the Wednesday following

. . . .

........Drennan the friday following

Nikell / George of Robt Nikell born 30 March in the Contey of Doien

Carnahan / Samuel of Samuel Carnahan farmer born the 9th of Agust 1756

Carnahan / mary of Samuel Carnahan farmer born the 14 of march 1759

Getty (John) of James Getty born Wednsday the 18th April & Babtised by The Revd Mr Drennin the 25th

Wallace (Grace) of Joseph Wallace, Born Wednesday The 23d May, 1759 & baptiz'd by the Revd Thos Drenna the 27th

m'Nealey (Alexr) of Hwe m'Nealey Born the 2 May 1759

Gordan (John) of Robt Gordan Marchant Born the 17 of March 1756

Gordan (David) and (Ursula) of Robt Gordan Marchant born the 31 of May 1759

Martean (Joseph) of Joseph Marten of Carmony born the 23 Jun 1759

Sloan / mearey of James Sloan Copear born the 6 of octr 1759

Sinclaire, Esther of Thomas Sinclaire born, Sunday 13 January 1760.

Clark margaret of Arthar Clark born the 12th of march 1757

Clark William Fredrick of Arthar Clark was born December the 15th 1758

. . . .

1765

Starleng / James of James Starleng born the 19 of Septembr 1765

Willson Elsebth Saley of Robt Willson born the 30 of Septmbr 1765

Morsion / John of Samcall Morsion born the 1 of Novembr 1765

Kirker / Marget of Wille...... born the 25 fevery 1766

Elder (Robt Higinbothom) of Thos Elder Born 15th January 1766 Babtiz'd By the Revd John Elder

Seales / John of James Seales Born the 9 of march 1766

Brown (John Meredith) of William Brown Born 11 March 1766 Baptised by the Revd Thos Drennon

Macaxell / John of James macexell born the 18 of maich 1766

Balley / Jarge of Tomeas Balley born the 26 of April 1766

Logean Jamias of Wilam Logan born the 20 of Jun 1766

Lucinda of William Mussenden born at Bath in England . April. 25th 1764

Arthur Johnston Mussenden of Willm Mussenden . born. August. ye 26th 1765

Saml of John Galt Smith born 15 May 1766

Catherine of Hugh Donnoldson 20th September 1766 Baptized by the Rev'd James M Kay

Elizth of Henry M Kedy born 1st October 1766

Stuirt William of Arter Stuirt ...... 8 of Nofbr 1766

..................st Decer 1766

..................laire born Taursday morning......... 67 baptizd by Mr Drenan 23d

Issabella of Thos Elder Born 4th Febry 1767 Babtized By the Revd Mr Drenan

Mary . of John Galt Smith born 2 May 1767

William of Hay Bron born the 10 of Juley 1767

Marget of Thomes Gustes born the 13 of Septr 1767 [Gustes = Justice]

Ann of John oNiell born Septr the 26 1767

Jean / of James Logen born octr the 8 1767

Brown / William Brown of Willm Brown Siptember the 13—1767

James of James Starling of the fales born the 17 of octber 1767 and Babisted by the Revd Mr Drenn

Hughes Stephson was Born Jen'y 17th 1768 of James Hughes

Ewrdy of Alexandr Dlap born the April 2 1768

Sunday May 15th—1768 Wm Dawson of Monkstown in the parish of Carmoney, his Daughter was. Babtized this Day, by the Name of Agnes. & was Born the 9th Inst

James Miller the son of Isaac Miller in town mercht Born ye 3d Day march 1765
John of John Defsion born Jun the 5 1768 helegomrtion [Defsion = Davison]
Ann of Henry M'Kedy born 18th May 1768
Genet of Wileam morlend born the 8 of July 1768
Cathrine / of Thos Elder Born the 14th July 1768 —Babtiz'd By the Revd Mr Drenan
Ross of Thoms Defsion born Agest the 21 1768
Marget of John M'Kulliem born Agest the 29 1768
Robt of Thomes Wilsiom born September the 21 1768
Arthur / of James Park born the 30th Octor 1768
Valentine / of John Galt Smith the 26 Sept. 1768
Thoms of thoms Dorean born Jnrey the 25 1768
Mearey of Alexander Dlap born May the 6 1769
Callwall (John) of Robt Callwell born April 7 1757
Wm Callwell born Sept 1 : 1758
Jane Callwell born January 11 1763
Robt Callwell born May 31 1764
Nathl Callwell born March 11 1766
James Callwell born Nor 20 1767
Elizabeth Callwell born May 10 1769
Frances Callwell June 11th — 1772
John of Neal. white born Septembr the 29 1766
Marget | of Neal. white born may the 17 1769
John of Wileam m Clee born Agest the 3 1769
Willem of John Dlap born Agest the 28 1769

. . . .

marey of James Haml'tion born Sept the 18 1769
John Galt. / of John Galt Smith born 23 March 1770
marget of Wilcam Dawson born the 6 of may — 1770
James of Robt Herdman born the 30 of Apriel 1770
Thomas of Willeam Homeas born the 17 of Jun 1770
Goish / of James Sarling born the 21 of June 1770 [Goish-Joyce]
Andrey of John m'Kuilliem born the 2 of Noumbr 1770
Elizabeth / of John Gregg born 8th May 1771
Wileam Gregg of Robt Herdman born the 15 of July 1771
Mary Ann / of Jno Galt Smith born 27 July 1771—
mary Jane of Isaac Miller born 23d October 1771
Jane / of William Irvin born 11 Sepmr 1771 —
Agnus (Murlin) born April 7 1772

John of Defed Bodell born the 12 of April 1772
Willeam of Willeam Logean born the 17 of may 1772
Agness of James Cumming born the 26 of may 1772
John of John Gillion born the 29 of may 1772
Deneall of Sameall Morsean born the 7 of June 1772
Marget of John Dlap of the fales born the 11 of June 1772
Elizebeth / of Joseph M'Cammon Shoe Maker Born the 17th of June 1755 five
Joseph / of Joseph M'Cammon Dito Born the 20 of March 1763
hannah / of Josh M'Cammon dito Born the 22 of December 1765
Georg / of Joseph M'Cammon dito Born the 22 of March 1769
Thamos / of Joseph M'Cammon dito Born the 14 of June 1772 and Baptised by Mr Marshel of Baleyclaire
Sarey of Wileam Stueart boren the 14 of Juley 1772 and Baptised by the Revd mr Cromey &c
William / of Robt M'Cleary born 16 July 1772 Bapticed by the Reverend Mr James Crummey
Thos & Richard Born 8 Jany 1774
Robt M'Cleary Born 29 Decr 1774
James of Wileam Loggan born the 27 of July 1772
Mary (of Henry M'Kedy) born 5th June 1772 Seventy two
William of John Galt Smith born 26 Octr 1772
Robt of James Hameltion born the 19 of nofr — 1772
Thomas of James Starlen of the falls born the
Jean of Huee Bron born January the 24 1773 and Bapised by the Revd mr Cromey
Hue of willeam mertion born febr the 28 1773
James of Ramsey born april the 12 1773
Robt of Robrt Bron Born the 22 of may 1773
Ester of Allaxendr Sharp born the 25 of may 1773 And Rabistisd by Revd James Cromey
Ann of Gorge Rogers born the 30 may 1773
Sebaston of Robt Herdman born the 3 of June 1773
Nifen of Thomes willesom born the 27 of may 1771
Cristfor of Thomes willesom boren the 27 of Sept 1773

Nansey of Thomes parkhiell born the 8 of octber 1773

James patrick Withrespon of James Withrespon boren the 14 of octber 1773 and baptised by the Revd mr mckie

Jane Hathron of Ewardr Stuert boren the 27 of march 1774

marey of Defed Bodell boren the 29 of march 1774

Elenor of Henry M Kedy, born 28 March 1774

Margaret. of Jno Galt Smith born 2 June 1774

Egnas of Wiml Teate born 22 June 1774

David of James Park born 27th June 1774

Jane, of Hercules Heyland born 4th Septr 1774 —Baptized by Mr Crombie—

Jennet, of John Holmes Junr born — 9th Octr 1774

Richeart of John Dinin born the 26 of march 1775

James, of James Crombie born 19th March 1775, baptized 26th of said Month by the Revd James Mackay—

Mary of George Young Born May ye 15th Baptized Said Day By the Revd Mr James Crombie

David of David Tomson Born—Sepr 22nd 1774 Baptized by the Revd Jas Crombie

Ivan (?) of James Kirk born the 24 of may 1775 and bapidzid by the evd mr James mackey

Mary of Robert Herdman Born 5 Septmber 1774 baptized by the Revd Jams Crombie

Jane of Allexander Sharp born the 25 of July 1775 and bapissed by the Revd James Crombie

Mary of Allexander Kentoul Born the 24 of Aprile 1775—and Baptised Augst 16 1775 by— the Revd Mr. James AberCrombie

Elisbeth of Defed Bodell born the 24 of Agust 1775

Elizabeth, of John Holmes Junr born, Wednsday 11th Octr 1775 & Baptized The 13th of same Month by Revd James Crombie—

Lyle (Thomas) of Musenden Lyle born 15th August 1775 and baptized next day by Revd Jas Crombie

Cochran (John) of John Cochran born Friday 22 day of May 1772 and baptizd Monday following by the Revd Wm Nevin Downpatrick (Joanna) of John Cochran born Mond Septr 27th 1773 and baptizd by the Revd James Crombie

Wileam of Robt Broen boren De'mber the 6 1775

James of John Shenkes born Nofmbr the 9 1774

Gilbert of John Shenkes born Jnunrey 29 1776

James of Alexr Dlaep born nofmber 20 1773

Jane of Alexandr Dlap born fabrey the 13 1776

John of John Defsion born fabrey 15 1776

Isabela m'Cleary Daughter of Robt M Cleary Born 8 Decr 1775 Baptised by the Revd Mr Crumbie

Joseph of James Crombie born the 1st of March 1776, baptized by the Revd James Mackay—

John of Will: Rainey born the 14th March 1776 was Baptised by the Revd J: Crumbie

Henry Johnston, of Henry M Kedy born 31st March 1776 Baptized by the Revd Jas Crombie

Marget of James Roney born Apriel the 20 1766 And Baptized by the Revd Jab Crombot

Alexander of John Clide born Juley the 24 1776

Alexander Faulkonder of Belfast

Robert	Faulkonder born June—11—1758
Elisabeth	Faulkonder born July 10—1760
Serah	Faulkonder born May 24—1764
Esibalah	Faulkonder born September 21—1766
Alexander	Faulkonder born December 11—1769
Rogers	Faulkonder born August—23—1775

John of James Starlen born June the 2 and baptized by the Red mr mackay 1776

Ewedeard of Eward Stuart born Jun the 4 1776

Burden (Mary Ann) of John Burden was born in Lisburn the 30th of Novemr 1775 and baptized the Sunday following by the Revd George Kennedy Minister in that Parish.

Lyle (Mussenden) of Mussenden Lyle was born the 18th Jany 1777 & Baptized the next day by the Revd James Crumbie

William M'Cleary of Robt M'Cleary Baker Born 16 July 1772

Thos and Richard Born 8 January — 1774

Robt M'Cleary Born 29 Decr — 1774

Isabela M'Cleary Born 8 Decr — 1775

Robt M'Cleary Born 5 febry — 1777

All Baptised By the Revd Mr Jas Crumbie

James, of John Holmes Junr — Born Sunday 9th febry 1777 & Baptized the 13th of Same Month, by The Revd Jas Crombie

Wm Simson, of Jas Crombie—born Sunday the 16th of febry 1777 and baptized the 23d of same month by the Revd Jas Mackay

Andrew of Efream M'Docall born April the 7— 1777 Baptised by the Revd Jams Cromibe

Ketren of Willeam Hanley born Genry the 3 1778 and Baptised by the Revd Mr James Cromibe

Lyle (Thomas) of Thomas Lyle born on friday 23rd Janr 1778 & baptised the 25th of said month by the Revd Jas Crombie

Nansey of Edwartt petecru born the 13 of febrey 1778—baptised by the Revd Jas Crombie

Jean of John Diemen boren Febrey the 18 1778 and Baptised by the Revd mr m'kiee

Sarey of John m'Gineas born march the 25 1778 and Bapised by the Revd mr m'kiee

James of Joseph m Krea born April the 9 1776

John of Joseph m'krea born April the 1 1778 and bapised by the Revd mr Crombie

Elibes of John Defson born Apil the 3 1778—

Isabella Maria of John Brown born the 1st of April & baptised the 15th of the same Month 1778 by the Revd Mr James Crombie

Briget of James Roney boren May 20 1778 a baptised by the Revd mr Leard 1778

Henry—of John Holmes Junr born Wednesday the 3d of June 1778 & Baptized the 7th of Same Month—by Revd James Crombie

Catharine Hellen—of the same—Born 4 July & Babtized by Mr Crombie the Augt

Hugh of James Crombie born the 9th of September 1778 baptised by the Revd James Mackay

Henry Johnston of Henry M'Kedy born 31st March 1776 Baptized by Revd James Crombie

Kathne of Henry M Kedy born 26 March 1778 Baptized by Revd James Crombie

Charlott. of Jno Galt Smith born the 16 Novr 1778 Baptized by the Revd Mr James Crombie

Eweard Bron born the of the 15 1779

Alexnder of John Klied born Agest the 2 1777

John of John Klied born march the 22 1779 and bapised by Revd mr James Crnbie

Mearey of John m'Gineas born octber the 6 1779 and bapised by Revd James Crnbie

Wileam of John Watt born octber the 21 1779 and bapised Revd James Crombie

Robert of Alexandr Dleap born febrey the 6 1780

Wileam of Alexander Dleap born Decembr 9 1782

James Mecrory of wileam hanley Was babtised 12 of Martch—1780

Robrt of John Dinean born octber the 19 1780

Elisebth of Vileam hanley born April the 11 1782

wiliam of John wilson was Born the 17 September 1782

Sarey of Dafed Bodeal born July the 1—1783

Martha Daughter of Wm Rainey was Born July 19th 1778 Eight Baptised by the Revd J. Crombie

Wm Henry Son of Wm Rainey was Born Apl 22d 1780 Eighty Baptised by the Revd J: Crombie

marthey of James Roney born July the 8 1780 and bapttised by the Red m Leard

Thomes of Dafed Bodell bern July the 24 1780

Edwd Jones of Jn Galt Smith born the the (*sic*) 15th Augst 1780 Baptized by the Revd J Crombie

Mary Elizabeth Crombie of Jas Crombie born 26 May 1781. Bapt. by Mr Beattie

James / of David Dunn, born Thursday—11th July 1782—and Baptized the Thursday following by the Revd James Crombie

Robert . of John Galt Smith born 20 Novr 1782

David of David Logon Born the 2 of January 1783

Hugh of James Rony Born the 2 of Janur 1783

Maria / of James Holmes, born 17 June 1783 and baptizd the Monday following by the Revd James Crombie.

James / of Wm Magee, born 16th September, 1783 —and baptized the 25th of the same, by the Revd James Crombie

Sarey of John Dinean born octber the 21 1783

Uiliam of Richard Getggood Born December the 5 1783 and Baptised By the Revd James Crombie

Marget of wiliam Logan Born December the 8 1783

Margarett /'of David Dunn born Sunday the 4th. January 1784 and baptized the Sunday following by the Revd James Crombie

Isbell of Huie Cples born the 9 of fbry 1784

John of Alexander Sharp bor'n march the 12 1784

Charles / of Alexr Sutherland . born Saturday the 24th of Apl 1784. and Baptized the Wednesday following by the Revd Jas Crombie

William / of Wm Magee born the 2d September in ye year 1784 and Baptized the 9th of said Month, by the Revd James Crombie

Elizabeth / of Henry Bamber Born Saturday the 28th of Augt 1784 and Baptized the 29th by the Revd James Crumbie

David of Wiliam Logon Born Janury the 7 1786 and Baptized by the Revd James Crumby

Elizabeth—of Thos Brown. born the 27th July 1782—

Sally, of the same—born the 27th October 1783.

John, of the same, born the 10th October 1784. all baptized by the Revd Mr Crombie

James of John wilson Born the 14 of May and Baptised by the Revd Jams Crumby 1785

James of wiliam stewrt Born the 29 of May and Baptised by the Revd James Crumby 1785

Elizabeth / of William Sinclaire born 17th June 1785 & baptized by the Revd Jas Crombie

Elonar of James Rony, Born Agust the 30 1785 and Baptsed by the Revd James Crunbe

Catherina of Thomas Savage born the 18th May 1785 & Baptized by the Revd James Crombie

Elizabeth / of Wm Magee, born 13th October, 1785 —baptized Thursday, 27th October by the Revd James Crombie

Margret of hugh sailes born the 16 of Decembr and Baptized by the Revd Mr James Bryson 1785

Thomas of Richard Getgood was Born the 7 of March 1786 and Baptized By the Revd Dr Crombie

Aun—of David Dunn born the fourth of April 1786 —and Baptized, the 8th following—by Revd James Crombie

John of John Dunn Born the 18 of July and Baptisd by the Revd Mr James Bryson

Isabella of Thos Brown born the 14th July 1786 and baptized the 31st of the same Month by the Revd Mr Bryson—

Catherine—of Wm Magee, born the 18th May 1787 —baptized the 27th of the same—by the Revd Jas Crombie

Eliza (of R Wallace) born 14th Decr 1787—bap-tiz'd 1st Jany '88 —by the Revd. James Crombie

Elanor Ann / of Wm Mylrea Born the 3d of Janyary 1788 And Babtised the 7th of same month By the Revd Jas Crombie

Elizebeth Agnes Daughter of Richard Getgood was Born Aug the 31 of 1787 and Baptized By the Revd Dr Crombie

Ellanah (?) of Alex Delap born the 15 of Janury 1778 and Bapt by the Revd James Crumby

Jane of Thos Brown born the 2d January 1788 and baptized the 13th of same Month by the Revd Doctor Crombie—

James of Jams Rony Born the 14 of April 1788 and baptised by the Revd James Cromby

Richard M Clur / son of Richard Getgood was Born November the 18 1788 and Baptized By the Revd James Bryson

Margaret, of James Carson Born Friday 6th June 1788 and Baptized the 15th following, By the Revd James Crombie

Samuel of Hugh Saill Born the 12 of Septmb and baptised by the Revd James Cromby

Jane—of Wm Magee, born Sunday 15th March 1789—babtized the 22d of the same by Doctor Crombie

William—of Thos Brown born on Thursday the 30th April 1789—baptized the 17th May following by Doctor Crombie

Thomas Dinnem Born 11 of July 1789

Ann of William Gordon Born march the 23d 1790 and baptised April the 7 by the Revd James Bryson

Frances—Daughter to Thos Brown born On Monday 24th May 1790. baptized the 13th June following by the Revd Dr Bruce—

Elizebeth Agnas Daughter of Richd Getgood Born the 11 of June 1790 and Baptized the 4 of July By the Revd Doctor Bruce

[This exhausts the earlier portion of the existing Baptismal Register. From 6th May, 1790, the Register of Baptisms has been duly kept by the Ministers. The irregularities and imperfections of the record printed above are apparent on the face of it. Its incompleteness may be estimated by the following circumstance. Between 6th May and 4th July, 1790, only *two* entries of baptisms by Dr. Bruce are recorded in the Register as kept by the sexton. But during this period Dr. Bruce baptised *eleven* infants, as shown by his own methodical entries, which begin on the leaf immediately following the last entry given above.]

FUNERAL REGISTER, 1712-1736

[This book was begun 10th June, 1712, but the page containing the first entries is lost. It contains 171 pages of Funeral Entries (the last being dated 19th October, 1736), and 58 pages of accounts connected with them. The entries to 29th July, 1718, are in the clerkly hand of Thomas Swendill, sexton of the First Congregation, to whose widow eight shillings was paid for the book, on 20th Oct., 1718. Swendill was succeeded as sexton by David Ferguson (till 5th Feb., 1720), and Ferguson by Samuel Pentland (or, as he writes his name, Samull Pentelan). The entries do not give the dates of deaths, but of burials, with an account of the mort cloths (or palls) and cloaks used at the funeral. These funeral trappings were originally the property of the First Congregation, and afterwards the joint property of the First and Second Congregations, and were lent on hire. The entries show that they were often let out for funerals in connection with other congregations, sometimes at considerable distances from Belfast. The following is an exact copy of the earliest extant page, omitting only some later scribblings.]

2.	Acct of what is Given out.	£ s d	ye Day and Month when paid.	£ s d
1712.	Caried over	9 . 12 . 6		
July : 12.	. Bealy Adam's his Wife's ffunnerall . Best Mar Cloath - - - - - - - - . to 1 Clocke - - - - - - -	... 7 . 6 ... 1 . 6	paid : July 21. 219.*	... 9 ...
16.	. mr William White Ship-Carpinter his ffunerall . pr Salt Jno Park—Best Mar Cloath - . to 11 Clockes at 1s: 6d: pr Clocke -	... 7 . 6 ... 16 . 6	paid : Janry : 10. 221.	1 . 4 ...
	. mr Jas Reed poathicarrey his Childes ffunnerall . to 1. Clocke - - - - - - - - - -	... 1 . 6	paid : July : 22. 219.	... 1 . 6
21.	. Thos Tayler plantation his ffunnerall . Cloath Mar Cloath - - - - - - -	2 . 6	paid : Agust : 4. 219	... 2 . 6
26.	. mr Jas ffarrly Dr his ffunnerall pr mrs mcBride . Best Mar Cloath - - - - - - - - . to 8 Clockes at 1s: 6d: pr Clocke - -	... 7 . 6 ... 12 ...	ffforgiven : June 15. 383.	

2.		Acct of what is Given out.	£ s d	ye Day & Month when paid.	£ s d
July	29.	. mr John Anderson Doctr his ffunnerall . Best Mar Cloath - - - - - - - - . to 14. Clockes at 1s: 6d: pr Clocke -	... 7 . 6 1 . 1 ...	paid : Agust : 4. 219.	1 . 8 . 6
	30.	. Heugh Agnew Couper his ffunnerall . Best Mar Cloath - - - - - - - - . to 3. Clockes at 1s: 6d: pr Clocke -	... 7 . 6 ... 4 . 6	paid : Agust : 4 219.	... 12 ...
	31.	. mr William Rodger Marchnt his . Mothers ffunneral—Best Mar Cloath . to 15 Clockes at 1s: 6d: pr Clocke -	... 7 . 6 1 . 2 . 6	paid : Agust : 9. 219.	1 . 10 . 0
Agust	2.	. mr Goudy Minister Belliwalter his . Son's ffunnerall pr mr John Cloug'ston . Childers Mar Cloath - - - - - - -	... 5 ...	paid : May . 6. 221.	... 5 ...
			16 : 4 . 6		

The prices were subsequently reduced, as appears from the subjoined entry of 5th December, 1716.

1716

Xbr 5. Memorandom this Day Both Session Meet Together & haue Concluded that ye pricess of ye Clockes & Mar Cloathes be as ffolloweth—viz.

Best Mar Cloath in Town	.........5.........in	ye Cuntrey	.........10.........	
Second Mar Cloath in Town	......3.........in	Ditto	.... 6.........	
Cloath Mar Cloath in Town	......2.........in	Ditto	.... 4.........	
Childers. Mar Cloath in Town	......2.........in	Ditto	.... 4.........	
Childes Mar Cloath in Town	......2.........in	Ditto	.... 4.........	
pr Clocke in ....in Town	......1.........in	Ditto	.... 2.........	

The lost page 1 contained eight entries, relating to the families of Samuel Smith, senr. (10th June, 1712), Carrouth (12th June), Rev. James Kirkpatrick (12th June), James Smith, senr. (18th June), John Shadges (19th June), Colinwood (28th June), John Reed, of the Plantation (7th July), and Orre (9th July).

In the following extracts (taken from page 3 onwards) the name, where no italic letter precedes, is that of the person buried. The italic letter shows what member of the family was buried, whether described as father, mother, brother, husband, wife, son, daughter, child, or grandchild (*c.s* is male child, *c.d* female child, *si* sister) of the person named. A comma has been inserted between the name and trade or place of abode.

1712

Agust. 3 *w* James Clark, Laberour

11 *c* mr John Shadgs, Marchnt

21 *w* John jordgan, Northstreet

Sept 1 *w* mr Robert Agnew, Mariner

4 *c.d* mr Heugh Dayet

6 mrs Ann Buttle, pr Mr George

9 *c* mr Androw Agnew, Couper

Sept 10 David Bucher, Barber

13 mr ogilbe, Minister in Learn, pr mr John mc Mun, Marchnt

14 *c* William mc Cree, Shew Maker

21 *c* Isaac Monipenny, Beaker

c William Liget, Weaver

22 *b* mr John young, junr

29 *c* mr Hennery Duncan

* These figures refer to the page in the statement of accounts later on.

Octr	11	c	Allexdr David'son
	12	c	mr Jas Stirling, Malster
	29	f	mr Robert Boyde
Nov:	4		George Dunlap, Beaker, Sener
	5		mr Thos orr, Minister in Cumber, pr mr Gilbert Moor, Marchnt
	8	c	mr John Kennidy, Cultra
	9	h	Widow Mathiss
	13	w	Archbald mc Mulin
	22	h	Widow Spear
	30		Doctr peacock, pr mr Sam: Smith, Sener
Xbr	15	w	mr Jas Smith, Sener
	28	c	mr John Armstrong, Marchnt
	29		mrs. Elener Hoge, Near Banger, pr mr Hennery Duncan
	30	c.d	mr William Dinn, Marchent
1712/3			
Janry:	3	d	mr Robert Millikin, Marchnt
	4	h	Widow mc Ilroy
			James Donnalson
	5	h	Widow Alexdr
	11		Edward Nowals, pr mr Sam: Smith, Sener
	12	m	mr Ross, at ye Lodge
	16	h	Widow Kearnss
	17		Widow Blear
		s	Mr John young, Sener
	19		Elez: Harbison, pr mr Sam: mc Clinto
	20		James Realy, Carpinter
	23		mr John Ross, Marchnt
	27	f	Heugh Glenhomes
	28	w	John Torbourn, Tabacco:
	29	s	James Hamilton, in Church-Lean
ffebery.	7	w	mr John Smith, Potter
	16	w	mr William Willey
		c	mr patterick Kennity
	17		mr Heugh Boyde, Marchnt, pr mr Sam: Smith, Sener
	24	w	Thos Clemanss, Carpinter
March	3	w	James Homes, Barber
	7	d	Widow Carther
	10		mr Heugh White, Banger, pr mr Jas mc Clewar, Marchnt
		w	John mc Gouan, juner, Milstreet
	13		mrs. White, pr mr Androw Hutcheson
	14		mr John Begly, at Antrim, pr Jas Brown, Sadler
March	20		Doctr Correy, pr Doctr fforguson
	21		mrs. Cambeage, pr mrs. Peacock
1713			
	26	c	Richard Whitesid, hatter, Northstreet
Apr	1		Gilbert Marrow, Car-Man, pr mr William Rainey, juner
	21		John Parkhill, pr mr John Armstrong
	25		Capt Richardson, Near Armaugh, pr mr Jno Chambers
	26		Widow Marrow, pr Gaven Marrow
	27	c d	mr Heugh Dayet
May	3		John Chambers, pr Son James
	8		John parker, pr Son John
			Adam Johnston, Milstreet, pr Son George
			Capt Stevenson, pr mr Isaac mc Cartiney
	13	c	mr Heugh Sharp, Marchnt
		f	James Tood, Carr-Man
	26		mrs. Saffage, in New-Toun, pr mr Jno Shadges
	27		Margeratt Rodger
June	3		mr William Johnston, pr mr Thos Bigam
	8		Left William Manson, Near Maheralin, pr mr Jno Chambers, Marchnt
	14		mr Androw Maxwell, Marchnt, pr Son William
	20	c	mr John Smith, Marchnt
	21	m	Archbald Hunter
	24	m	James Tood, Carman
		c	Androw Johnston, Northstreet
	27	c	mr Hennery Duncan, Doctr
	29	c	George Prat, Couper
July	6	w	Colonneill Mountgomery, pr mr Sam: Smith, Sener
	10	d	mr John Black, Marchnt
	12	h	Widow Skeets
	23	h	Widow Lashley [*Leslie*]
Agust	4	c.d	Robert Calinder, shew-Maker
	11		mr Edmond Staford, pr mr Sam: Smith, Sener
Sept	2	s	mr Heugh Dayet
	3	c	mr Robert Wilson, Marchnt
	6		Hakens mc Gill, Esqur — Gill-hall, pr mr Sam: Smith, Sener
	7		James Staford, Long-Cassey [*causeway*], pr Malkam mc Bride

Sept 14 Bealy Addam's, pr mr John Bell, Marchnt
15 mrs. Maxwell, at the Drum, pr mr William Rainey, juner
27 John Cotter, at the pound, pr mr Michell Greg'ston
Octr 7 mr Alexdr Hanna at Antrim, pr mr William Hanna
25 John Brown, Tayler, pr mr William Mitchell, Marchent
Nov. 9 mr John Moor, pr mr John Boyde
14 George ffleming, pr Alexdr henderson
12 (*sic*) The Scots Leard, pr David Potter
26 *w* mr Heugh Dayet
Xbr. 7 William Neilson, pr Brother Thos
9 mrs. Addair, at Loughan-More, pr mr Sam: Smith, Sener
10 John mcffarling, pr Thos Neilson
11 Margerat Laughling, pr Jas ffrizell
26 mr ffutt's, at Belliclear, pr mr Brice Blear, Marchnt

1713/4
Janry. 1 mrs Boyde, pr mr ffran Boyde, Marchnt
5 Madam Upton, pr mr Sam: Smith, Sener
13 *h* mrs. mcMinn, pr mr William Craford
15 *c* mr James mcClewer, Marchnt
16 Robert Malkcam, pr mr Robert Millikin, Marchnt
20 mr William Martine, pr Daughter Ann
c mr Sam: Smith, juner
21 mr Androw Hutcheson, pr Wife
23 *d* mr Alexdr Teate, at Cordonall, pr mr Gilbert Moor
24 Cornall John Hamilton, at Laughnavernass, pr mr Brice Blear, Marchnt
ffebery. 19 mr Thos Stewart, at Bellimarrin, pr mr Sam: Smith, Sener
21 mr Thos Winter pr John mcCammon
27 William Murfey, Long-Cassey [*causeway*], pr Wife
March 1 mr Cloud'sley, pr mr Joseph Dabson
7 *m* Margerat Miller
17 Lord Mussrain [*Massarene*], at Antrim, pr mr Sam: Smith, Sener

March 20 *c* mr ffran: Boyde, Marchnt
22 mr Robert Hamilton, at Cordonall, pr son Alexdr
Apr. 3 *s* mr James Smith, Sener
11 *w* mr William Sinkler, Milstreet
Capt James Dalben, at Dinnean, pr mr John Black, Marchnt
27 Widow Hogge, pr Thos Arthur, Sener
d John Johnston, Tayler
30 *c* mr James Adair, Mariner
c mr Alexdr Adair, Marchnt
May 1 *c* mr John Armstrong, Marchnt
3 *c* mrs. mcMinn, Widow
w John Pamer, Milstreet, pr mr Jno Heasilton, glover
6 *h* Widow Speaven
8 *c* mr Robert Lennex, Marchnt
9 *d* mr William Sharper, Long-Cassey
10 *s.c* Adam Tonnough, pr mr John mcMunn
13 Thos Tobey, Tidweater [*tidewaiter*], pr John Thomson, juner
14 mr William Hennery, pr mr Robert Millikin, Marchnt
18 *d* mr Edward Wilson
mr John fforguson, poathicarrey
mr Johnston, pr Doctr fforguson
19 *w* George Johnston
20 *c* mr Robert Millikin, Marchnt
mrs. Jean Stevenson, pr mr William Stevenson, Marchnt
21 Widow Bear, pr Androw Logan, Couper
h Widow Dounalson
28 Widow Beggs, pr David Sleater, Weaver
June 1 *c* mr James Adair, Mariner
9 *s* George Lashley [*Leslie*]
15 *c* Edward Riden, Putter
Joseph White, pr mr John homes
16 *m* Alexdr Hamilton, at Cordonnall
28 mr Patterick Isaac, at Beliwalter, pr mr Hennery Duncan
July 4 *c* mr James Adair, Mariner
c mr David mcKnight, Marchnt
5 mr William Shaw, at the Bush, pr mr John Mountgomery, Marchnt
17 *c* mr William Stevenson, Tabacco:

July	17	c	mr Michell Menkin
	18	c	The Doctr of the Armey
	25		mr Androw Mountgomery, gleaser, pr Wife
Agust	4		Widow Nesmith, pr order of Sessions this Day Meet [*The day was Wednesday.*]
	5		Marrey Grăm, pr mr John young juner
Sept.	8	w	mr Thos Lyle, Marchnt
	19		mrs. Margerat Euless, pr mr John Blacke, Marchnt
		c	mr John Smith, Marchnt
	26	w	John mcffarling
	29		mr Benj: Leggit, Near Carickforguss pr mr Robert Craig
Octr	9		mr Thos Henderson, Tabacco: pr mr John Tayler
	15		David South, pr John All, Loder
	22	st	Archbald Hounter, Smith
Nov:	2		mr John Bell, Tabacco: pr mr Jno Smith, Tanner, & mr Hennery Duncan
		w	mr John Tayler, Tabacco:
	3		Widow Loudan, Couper, pr Son Thos Loudan
	4	c	mr ffran: Stewart, Mariner
	5	c	mr Jas Robison, Marchnt
	23		Marrey fforman, pr Doctr fforguson [*This was a child.*]
	27	w	James Tho'mson, pr John Heasilton, glover
	29		mr James mc Cappen, Ministr, Belliwalter
Xbr	6		Robert Gib, pr mr Robert Agnew
			mr John Ewing, pr mr ffran: Davenport
	9	cd	John Logan, Couper, juner
	13	w	Michall Tayler, in Millone
	17		Alexdr Teat, at Cordonall, pr mr James mc Clewer, Marchnt
	20		mr Alexdr Stewart, Marchnt, pr Wife
	24		mr James Hamilton, at Cumber pr mr Jno Shadges
	25		mr David Buttle, pr Son George & mr William Cuningham
	27	w	Robert Hay, Schooll Master
	30	c	mr Heugh Linn
		c	William Sharpley, Tanner
1714/5			
Janry	4	w	William mc Cree, Shew Maker
		c	William Sharpley, Tanner
	5	c	Thos Ergillson, Weaver, in Cow lean
	12	s	Widow Richardson, pr Both Sessions—this Day meet [*The day was Wednesday.*]
	16		Thos Wilson, pr Doctr fforguson
	20	w	David fforguson, Sexton
			Widow Gilmor, Plantation, pr Daughter
ffebery	7		mr James mc Gee, beyond Holiwood, pr Son Robert
	8		John Stewart, Dunmory, pr mr William Smith, Marchnt
	9	w	Androw mc Laughling
		c	mr Robert millikin, Marchnt
		c	mr James Adair, Marriner
		c	Doctr of The Armey
		c	mr Heugh Linn
	15	d	Daniell fforguson, Mariner
	21		Widow Sinkler, pr mr David young, Marchnt
March:	15		Marrey Lum, pr Robert Glover
	24		mr John Shaw, pr mr Hennery Shadges
	28		James Bucher, Mariner, pr Robert Thomson, Ship-Carpinter
Apr	3	c	Thos Sturgan, Glover
	6		mr Thos Poringer, pr mr Patterick Treall
	8		mrs Margerat Dayet, pr mr John Chambers [*This was a child.*]
	13	c	The Doctr of the Armey
	27	c	mr John Elsmor, Colectr
	30	c	mr Alexdr Stewart, Mariner
			mr John Gaat, Marriner, Bellicloughan, pr mr Robert Androw
			Hennery Carr, Cave-hill, pr brother Jas
May:	1	c	mr James Whitelock, Bucher
	2	c	Robert Calinder, Shew-Maker
		c	mr Heugh pringell, Marchnt
	19		Madam Duntreath, pr mr William Smith, Marchant
	21		Alexdr King, pr Moses Carr
	25	w	Arthur mc Kann, pr Son: Sam:
	28	c	William Simm, Carpinter

June 15 *c* Cornall Hamilton, [per] mr James mc Clewer
Capt Sam: Mountgomery, at Spring-Vaill, pr mr Jno young, Sener
cs Madam Hamilton, pr mr Jas Hamilton, Marchnt
July 11 mr Patterick Shaw, pr mr William Smith, Marchnt
12 mr Thos Stewart, Ballidrean, pr mr George mc Cartiney
13 mr Hance ffearly, Near Tonnough-neif [*i.e. Saintfield*], pr mr Jas mc Clewer
24 mrs. Lamb, pr John Porter
Agust 11 *c* Patterick fforguson, Mariner
c Thos Eagilson, Weaver
24 *w* mr John mc Knight, juner
26 *c* William Sharpley, Tanner
27 *cd* mr Michall Wood's, at ye Keey
28 mr William Dinn, Marchnt, pr mr Thos Bell
Sept 3 mr David young, pr mr John young
4 mr James Gambell, pr Thos Warnock
5 Mr ffreeland, Minister, pr mr uchtred mc Dooll
Thos Scott, pr mrs Ann Martine, at ye Keey
11 *c* mr John young, juner
27 Thos Morton, pr mrs Morton, at Dunmorey [*This was a child.*]
Octr 1 *c* mr Patterick Kennidy, Marchnt
17 John Jorgan, Northstreet, pr David fforguson, Sexton
28 old James Tayler, in Broad Street, Mariner, pr mr Robert Agnew
Nov: 2 *w* James Adair, Shew-maker, pr Jno mc Connall
10 *cd* John Mean, Mariner, pr David fforguson, Sexton
21 Marrey Harbison, pr mr John mc Bride
30 Salt John park, pr James parke, Marchnt
Xbr 3 James Adair, Shew-Maker, pr John mc Connall
5 Squr Dabb, pr mr Sam: Smith, sener
15 *c* mr patterick fforguson, ye Cornour [*coroner*]
Xbr 18 mr John Stewart, at Bleariss, pr mr Sam: Smith, sener
27 mr patterick Hamilton, Craig-boy, pr mrs. Coug'ston
29 mrs. Jean Shean, Near Gleneafey, pr mr Jas Blow

1715/6

Janry 27 *d* Archbald Craig
John Williamson, pr Brother Jas
28 Heugh Liggit, Weaver, pr Wife
ffebery 2 Thos All, Carr-Man, pr Brother Jno
4 Widow Maxwell, Huxter, pr Daughter Margerat
7 *c* mr John Smith, Potter
8 *c* Katherin Scot, Broad street, pr David fforguson, Sexton
11 *w* Robert Maxwell, at ye Keey
13 James Nickels, Barly-Bumper, pr David fforguson, Sexton
14 Widow Mean, plantation, pr Jno Mean, Couper
18 mrs. Orre, pr mr Geo: mc Cartiney, Marchnt
19 John Loggan, Couper, sener, pr Robert peagin
20 William Walker, Barber, pr mr James Blow
22 Margerat Eldrage, pr Thos Heaslap, Weaver
25 *c* mr John Johnston, Tayler
28 Joan Ballintine, pr Archbald
James Gillcreass, pr William Garrick
March 18 mr George mc Knight, pr Jno mc Knight, Sener
27 *s* Brice Tayler, horse-jokey
Apr 7 *c* mr Hennery Duncan, Doctr
15 John Stote, pr Son William, ye Couper
28 John Johnston, Barber, at the Keey, pr mr Thos Martine
22 *cs* mr Isaac mc Cartiney
23 mrs. Gamble, Petters-hill, pr Thos Warnock
24 *w* mr John Mearss, Minister, in New-town, pr John Thomson in Ditto [*i.e. Newtownards.*]
29 mrs. Kitchen, in Skigineaill, pr mr Robert Wilson

Apr 30 Widow Stote, pr Son William, ye Couper
May. 2 mrs. Joan Hill'ss, pr Joseph Bigers Wife
8 William ffrishell, pr William Blackly
10 Capt Gallant, at Gillgorme, pr mr William Smith, Marchnt
14 *c* William Dunn, King's-Arm'ss
18 Margerat Leass, in Cow-Lean, pr Widow mc Kinney, at ye Keey
June. 8 *s* Duncan Lamon, pr Jannet Rain
10 *cs* John Thomson, Mariner, Milstreet
13 James Williamson, pr Jno Mountgomery, Marchnt
John mc fferran, pr Wife
14 *c* Androw Love
James Wattson, pr Son James
15 *c* David Potter
18 John Vent, Sleater, pr Jno Noulty
22 mr Heugh Walliss, in Beliobikin, pr mr John young, sener
25 mr ffran: Shean, Near Gleneafey, pr mr Jas Blow
28 mrs. Walliss, Widow, in Belliobikin, pr mr Jno young, sener
July 1 *c* Widow Scot, pr John Simson
13 mrs. Jean Mushit, pr mr Sam: Smith, sener
w mr William Rainey, sener
14 mr William Craford, pr son David
15 Doctr Alexdr, pr mr Jas Blow
17 mr John Boyde, Mariner
mr Lason, pr mr John Euless, Marchnt
Agust 19 mr Jas Purvess, pr Androw Loggan, Couper
20 mr ffolk White, pr mr William Smith, Marchnt
Sept 24 mr Thos Lowarss, at Donnougha Dee, pr mr Sam: Smith, juner
27 mr Sam: Henderson, Tanner, pr wife
Octr 12 mr James Houd, Minister, Learn, pr mr Jno Mountgomery
25 Widow porter, pr John porter, Couper
Nov. 1 mr Alexdr Adair, Marchnt, pr mr Jas Adair
10 mr mc Mulin, pr mr Hadock, Esqur
Xbr 7 Morion Strong, pr John ffiemin, Marchnt
11 *m* mr Haking, pr mr Sam: Smith, Sener
17 James ffite, Chanler, pr Jas Jackson
27 *c* Widow Adair, pr mr Jas Adair
28 *c* mr patterick Kennidy, Marchnt
29 Mr Heugh Moor, at Carrickforgus, pr mr Robert Millikin

1716/7

Janry 9 Major Daben Dinnean, pr mr Gilbert Moor, Marchnt
22 John Hamilton, pr Son Jas
27 mr William Dinn, King's Arm'ss, pr Wife
ffebery 4 James Stirling, Malster, pr mr Alexdr Moor
7 mr John Craig, pr Brother Robert
14 *c* mr Robert Lennex, Marchnt
Lord Mount Alexdr, at Cumber
20 *c* John young, juner
March 4 *c* John porter, Couper
5 John Stevenson, Malster, pr mr John Greeg
8 *c* mr David mc Knight
10 *c* mr William Smith, Marchnt
c mrs. Adair, Widow, pr David fforguson, Sexton
17 *c* William Stot, Couper
27 *c* mr John Smith, Suger
mrs. Mountgomery, at Rosment, pr mr Sam: Smith, Sener
30 *ed* Thos Swendill
ge Nichless Thedford
Apr 2 *c* mr Robert Stewart, Mariner
3 mr John Bell, Marchnt, pr Wife
c mr John Brown, Deary [*dairy*]
11 *c* mr Sam: Smith, Tanner
John Marke, Watter-Carier, pr Jean ffulerton
17 mrs. Roan, at Laughmore, pr mr Sam: Smith, Sener
23 *c* mr Sam: Smith, juner
24 *c* mr Robert Millikin
25 *c* William Sharpley, Tanner
30 *w* Heugh Blackwood, Carpinter
c ffran: Kirkly, Ship-Carpinter
c William Sharply, Tanner
May 9 *c* mr William Woods, at the Mill-watter

May 9 John Martine, at Bearss-Mill, pr Robert Herron
12 cs Widow Bell
19 cs mr John Johnston, Marchnt
21 c mr patterick fforguson, Cornnour
c William ffife
22 c David Marrow
c John Johnston, Marchnt
24 c John Boyde
28 c mr James Blow
c William Boyde, Barber
29 c Thos Warnock
June. 1 c William Reed, Mariner
2 c Robert Donnalson
3 c mr Sam: Smith, juner
4 c mr William Ringland
John Robb, Mariner, pr David fforguson, Sexton
8 gc John Thomson, huxter
9 c Robert Craig, Marchnt
10 c mr James Blow
c Thos Warnock
13 mr patterick aDair, Minister at Carrickforguss
15 c mr Isaac mcCartiney
16 c John Reed, Mariner
17 c mr John Mear'ss, Minister, New-town
c John Malkam, Tabacco
c mr John Armstrong, Marchnt
July. 2 c mr Robert Lennex, Marchnt
8 d John Kain, at Carickforgus, pr mr Jas Adair
10 gc mr Brice Blear, Marchnt
14 mr Thos Bigam, Merchnt
c mr patterick fforguson, Cornour
c mr Kennidy, of Cultra
17 c George Pringell
22 mr John Smith, Tanner
23 d David Loggan, Shew-Maker
Agust 5 John mcHallam, at the plantation, pr Thos whiteside
6 w mr John Heasilton, Glover
11 Christifor Strong, pr mr Jno ffleming
31 c William Stote
Sept 5 Alexdr Smith, pr mr Sam: Smith
John mcKenndery
6 Agnouss Smalchey
8 Alexdr Speaven, pr Robert hunter
9 Androw Loggan, Couper

Sept 30 c Widow Adair, at Carrick forgus, pr mr James adair
Octr 2 d mrs. Ross, pr order of Session
3 Katherin Camphle, pr Mother
15 w Charless Gordan, Back-ramper
27 Mathow Ronan his Mother in Lawes ffunerall
Nov. 1 mrs. Margerat Gattey, at Learn, pr mr Robert Androw
6 Robert ——— Whiteside, pr mr John Heasilton
13 mrs. Rachell Boyde, Widow, pr Daughter Jean
Sam: Henney, penter, pr mr Brice Blear & mr Jno Smith
18 w James Guttery, Gabert-Man [*lighterman*]
23 Mr William Rodger, pr mr David Spence
25 mr John Rainey, pr Wife
26 mr Thos Bell, pr mrs. Bell, Widow
Xbr 1 David Sharpley, pr Son William
7 cs Widow mcDouall, at the Corn-Mill
14 s mrs. Jones, at Mill-Loon, pr mr William Legg

171/8

Jany. 3 George park, Breaser, pr Daughter
7 w Heugh Linn
9 c Mr Sam: Reed
20 mr Jas park, Marchnt, pr Son Jas
21 d mr Geo: mcCartiney
27 c ffrancis Boyde
ffebery 2 m mr Sam: mcKitterick
7 c mr Isaac mcCartiney
8 mrs Boyde, pr mr Sam: Smith, juner
Alexdr Doliway Esqur, pr mr Jas Adair, Marchnt
10 c Capt Denty, per mrs. Bealy
gc Widow ffife, pr Robert Jackeson
23 w John Clark, Marchnt
25 w William Steuard, of Cloghog, pr mr Brice Blear
w John mcCammon
27 William Walliess, at Bely-misca, pr mr Jno Young, Sener
March 3 c mr William Mitchell, pr mr Gilbert More
mr John Tomb, Minister, at Mahera-felt, pr mr Joseph Innes

March 4 mrs. Dayet, pr mr Hugh Dayet

12 *w* John patterson, pr David fforguson

17 *c* Robert Deiyeall [*Dalziel*], Carpinter

24 *d* John mc Donnall, Glover, pr mr Jno Heasilton

26 mr Stafey petticrew, Minister in pr mr Brice Blear, M rchnt [*Rev. Stafford Pettigrew, Ballyeaston*].

29 mrs. heterige, Widow, at Marheriball, pr mr Isaac mc Cartiney

Left Stevenson, at Killyleah, pr mr Sam: Smith, Sener, Marchnt

Apr 5 William Sharper

11 *w* John Thomson, huxter

15 Widow Hutcheson, pr mrs. mcKnight, juner

23 Jean Bodan, pr mr William Mitchell

25 *c* mr Patt: Kennidy, Marchnt

28 mr John Knox, at pr Son Thos

May 7 Michall Bigger, Smith, pr Wife

June 1 John mcDonall, pr Doctr fforguson, mr Jno mc Bride order

9 *w* mr John Brown, Derrey [*dairy*]

12 *w* mr John Chalmbers, Marchnt

15 *c* Mr Sam: Reed

July 1 *w* mr Sam: mc Clinto, juner

2 *c* mr John Mathers

c mr John young, juner

c William Colbart, Bucher

c mr Hugh Dayet

c William ffife, Skiper-Lean

w Jas ucher, Back-ramper, pr mr Jas Adair

23 Mr John mcBride

29 Jno mc Knight, juner, pr Wife

c Jas Brown, ye Sadler

[Here begins a new hand, apparently that of William Dick.]

Sept. 3 wdd Loggan, in norstreat

3 *c* Mr. Daniel Musindin, Marchnt

Octr. 10 wdd Davesonn, in the Loang Lean

14 *c* Mr. Donelson, in petersill

16 *c* Mr. Mrsell, the MarChait [*Market*]

Nov. 1 Mr. Stafford, in portglenon, pr Mr. Joseph Innes

2 *s* John mcbide, in Beleygoemarten

3 *c* Mr. Thomas Miller, MarChant

6 *w* Mr. Stnson, in petersill

Nov. 8 Mr. walles, in Celenchey [*Killinchy*] pr. Hugh Walles, MarChant

11 John Johnston, the Tealear

13 Samull Mafet, of bangull

13 *c* David Mcneight, in petersill

13 John Lusk, Sealor, Living in varen streat

15 Robert Holmes, in Skepers lean

16 wdd Kirkwood, Living on the Kie

16 Sorgen Finlay, to the Contre [*i.e. some funeral in the country ordered by Surgeon Finlay*]

18 Mr. Muntgomrey, of nutan [*Newtownards*]

19 *cs* Macomb mcbrid, in beleyGomartin

21 *c* wdd Anderson, in Millstreat

26 *w* William Hosocke

28 wdd Singelton, in Millstreat

28 *c* Mr. James Adaire, MarChant

Decm. 29 the Revd. Mr. ffillop Meares, in nievtand [*Newtownards*]

29 Mr. Samuell M ane

30 wdd bell, in broad streat

1719

Janr. 18 *w* Alexander Blear, liveng in norstreat

19 *d* Marey Sorely

30 Annes Muntgomrie, in Church Leain

ffebery 7 John Marten, in the planteshon

9 *m* John Mathies, in the plantteshon

11 *c* Hugh blackwood, Carpenter

13 *c* Allexander Carson

16 *s* old James bigger, the Cotelar

March 1 *c* James Munceye, in varen Streat

21 Majer norie, in poartGonon, pr. Joseph Innes

23 Mr. Boyd, of the Glastry, pr Margret neven

24 *d* Mackom Mcbrid, in beleygomerten

26 Agnes Miller, in the planteshon, pr hir son Alexander

28 *s* wdd Cearnes, bookbinder

29 *c* Mr. James Cobame, in brid eland [*i.e. child of Rev. James Cobham, Broadisland*].

29 *d* William Stevart, in the Loang Casay

Apr. 1 *s* Mr. Dallrumple, MarChant

14 Mr. John McCallpen, the Taner, in Melstreat

15 *s* Macomb Mcbrid, in belego Marten

Apr. 28 Moses Carr, osler, Samull M'Clentons
29 *cd* Mrs. Macerthney, the wdd
29 *c* ffranses Stwart, in Skepers Lean
30 *c* James browne, the Sadler
30 *c* Hugh blackwood, the Carpenter
May 1 Moses Hill
4 *w* Mr. oahtrie M'Doule, MarChant
6 Mrs. Leadeland, pr mr. Will Smith, MarChant
8 *c* Abel Hodskis, mealor
10 *c* Robert Heayes, SColemaster
16 *s* Mrs. Jones, at Milltoon
16 *c* John Mean, in the pantteshon
22 *w* Mr. Hendric Ealles, sufren [*Henry Ellis*].
27 Mr. John Sanders, in bangul, pr James M'Clure
28 *c* Pat fforgeson, at the sin of the son
June 4 John Smith, poater, pr his wife
4 Mr. Robert Agnew
5 Mr. James Muntgomrie, of port Aferey, pr John M'Camond
July 2 *w* Mr. walles, in Cekkenchey [*Killinchy*] pr Hugh Wales, MarChant
5 *w* Thomas Qay, in the Church Lean
6 *w* Alexr. Spear, in the Loang lean
7 *c* John beles, in norstret, pr Thomas Martin
9 *c* Mr. James boayd, in learn [*The child appears to have been grown up, and living in Church Lane*]
9 *c* James Moor, in noar streat
17 *c* Mr. Robert Wolson, in broad streat
20 John Shaw, in peterhill, pr Charels Rameg and Gaien Mora
30 *c* Mr. Daniel Musindin
Agust 4 Mr. John Greeg, in norstreat
6 *w* Adam Quacy, Telcar
6 *c* Mr. of neall [*O'Neil*] one the Kie
13 weado Clark, in Millstreat, pr hir son
13 Mr. Kill, in Comber parish
17 Mrs. ffeitts, of beleyClear, pr Mr. Wolson, minester [*i.e. Rev. Thomas Wilson, of Ballyclare*].
20 *c* Mr. bankes
26 John M'Creath, Carman, in HarClus lean
Sept 4 Mr. ffranses Heslip, in Milstreat, Ealseler [*ale-seller*]
Sept 9 *c* William Willey, Caper smith
17 *aunt* Robert Deall
18 John boyd, on the kie, pr his wife
18 Mr. Earter [*Arthur*] Kennedy, of Coltra, pr Alexr Stewart
20 Mr. John wacker, in poartAferey, pr William Stenson
21 *c* Mr. Ringland, gold smith
26 *gc* Thomas Jaslip, Cloath MarChant
27 *s* William Willey, Capersmith
Octr 3 Mr. David Chalmers, MarChant, pr Daniel Musindins
7 *c* Robert Garner, prenter
12 *c* John Shads
15 *s* Mr. John Greer, in Hoalewood
15 *servant* wdd blear
19 Mr. ffranses Ash, in keleaD, pr James bow
26 *d* Edward pearse, Corier, pr Daniel Musind
27 *c* John Suter, Eeal seler, in the Adem and Eave
Novr 1 John m' ffarlien, in the planteshon
1 Samuel Miller, Elseler, in the Egel and Chill [*Eagle and Child*]
2 *c* William boyd, Carman, at the pown
5 Cornl. William Shaw, of the bosh [*Bush*] pr william Smith, MarChant
16 *c* yovng Samull Smith
17 John nowland, his mother, the powlster, pr Mr. Andrew
Decmb 2 Mr. Coalvien, in Dromor, [*i.e. Rev. Alexander Colville, the elder*] pr James M'Clure
2 Mr. Colena Shaw, of Mahrhoahel, pr Mr. M'Clure
5 *c* yowng Samuel Smith
9 Mr. James Carr, of Learn, pr James bordges
13 *c* James Snieth, Elde, in nor Streat
16 John Shaw, Esqr., in the bosh, pr Mr. William Smith
23 *w* Daniel ffisher, in the planteshon, pr his Doaghter
24 *c* Thomas Jowdan, Couper, in norstret

[1720]
Janry 2 *c* Mrs. Garner, A streanger in town, pr Mr. ffimen

Janry 5 *w* Mr. William Jonston, of Celeleah [*Killyleagh*] pr Mr. James M lure
7 *w* Abel Hadskis, the nealer
18 *gc* Mr. Tatfor, at the Corner
23 *c* Mr. Allexr Chalmors, in peterhill, MarChant
25 *servant* Doct. M'artnay
ffebry 5 *w* Alexander Hamelton, weaver, in Roes Marey lean

[Here begins a new hand, that of Samuel Pentland.]

1719/20
15 *c* Gain Hamelton
19 John Carr, his Mother in Lawe
25 John Loggen, Couper, in Rose mearey Lean
28 *c* Andrew Loves, barberr
Mar 1 Mr. Samull Smith, taner, in norstreat
2 *c* Wuld Mathise, in the planteshon
4 Madam Poack, in Coltra
4 *c* Mr. Andrew Agnew, MarChant, in Church lean
5 Gaien Hamelton, Couper, in nor. streat, pr Will Stenson, MarChant
7 Daniel fforgeson, in in norstreat, Mariner, pr his wife
11 *c* Alexander Cilles, Maltmen, liveng in Melstreat
15 wdd Ross, Scoullmistres, in wdd nessmiths Entrie, pr Mr. Kill-patricket [*i.e., Rev. James Kirk-patrick*]

1720
Mar 26 Andrew Hunter, Cuper, Living in the back of the MarCet House
26 Saruant of Mr. Wales [*Wallace*] MarChent, in neweary, Died in Rowland M'Giles
27 *gc* Thomas Haslipe, weaver, in norstreat
30 *c* Joarg Ashmor, Glover, in Milstreat
31 Docter Weare, in Antriam, pr Joseph Innes
Apr 15 oJeam Campel, pr his son John Campel
16 Mrs. ffeearfield, liveng in the County of Down and pariesh of Cell meagen, pr William Walles, MarChent
22 *c* Anntoney Thubrow, Sealowr, in the planteshon
Apr 30 *c* David Kennedy, MarChent, in broad streat
May 2 wdd Knowles, pr Hir Doghter
4 *w* Mr. Jonston, in Reedamon, pr Mr. Arbockels, MarChent
4 *c* Andrew Love, barber
7 wdd Holmes, in scepers lean, pr James Muncey, yonger
8 John M'rire, tealowr, in roes Mearey lean
8 *c* Mr. William Stenson, MarChant
9 wdd Adaire, in Caregforges, whose boriel was in holewood, pr James Adaire, MarChent
11 Mr. Ritchard Ashmore, pr his wife
12 A jurneymanes of Mr. William Ringland, one the Kie
19 Mr. Hugh Muntgomry, in the Cnoak paries, to his wife
20 James Gutrie, Gabert man [*lighter-man*] Living in the planteashon
21 wdd watt, in Jolewood porish, pr hir son James wat, MarChent
27 *c* William walles, tealowr, in mr. Arbockels Entrie
Jun 1 Mrs. Campel, in Antrom, pr Robert Creag, MarCnent, in norstreat
3 John Drennan, Ropp macker, pr Samuel M'Kitrocket
5 *w* Andrew ffiev, in the Long Casae
6 *c* Thom warnocke, in peters hill
7 James Rudeman, in the norstreat
12 James pinkerton, in the loang lean
13 Thomas Gibson, Glower, in Melstreat
18 Rowland M'Gill, osler, in Mr. M'intons
18 Wdd whitt, on the Kie, pr franses Kirkland
July 1 Wdd Gregg, in HarColes lean, pr Mr. Andrew Agnew, in Church lean
1 Mr. M'Culoah, in ronels, Esqr., pr Mr. Brise blear
12 Mr. Blackwood, in bangwol, pr David park, MarChent
18 *c* James Warkes, leabrower, in the long lean
20 A sister in Law of James Whotels, in warens stret

Agust 14 Mr. Samull McClinton, at the sin of the Crown, pr his son Samull McClinton
20 *w* patr Crow, in peterhill
23 Mrs. Catraien balief, in the new boldings, pr Mr. James Martien, in Lesburn
27 patricket brown, in peterhill, pr his brother, John brown
29 wdd brumfild, in scepers lean, pr hir neas, Elisebth Thomb
29 wdd Harper, in broahshan, pr Mrs. Harper, MarChant, in broadstreat
Octr 12 *d* Edward Mcleaney, in the ffalles
22 *c* John Cunigham, in the milfeld lean
26 Wdd Simson, MarC, per hir son William
27 *c* John Jonston, MarChent
29 Mr. Joseph Chochren, MarChent, to his wife pr. Samull MalCom, Tobaco Spener [*spinner*]
Novmbr 1 Robert peagon, at the Corn mill, pr his son Robert peagon, beacker
15 Wdd ffinlay, pr William paterson, in norstreat, showmacker
18 Mr. Loang, MarChent, in Mahrihoohel, pr Mr. James Mclure, MarChent
Desmb 1 Mr. Eatten Euwat, Minester in the parish of Cloagh milles in the County of Antrim, pr Docter Mcneall
1 *c* Thomas Miller, MarChent, at the Stonbridg
15 Andew Mckie, truper, pr his wife, the stamper
15 *c* John Stockman, Sealear, pr his wife
19 William Grriear, in Holewood, pr his brother
30 *d* John Cille, in the Loang Casca, pr his brother Samull Cille
c Edwar whittlocke, Marchent

[1721]
[Jan] 6 A step Doghter of Robert Crofords, on the Kie, Maroner

1720
Janr 9 *s* Macom Mcbride, in belegomartien
9 *c* Mr. William Muntgomry, MarChent, in norstret

Janr 14 Mrs. balentine, in Millstreat
17 *c* David Kennedy, MarChent, in broad streat
21 *c* Allexr. Henderson, Gleasowr, in norstreat
21 John woodes, at the fowr Lone Ends, melone, pr Joseph innes, MarChent
31 David Stoormie, in belegomarten, pr William Stenson
31 *w* John Gelston, in Cnoack parish, pr James Hamelton, in Caselreah

1720
1
ffebr 3 *c* Samull Gillmor, in the loang Casea

[Here begins another hand, apparently that of Andrew Agnew.]

h Wid Callinder
wid English
mr Jno Smith for Hugh Wallace
Tho: Lawry
Wm Rainey, for Arthur Maxwell, Esq.
c David Murray
c Ed: Whytelock, some time before

1720
1
febry 17 Jno Semple
18 *w* Jno martin
25 Wid: Greg, Glenavy
mar: 2 *w* Jas Smith
7 Wm Whytler
12 Wm Martin
13 *c* mr Joanes
14 James Connyhy (?)
23 *c* mrs. Loe
24 *w* Jno Barre
25 *c* mr negam (?)

1721
apr 5 Wid mcWilliam, by Jean Willson
12 St John Johnstone
16 Janet Demster
18 *d* David Logan
20 Jno mcGlochlin
c Richd fferralls
25 mr Kennay, widow
27 *c* Wm ffife
may 3 James Boyd
Agnes Hethington
7 Adam Quae
16 *d* Jno mitchell

[Here begins another hand.]

1721

Jun 12 Mr. Cunnigham Esqr., in the Count of Dearey at Springhill, pr Mr. Samull Smith, MarChent, yownger

12 Thomas blayen, Eallselar, in noarstreat, pr his wife

13 Jean wolson, in Churck lean, pr John Charters

29 Mr. Hamelton, that was Cast Away on the Dock, pr Robert hamelton, MarChent

30 widdo brown, in the falles

July 1 *c* William Roper

7 *d* John ffisher, sawer, in the loang leain

8 *c* Docter Doncan, potegar

12 *w* William Simson, sealDler, in norstreat

21 *s* James Cowter, in the Loang Casae

22 william Simson, the sadler, pr John Ros, David morrey

26 *c* John Stowart, living At the browrie [*brewery*]

Agest 4 *d* Mr. M'murlian, living in Dene Goar [*Donegore*]

5 *w* ArCheabel Mintgonry, taner, in noarstreat, pr Mr. Hamelton, in Holewod

9 *c* Hugh backwood, Carpenter

11 *c* Hugh Qacy, Teallowr

12 William M'rea, Showmaker, pr John poarter, Coper

18 *c* John Smith, MarChant, in broadstreat

19 *c* yowng Charels Ramage, in peterhill

29 *w* Hugh Muntgonre, in Dinygor, who Died in petterhill and was boried in Shankel, pr his son Robert Muntgomrie

Sept 3 *c* John Gregg, the Smith, in norstreat

3 *c* John Cloirdy, botcher, liveng at the Melgeat [*Millgate*]

8 *w* Mr. Robert Hamelton, pr brown Joarg M'Cartnay

14 *c* Mr. William gowane, in peter Hill

18 *c* Mr. Joarg Gutrie, MarChent, in broad streat

24 *c* Mr. ffearol, in peterhill

27 *c* Pat Kennedy, the MarChent

Octr 3 Mr. Killoe, in the Cumber pearish in the Cownty of Down

9 *c* Mr. warnock, in peter hill

17 *b* Robert M'Gee, in Holewod, pr Robert M'Gee, in waren streat

17 *c* Mr. Joannes, Exise Man

18 *w* Edward pearss, the Correr [*currier*] in nor Streat, pr Mr. Lille

24 *w* John Scoat, in the ffalles

30 John Sharpe, the Smith, pr Mr. Sharpe, the MarChant

Nobr 5 *c* John M'Gown, in Melstreat

8 Madom paotenger, in Careforgous, pr Capt Jmes Maxneel hamelton, in the Drum

9 *c* Robert tamson, Sealer, liveng in Melstreat

9 John Suoters, Elseler, pr his wife

10 *c* Mr. John fforgeson, potegar

12 John bowman, the Meason, pr his wife

10 the Colectors leady, pr Oabedia Groaves

16 *c* John M' Lonehan, in norstreat

17 *c* Mr. Robert Hamelton

22 David Staford, in the ffalles, pr his brother Alexr

22 *c* Mr. Middelton, Eall seler, in norstreat

23 *c* James Muncie, in scepers lean

Desm 2 *c* David Kenedye, in broad streat

8 *w* ffransess Malcom, peterhil

11 William Arther, in norstreat

21 *c* David potter, in town

30 James Stafor, at the fforth River, pr his brothe Alexr

[1722]

Janr 2 *s* the Revd Mr. M'craken, in lesburn, pr Mr. Cornel brise

3 Mr. Orr [*Rev. Thomas Orr*], in Combar, pr his Clark

3 *c* Thomas Qua, in Church lean

6 *c* Joarg Ashmor, in melstreat

10 *c* Mrs. Smith, in the Shogerhovs, pr hir son John

11 Mr. briss blear, pr John fforgeson

26 Thoomas Stowart, prentise to Mr. Arbockesl, pr yowng Samull Smith

Janr 27 wdd Gregg, pr Mr. Willson [*Rev. Thomas Wilson*] Menester in belley Clear
27 *c* Mr. James Adair
27 *c* John Mc Gown, living at the Melgeat
28 William Gaieit, Living in beley Esten, pr Samull Smith, Siner
30 *c* William Carsan, in Mellstreat

1721
22

ffebr 6 *c* Mr. Ree, Ship Carpenter, in waren streat
8 Mrs. M Gill, in lurgan
9 Mrs. Ashmor, in Mill Streat, pr hir Son John Ashmor
23 Mr. Mathis, weater on the Kie, pr obedia Groaves
23 Mr. Talford, pr obedia groaves

Mar 10 *c* Mr. Hugh Lin
10 *c* John stoakman, Marioner, pr his wife
14 Capt whitside, living in Mellone, pr his wife
16 *s* the Revd mr. Mccapien [*Rev. James M'Alpine*] Minester in beleynehinch, pr William Stenscon, At the Ston bridge
20 *c* John Daben, Liveng in peter hill
21 *c* Thamas warnock, in peter hill
21 widdle Campbel, in melstreat, pr Mr. Craford, Minester [*Rev. Andrew Crawford, of Carnmoney*]
22 Samuel M kitterick, in norstreat, pr his wife
29 David Kennedy's brother, taner, in norstreat
29 A brother of Archelb Miler, ffidler, living in noarstreat, pr Martha ward
30 *c* James Moor, Sealler, in warean streat
31 *c* David Spence

Epr 1 *c* John Goarden, MarChant
1 *d* Robert Sinkler, in the loang lean
2 *c* Hugh Linn
3 *d* wdd ffisher, in Casel streat, pr hir son
5 old Mr. Innes, pr his son, Mr Joseph Innes
6 *c* Thomas whitsid, Ship Carpenter, on the Kiee

Epr 8 *c* Mr. Eddmeston, pr Mr. James Adair
8 John Haselton, Elder, pr his wife
9 *c* Capt M Coloah
10 A saruant of Mr. blow, prenter
12 Mr. Lankes, pr Mr. Obedia Groaves
14 *c* Staford Millford, Tealowar
17 Henery Poater, barber, in in mill streat, pr David Poater
26 *c* Mr. John Clark, MarChant
27 Mr. William Roadgers, Potegar, pr David Spence
28 *c* Pat fforgson, at the fowr Corners

May 2 Mrs. Clamens, pr Docter Donkan
6 *c* Joarg Rosbrogh
9 olld Mr. Reanney
10 *c* John M amon
12 *c* Gorge Ashmor, Glouer, pr John Ashmor
14 *c* Docter Donckan
(*sic*) 91 *s* Robt M Gee, in waren Streat, who was boried in holewood
26 *gc* brown Gorge M Cartnay
28 *c* Hugh Pringel, MarChent
30 *s* wdd Campbel [*three cloaks apiece were ordered by* the Capt of the tealoars, the Capt of the beackears, *and* the Capt of the Show-mackers]
31 Mr. Hendrey Doncan, tothe ffunerall of his Mother in law

Jun 3 *c* Docter Doncam
4 Mr. David spence, MarChent, pr his wif
4 *c* James Dicke, Miller, of the Mallt mill
7 John browns Mother in Law, Chanelar, in Mellstreat
9 Leard Hamelton, Living at Holewod, pr James Mc Lure, MarChent
9 *c* James Mafert (?), the beacker
13 *c* James Grear, Shoemacker, pr Mrs. Agnes, botcher
16 *c* Antoney Conegham, sealler, living at the browrie
21 *w* John Hathorn, Cornmill
26 *w* Mr. Mcquearn, in beley Manoh [*Ballymena*], pr Alexr moar, peterhill

July 3 Robt Adams, Ship Carptenar, pr James Wear, Mariner

July 9 Mr. Baniam Patterson, MarChant, pr his wife
11 brise blairs wdd paid 12 shilings that she had in her hand for the Revd Mr. Cowters [*Coulter*] Doghters funerall
12 *c* Andrew Skellin
13 brown Gorge M'Cartnay, pr his son George
14 *w* Will Arter, pr willam Stoatt, Copar
16 *w* Mr. Teatt, potegar, in Lesburn
17 *c* John Maxwel, hoxter, norstreat
21 wdd Cawall, in hallewood, pr Mr. M'Clure
Agst 5 *c* wdd M'Gill, Elseler
6 Mr. Robert Andrew, MarChant, pr his son Gehrall
8 Mrs. Ann Martin, pr Mr. ffransess Joy (son in law)
11 John ffreaser, in beley Gomarten, pr John brown his Stepson
11 Samull beggs, Showmacker, Long lean
17 *c* Mr. Ardbockel
17 Robt Hamelton, Copear, one the Kie, pr his wife
29 Mr. Black, Combar, pr Doctr Donckan
Sept 15 Mrs. Maxwel, pr Patricket Maxwell, who Died in beley Manoh and was boried
17 *c* yowng James Smith, malltman, in norstreat
20 Mr. John Kennedy, of Coltra, pr yowng Saml Smith
24 James Iralland, in tempell patricket, pr his Son John Iralland, in the fall
Oct 7 *w* George Roasbrogh
14 *w* James brown, SeaDler, in norstreat
23 *s* Alexr Moor, peterhill
23 wdd Deaveson, warenstreat
24 *c* Mr. Danield Mussenden, MarChant
25 James Creaghton, Ropwack [*rope-walk*]
30 *c* borbra M'Gill, hole of the wall
Novr 3 widd M'Cadam, longeasa
3 Mr. Edward Whitloack, MarChant
15 James M'Tear, MarChant, pr his brother Sam M'tear
Novr 18 Mrs. Sharp, fowr Corners
18 *c* Hugh Pringel
27 Neall boy M'neall, who Died in Doctr M'nealls, pr EarChabld [*Archibald*]
30 Mrs. Gallant, Gelgoram [*Glengorm*] pr ArChebl M'neall, potegar
Desm 11 Mary Millen, melstreat, pr David Kennedy, taner
22 *c* Mr. boyd, of the Gleasrie [*glasshouse*], pr Mrs. Marget Neven
22 *w* James layon, Ship Carpenter, plantesion
27 *c* Mr. John Johnson, MarChent
27 will Anderson, Fall selear, in broad streat, pr Mr. James blow

1723

Jan 7 *c* Robart Haye, Scolmaster
10 Mrs. Lee, in learn, Pr Joseph Innes
11 David Park, pr his brother James Park
12 *c* Antoney Coke, Sealer, Roas Marey lean
19 ball Jean
20 *d* Temothy ffulertan, Stronmilles
24 Margrat Cambel, Long lean, pr Thomas M'onall, Shomaker, norstreat
28 *c* John Clark, MarChent
28 *c* Robart Hamelton, Hoxtor, Norstreat

1722
3

29 *c* Robt Hay, Scolmaster, Market house
ffab 3 Dauid beggs, Carman
6 *c* Mr. Pat Smith
7 *c* Clamens M'Cadam, peterhill
12 *w* Hallbert Carr, in peterhill
13 *c* Robart Dalzel, Carpenter
16 *c* will walless
17 *s* Thomas bornsid, whelwright
24 wdd MallCom, pr wrs blear, broad streat
27 Archabld Creagg, pr his wife
Mar 8 Thomas Arther, Norstreat, pr will Stoat, Copar
14 Hanna Jolmbes [*Holmes ?*], hoxter, in norstret, pr brother James Holmes, wiggmaker
16 Mrs. Neall, Kerkdonall, pr hir son ArChebld Neall

Mar	23		Captr Treall, pr Joseph Podgenar
	24		Mr. Edward Whitsid, Melone, pr his son John whitsid
Apr	3		Mrs. Andrew, pr hir Son Gebrall Andrew
	3	*w*	Daniel ffisher, pr him Selfe
	7	*w*	Sam M'kelvey
	12	*c*	John Johnston, MarChent
	18		Neclous Sharp, preanties with Mr. will Mitihel, MarChent, Pr his brother John Sharp
	21	*c*	Thomas M'lune, Glover
	24	*w*	Joohn Anderson
	28	*c*	william Lason
	29		John beard, Loang Casa, Smith
1723			
May	13		Richard Lamb, pr John poarter, Couper
	13		wido Johnston, Waller, pr John brown, Chanler, Melstreat
	13		Mr. Gordan, bandbridg, pr John Gordan, MarChent in town
	13		A Scoatch Man that Dayed in town
	19		Alexr M'mun, pr Mr. John M'mun, MarChant
	22	*c*	John Alld, Cloath MarChent
	23	*si*	William Colbart
	24	*c*	Joseph mines, Sealler, Potengers Entrie
			James Carithers, Glover
	31	*c*	John Geades, Carier, Norstreat
Jun	2	*w*	David Kennedy, MarChent, broad Streat
	3	*c*	will Maxwel, MarChent
	5	*w*	Mr. Roase, Lodge
	10	*w*	Sam boman, gleaser
	16	*c*	Doctar Duncan
	16	*c*	James white, Copar, Roos Marey lean
	18	*d*	wdd Cearns, pr hir mother
	21		Margrat Robeson, Scepers lean, pr hir Sister, widdo M'lelan
	22	*si*	Squear Dason, Dasonds bridge, Pr Joseph Innes
July	3	*c*	John brown, Norstreat, Meallman
	8	*w*	William Combe, at millwater
	11	*d*	wdd boyd, glesrie, pr Margrat Neven
	16	*w*	Mr. Dickson, Cerkdonel, Pr franses boyd, ChurChlean
July	17	*c*	John M'Dowal, heresons lean
	17	*c*	william M'Conoah, tealowar
	20		Joseph barklow, Carpenter, Pr his wife
	27		Robert M'Geies Mother, who was boried in holewod
	29	*c*	John M'Dowall, Carrman
Agest	3		Thomas Miller, MarChent, pr Pat forgeson
	5		John Means, Sceper, planteson
	6	*c*	John M'Dowall, Carman, Harklors lean
	6	*s*	Mr. M'Cen, helsborow, pr E.Adam M'Cen, prentis Mr. Eeels (?)
			Mr. Shavegg [*Savage, per*] Mr. Sam Smith, junr
	9		Agnes Hunter, Church lean, pr Hilley Hunter [*her brother*] Retrney [*attorney*]
	18		wdd Hogsid, pr hir Doghter Reachel
	21	*w*	Mr. Neagen, pr obedia Groave
	26	*c*	John M'Cart, taner, peterhill
	31		Mr. William MuntGomry, pr his wife
Sept	9	*c*	Mr. Dunlap, living in Mr. Andrews house
	9	*w*	Mr. Stoward Esqr., Celey mon [*Killymoon*], pr yowng Sam Smeth
	24	*c*	Sam M'Clentow
Octr	1	*w*	James wright, Tealloar
	2	*c*	Mr. John wallas, MarCent, broad streat
	9	*c*	David Dunn, Mariner, in scepers lean
	20		william Simes Mother in Law, Carpenter
	28		olld Doctor fforgeson, pr Capt M'Coloah
	29	*c*	John M'gown
	31		Mrs. M'Glahlen
	31		A sarvant of Mr. Maxwels of feney broag
Novb	2		ffransis boyd, Church lean, pr his wife
	5		Mr. Carr, in belymanoh, pr Mr. wason, broad streat
	9	*c*	Mr. will Leg, in Mellon
	11		Thomas Allan, at the brurie, pr Patrick Smith, browrie
	13		wdd M'Dowal, back Ramper, pr hir Doghter Agnes
	17	*c*	Isaac Ramag, peterhill

Novb 24 Mr. Stel', banger, Pr Mr. James M Clure
26 c Allexr Deaueson, Chanlor, in ChurCh lean
27 Jonathan Moor
28 c nathaniel Moarison, ChurCh lean
Desm 1 c Mr. James Adair, MrChent
8 Mr. John yowng, MarChant
5 c William Greage, Teallor
11 A Child who was A frind of Madam Dabes, pr Madam Dabes [*Dobbs*]
12 c baniam M Dowall, Dunegor, pr Mr. M Lure
14 John Sherp, in hoolowod, Pr Mr. Rowland Sharp
21 c Jorg Carsan, waterman
22 wdd Thamson, pr Mr. Ramse
24 c Mr. John fforgeson, potegr
24 c Mr. Joarg M'Cartnay
25 warham Smith, Church lean, pr oabida Groaves
[1724]
Janr 4 Long Margrie, pr Mr. James blow
10 w Hugh blackwoo, Carpenter
17 c Cornall fforgeson
17 A streang [*stranger*] in town
21 s John fforgeson, potegar
27 w Robt Lawe
ffebr 2 John Shaw, Shoger howse, pr Mr. Jon Smith
1723
4
4 c Mr. will Mitchel, yowngcr, MarChant
5 the Leat Sr John Roding [*Rawdon*], in Mayorah [*Moira*], pr Mr. M Cartney
6 Samull Holmbs, broad streat, pr his mother
8 c John Gregg, Smith, in Norstreat
11 John Campbel, Lodger in Mr. John M muns, pr Mr. James burges
13 Thomas Eagelsom, weavor
13 b Mr. John Clark
13 d Willm Hasock, melfild
14 c James Moor, Miller, ffall mill
17 d Jon M Gown, Mill streat
18 Richard farels Mother in law, living in tempelpatricket
21 c Mr. John Smith, Living at the sluse bridge
ffebr 24 s Mr. Colam, Returney
28 the Leatt Revd Mr. Sam getty in learn, pr Mr. gebrall Andreow
Mar 2 m Mr. John Clarke, the MarChent
4 wdd watt, pr Mr. John Hamelton, beleynefy
7 w Thomas warnock, peterhill
7 w John Ashmor, Glower, Melstreat
8 the Leat Revd Mr. Williamson, in belenhinch, Pr William Ringland
9 Mr. umfres, pr Mr. John Holmbes
15 c John Ashmor, Glover, Mellgeat
17 c Alexr M Kown, Carman
31 wdd tultan, Millfeilld Lean, pr John Holmbs
31 c Jno Eggers, Smith, Rosemerylean
Epr 1 c william Delap, Last maker
4 Joarg boyd, in John Demster, pr Doctr M Cartney
6 c Capt M'Coloh
10 c David Craghton, Seallor
15 c the Revd Mr. Harper [*Rev. Samuel Harpur, of Moira*]
24 c Mr. John Colman
30 Willdliam Thamson, Seallor, planteson
1724
May 5 William M'Glathrie, in the Lang Casa, Pr Jon Cunigham
5 m Mr. Jon Stel, potgr, DonoGhiede [*Donaghcady*]
13 w Mr. Townsend, Mellgeat
15 Mrs. Cobam, in Hoolewod, pr Mr. Jon Smith, MrChent, broad streat
16 c Will Ringland, Gold Smith
17 c Andrew M'Comb, Millstreat
18 c James Thomason, sealler, Milstreat
20 w William stoat, Copar, norstreat
Jun 2 s widd Cearns
s Samull Gillmor, Long Casa
7 c Mr. will Maxwl, MarChent
13 w James Hamelton, peter hill
14 c John Eruen [*Irvine*], Millfieldlean
15 d Mr. James Cobam, Jolewood, Pr Mr. Jon Smith
24 c James Hamelton, Marinor, Pr Mr. James Hameton, at the bredg End
28 w Mr. Jon Gorden, MarChant
July 1 c Robt Dalezel, Carpentar

July 6 David Kennedy, North geat
8 c Mr. William Maxull, MarChent
12 Mr. Jon M'mun, MarChent
12 c Will Teatte, Glover, Millstreat
13 c Mr. William Townsend
15 Sam Carnchen, Long Casa
19 c Jon Sttel, potger
21 c Joseph Coahren, MarChent, at the stonbridg
29 Joarg Ashmor, Hatter, in Mill streat
30 w Mr. Oakes, in Glean Eauey, Pr William Sinkler, in Melstreat
Agst 8 c Mr. William Reany
8 c James Dicke, Miler, in the Malt mill
9 c Angos wacker, on the Kee
14 Dauid Kennedy, broad streatt, pr Jon Rose, potegar
15 c Mr. Hugh pringel, MarChent
18 c Mr. Mathies, in the ffalles
19 Will Tood, Carpenter
20 A saruent of Mr. Innes
22 Mr. Porter, in Kirk Donall, pr Mr. Andrew Agneow
23 d Mr. Mathies, in the ffalles
26 c Mr. James Park, MarChent
26 c Mr. William Raney, MarChent
27 William M'reight, Glouer, Mills streat, pr Alexr Kille
28 c Mr. Jon fforgeson, potegr
30 w yowng Samull Smith, MarChent
Sept 8 c Sam M'lento
8 c Richard Cowter
13 c Jon stowart, browrie
13 c the Reud Mr. ffatchard
14 c Abell Haskeson, nealer
20 Mr. David black, Pr his father Mr. Jon black, fowr Corners
28 c Mr. pat Kennedy, MarChent
30 c Mr. Henderson, Clark to Mr. M Culoahs
Octr 7 c Mr. Daniel Mosentin
8 c Edwar Harie, botche
11 Mr. Donelson, Gleneauey, Pr Mrs. Campbel, beacker
11 c Mr. Adam Gutrie, MarChent
14 w Alexr Craford, at the Maltmill
16 w Samull Marttien, in Hoolewod parish
18 c Jon Glean, in the hole of the wall
Octr 20 Mrs. Glespie, att nuttan [*Newtownards*], Pr Mr. Edward Whittloack, MarChent
22 c Mr. William Mittcheal, MarChant, at the stton bridge
23 c Mr boall, scallor, warenstreat, pr Mr Rea, scallor
25 c Mr Cobam, Retorney
28 c wdd miller, at the Sttonbridg
28 c Robt boall, in broad street
29 Mrs Eruen, Comber, who was boried in this town
30 c Widdo Miller, Sttonbridg
31 c Mr William Mittchel, MarChent, att the Stonbridg
Nour 1 old Mr Tattford, pr Mr Arther Tattfor
3 c Mr Robert boall, broad streat
8 c John Lawes, norstreat
9 d Andrew Derampel, MarChent
12 Mr Alexr Storvard, pr Mr William Ranie, MarChent
12 s Jon Garner, beacker, in Rosemary lean
14 c Mr Jon Walles, MarChant, broad streat
23 c Jon Sheain, in Gleneauey
Desm 1 Mr Agnew, of Celwaghter near Learn, pr Mr James burges, MarClent
2 m James Holmes, weauer, in Rosemery lean, pr Edward Loggan, Carman
4 James whitt, Copar, in Ross mary Lean, pr Mr Anttney Harenttion
5 c Mr Robert Creag, MarChent
6 c Mr Rusell, living in mellon, pr mr william tomsend
8 Mr Jon Porter, Copar, P. Mr Andrew Agnew
16 w Mr Andrew Delrumpl
22 c David M neight, in peterhill
24 Mrs Moor, who was Jonethon Moors widow, Pr hir son Jon moor
29 Mrs Gresell Reney, Pr Mr Jon Eccls
30 c Mr James Adair, MarChent
[1725]
Janr 2 c Mr James Mairs, Living in broad streat
4 c Mr Sam M Lento

Janr 9 *w* Hugh uansc, Labrer, Living in Rosemery lean
10 *c* Jon brow, in peter hill
13 *gc* James Law, Hoxter
15 Isack Ramige, Carman, Pr Chare's Rainge
28 *c* Jon Hana, Chanler, living in Norstreat
29 John M arttnay, Gabert man, Living in the plantesion
31 *c* Mr Robert M'Capon, living at the Mill geat
31 *c* Mr Richard ffarell, living peter hill
ffebr 6 the Leat Squeair Hatreckt, Pr Mr Isaac M'Cartnay
8 Samull boyd, Meall man, in Church lean, Pr Hugh Smith, in Church lean
11 *f* Mr Capt Maxwell
17 Mrs Petterson, MarChent, at the Market House, Pr Jon Johston, MarChent
18 *s* Mr James Hamelton, bridgeend
19 *c* Hugh Marteen, Pr John Thomson
20 Mr. Cromie, High Shieref, Pr Mr Jon Smith, Marchent, Juner
21 *w* Thamas Marten, Market House
22 *c* Mr Hugh Pringel, MarChent
25 wid M'Comeby, back Ramper [*Back Rampart*]
26 *c* Adam Patey, planteson
Mar 5 Mr M anse Kirkland, shipCarpner, living one the Kie
11 *c* Mr Cobam, Returney
12 James brown, in the ffales
12 *c* Edward whitloack, Mar Chent
15/14 Mr Jaremy Campbell, who was Loast in Garmoyle, pr his son
17 Enphams Rush, liuing in Rose mery Lean
17 *c* Mr William worthenton, living in Church lean
18 Mr Casky, who was lost in Gar moyle
19 *w* Mr Russel, in Hoolewod
24 *m* olld Sam Smith, living in Dunegoar, Pr Mr Pat Smith
30 Arther Kell, in Holewood, pr Mr James M' Clure

Mar 31 *w* William Anderson, living At the salt water bridge
31 Mr Roper, sealler, his Mother in law
Epr 2 *c* Jon Glen, hole of the wall
3 *c* Mr Cobam, Retorney
4 *c* Alexr Daueson, Selear
5 John M'Dowall, Carman, to his wife
8 olld John Adames, Norstreat
9 *c* Thomas ffeare, living in the Rosemary Lane, Marinor
10 *c* David Leathem, Gon Smith
13 Andrew M'Cone, Carman, Longlean, Pr Jon Ecles
15 *c* William yeward, tobackow Spener, in milstreat
21 *w* Antney Thobron, seaman
21 *c* Jon Chapman, Marinor, living in potengers Entrie
24 *c* Mr Jon Johnston, Marchent
May 15 *c* Jon Starlen, in the ffalls
19 *c* Jon Starlen, in the ffalls
19 *c* William bearrd, Marinor, living in the plantesion, Pr Mr Jon Carr, Elder
26 William Sallter, Living in the ffalls
26 *c* Mr Jon Stoakman, Marinor
28 *c* William Amblem, Coper, at the browrie
Jun 8 Jon neckelson, in the Long lean, baggman
16 *w* Mr Hugh Pringel, MarChant
18 *c* william Smith, Shogarhouse
22 Mr Hugh Cunigham, Clark to the old Mitinghouse
23 *c* Mr M'Clure, MarChent
29 Mrs Maxwel, of Obeday Groaues, of ffiney broag
30 Robert Skery, kie porter
July 1 Joarg Jhnston, Barber, in Mill streat
9 *c* Mr Jon M'Cartney, MarChent
13 *c* John Patterson, barber
19 Mr Greansheals, Carmoney
20 *c* William Geall, Shomacker, noarstreat
23 Mr M'Cologh, in Ronaldstown, Pr James M'Clure

Agest 6 *w* Mr Jon Johnton, in Norstreat, beacker
15 Mr John Challmbrs, MarChent, Pr his Son James
Sept 2 old Mathew Garner, Pr Mr Arther Tattford
3 *c* Sam Smith, Junr, who was boried in holiwood
5 *c* Mr Edr burt, sufron in town [*Benn gives the name as Nathaniel Byrtt; he died in office*].
14 *c* Jon Smith, son to olld Samull Smith
18 *c* Samull Smith, Ealle Selar, ffowr Corners
27 John Comack, in Mayrogh [*Moira*], Pr Mr John Jhnston
Ocbr 6 Robert Calhond, beacker, Pr John Rose
13 Mathew Garners wedo, Pr Mr Arter Tattford
13 Mr William Smith, Pr his brother Mr John Smith, Shogerhouse
Novb 8 Mr William Raney, MarChant
16 Cesie [*Keziah*] Tonough, back Ramper
18 *c* Mr Archbald M'neal, potegar
28 *c* Robart Thomson, ship Carpenter, plantesion
6 wdd Granger, Mill streat, Pr hir son in Law James Thonson
7 *c* William Hamelton, Cooper, in peter hill
13 Mr John Grrefen, Comber, Pr Mr Antoney Harenton
20 Robart Cauer, in Celead
25 *c* william Lason, smith, Church Lean
1725/6
Janry 5 *c* Thomas M'Clune, Glouer, in Rosemary Lean
12 John Ree, ship Carpener, living in waren streat
12 *c* Caluen Darlen, at the Sluse bridge
21 Patricket withers, Copper, in warenstreat, Pr Mr Andrew Agnew
25 *c* william M'Cologh, Telear
28 *c* Mr ffrases Cromie, MarChent
Febr 14 *c* Cornall Edward brise, who was boried in Balleycarey
Febr 18 *s* mrs Ross, at the ston bridge, Pr hir son John
MarCh 7 Cristian Poag, Living in Rossemarey Lean, Pr Mr Thomas Storgan
9 Mr Edward Willson, in waren streat
11 Archbald Moor, marioner, Living in waren Streat, Pr his wife
18 A Leftenanen of the man of war that is at Learn, Pr Mr James M Clure
29 *c* Mr William Staford, Marioner, in Clogstans Entrie
Aprl 2 *m* William brown, at the fforth River
7 Mr Antony Harenton, Rosemery lean
13 *w* John Brown, in peterhill
15 James Mcartnay, Sufron in Town, Pr his brother Jon M'Cartnay
15 *c* Mr John Smith, Son to olld Samull Smith
15 *c* John Hall, Coppar, in Sceepar Lean
17 Mr Jno black, Pr Mr James Arbockels
May 5 John Stwart, in Mellstreat, who was saruant to Mr Kelpatricket
7 *w* Mr Jon Sharp, MarChent, in broaD streat
7 *c* Jon fframe, weauor
8 *c* Edward Loggan, burnCarier
10 Mrs Arther, at the fowr Corners, Pr hir Granson, Arther Burt
27 *d* Mr Isaack Mcartnay, MarChant, on the Hanower Kee
30 *c* Mr William Walles, MarChent
Jun 14 *c* James Willson, butcher, in Rosemery lean
15 Alexander Hotcheson, at the millewater
15 *s* John Irwen, wever, in Jorges Lean
19 *c* James Weear, Marioner, at the ffott of Potengers Entrie
23 *c* Mr Maxwel, of ffeney Broag, Pr Corn Brise in Town
23 *b* Mrs Clogstan
27 *c* Docter Delap, at the Ston bridge
29 *w* Mr Woodside, Marioner, at the ffot of waren Streat

July 2 Daniel ffisher, Mariner, Living at the Kee, Pr his wife
4 c Moses Hill, butcher
8 c Robt Henderson, in beleninch, Pr Alexander Henderson, Gleser
14 d Mr ArChbld Stowart, in Comber
22 m Mr Samull McTearr, in norstreat
Agest 1 c Dauid morrow, Teloyr, livng in broad street
2 c margret Ruebery, in the Long Lean
5 c Dauid Layons, in the Long lean
11 w Robart McCapen, Taner, mel geat
16 w Dauid Morrw, Teallowe, waren streat
20 olld Mr James Smith, Pr his son James, norStreat
29 Mr Joseph Innes, Ston MarChant
Sept 1 olld Mrs yowng, Pr hir Son Hugh yowng
8 c Mr James Monsie, in Scepars Lean
10 w c Thomas Lowrie, beacker
13 c Capt James McCologh, in Waren Streat
26 c Mr James Moncie, in Scepers Lean
8br 11 c John yowng, Carppenter, living at the now Erexon Geat [*New Erection, i.e. Third Meeting-house, gate*]
15 c Mr James Moncie, in Scepers lean
27 c Mr Adam McCen, in waren Streat
29 c Alexr Henderson, Glesor, in norstreat
Nor 2 c Mr John Ald, MarChant, in the back of the MarCethouse
3 c Mr Robert McCapen, Taner, milli-geat
4 c Thomas McConel, Shoe maker, in norstreat
17 c will McDowaille, ffidler,
18 c David Pinkerton, beacker, in the Ston bridg
20 c Mr Willian Maxwell, MarChent, one the Hanouer Kie
29 c Mr John Seadg, one the Hanouer Kee
Desm 7 c Mr william Mettchall, Elder of the olld metting hous
8 Mr John Hamelton, beleny fey
10 f Ritchard Skerie
Desm 11 c william McCologh, Tayloar
11 c Samull mettchall, in noarstreat
13 c Robt Dallzel, Carpentar
27 c John boel, in harkels lean, weauer
31 s Mr John walles, at Doaggh, Pr mr John walles, in broad Streat
31 Mr James Smith, in Noar Streat, Pr his wife

[1727]

Jner 8 c Mr Sam McClenton, uentnar
10 c Samull willson, Stashenor, son in law to wdd Cairns
13 Mr MComb, in Doagh, Pr Mr John walles, in broad Streat
22 Mr John Eacles, MarChant, in broad streat
30 Mrs Grrean, in waren streat, Pr Mr Patrect Kennedy
ffebr 5 Henrie Jones, Pr his Sone Thomas, in Peter hill
6 c Robert Creage, Pr John walles, in broadstreat
15 John ffllemen, beyont the Long bridge, Pr his wife
3 Mrs beccerStaf, Pr Mr John Smeth, at the Sine of the Pecok
4 c Mr Arther Tetford
5 c Mr William Walles, at the bredg End
19 c Patreck Kenneday, MarChent
19 c Mr John fforgeson, Potegar
19 c Mr James yowng, MarChent
20 Mr David McCnaight, Peter Hell, Pr his wife
25 Thomas Mcneight, Teallor, Leiuing in Rosse marey Lean, Pr David Morrow
29 Mr Dickson, in Comber, Pr John Colbert
31 c Ritchard ofarel, in Peter Hill
Apr 1 Jean Marten, in ChurCh Lean
10 d Hugh Sharpp, in Kirk Doneall
13 d Mrs Manken, in veran streat
13 d John Gades, Corier
17 g c Allexr Moor, in Peter Hill
17 c William wyly, Coper Smith
(*sic*) 12 c wdd Smith, in nor Streat
27 c Mr ffranses Cromie, MarChent
May 2 s ArChbld Stwart, in Comber parish

May 6 *c* David Pinkerton, Living at the Ston bridg
9 *c* John M ffcran, Living in Rossemarey Lean, tealower
15 Mrs Mirifeld in Lisburn, Pr Mr Thomas Lill, MarChent
20 Mr Andrew Dalrumpel, MarChent, Pr Mr James Dallrumpl
20 *c* Mr James Parkes, marChent, at the Ston bridg
20 *s* Parson Hamelton, in banger, Pr Mr Sam Smith, junr, MarChent
20 Sara Mcneall, planteson
Jun 3 John M Dowall, Pr James mcDowll, in Holewood
3 *c* Mr Jon Moor, Scoll master
10 *c* John umfres, Scollmaster, in waren Streat
11 *c* Mr John Allde, MarChent, in Potengers Entrie
25 *c* mr John Macartney, MarChent
29 *w* Thomas ffeare, in Rose Marey Lean
July 11 *c* Jorg brakenrig, Gleaser, in Rossemarey Lean
15 Mr Ritchard Ashmor, hatter, in mell Streat
16 *c* Jorg brakenrige, Gleaser, in Rosse Morey lean
17 *m* John Irland
Agest 9 *s* John hamelton, Living in neow Combe
10 *c* mr Robert mcCapen, taner, in Mell Streat
24 *c* Mr John Johnson, MerChent
24 *c* mr James begger, marChent
26 *c* widdo Smith, in norstreat
26 *c* ArChbld mcneall
28 *c* mr James bigger
Sept 1 *w* williamson, in Caselreah
5 *c* Jorg Guttrie, MarChent
11 *c* George Gutrie
11 mrs Clugston, Pr hir son the sofren
Octr 6 *c* mr Sam Mclento
7 *w* James barnet, in melstreat
8 Dauid morra, Taylor, in waren Streat, Pr his wife
25 mr William Arbuckle, Pr his father mr James Arbuckle

Novr 5 *c* william Sinkler, in melstreat
6 Mrs Jean Clugson, Pr hir brother the Soueran in town
17 *m* Mr Cobam, Returnie, in Town
Desm 5 John boall, marinor, in waran Streat
14 A Streanger, living in Jorg Stevens Entrie, mell Streat, Pr Madam Dabb
23 *c* John willson, in Rose marey Lean, weauer
26 *c* Thomas wason, Carpeiter, in Rose Marey lean
27 *c* William Staford, marioner, in Clogsons Entrie
28 Robert Coper, in Hugh Pringels
[1728]
Janr 18 Mr Harper, Living in Glanarm, Pr mr Samull Allen
1727/8
ffebr 3 A Streanger that Dayed in the ffar End of ChurCh lean, Pr mr Joseph bigger
5 *b* Alexr orr
21 Mrs Donelson, Pr Hir Son in Law mr James McClure, MarChent
Mar 6 olld Mrs Ewens, in Peter Hill, Pr mr Jon Armstrong
12 *c* Allexand Henderson, Gleasor
14 A frind of Mr James blow, A yowng woman who Dayed in his House
15 *c* John bowall, weauer, in Harklos Lean
15 John fforgeson, son to olld Docter fforgeson, who dayed besides Dogh, Pr mr John forgeson, Potegar
21 Robert Morra, Taylor, in Rose mary Lean, Pr his wife
23 *c* mr wear, maironer, in the fut of Potengers Entrie
29 *c* Alexr Henderson, Gleasor, in norstreat
30 olld mrs Todd, Pr mr Thomas Lille & mr John Smith, in broad Streat
Aprl 4 olld william mclelan, in the Long lean, Pr mr mcDowalld and mr Robert mcGee, in Scepers lean
5 *w* Thomas Agnewe, scleater

Apl	6 *c*	William m Cologh, Taylor
	7	John Read, Labror, in the Plante-shen
	8	mrs Innes, Pr Mr Joseph Innes
	9 *c*	John M Dowall, Carman, in Peter hill
	11	mrs Comock, in Myroah parish, Pr mr John Smith, at the Pecoak
	15	olld James Orr, in Comber at the Dam, Pr Allext Orr, marChent
	17 *w*	Hugh Kennedy, in the Longlean
	19 *w*	William m Lelan, in the Longlean, Pr mr oahtrie m Dowall and mr Robert M Gee
	23 *d*	Mr James Moor, in the ffall Mill
May	1 *c*	William Moor, Chanler, at the Sluse bridg
	2 *c*	mr Jno Sttell, Potegar
	6 *c*	Jon Stell, Potegr
	6 *c*	william Endslie, Glower, in Rosse mery lean
	7 *c*	william Hanna, Taylowr, in Church lean
	14 *d*	mrs Camel, beacker
	17	Mr John Clark, MarChent, at the Market House, Pr his wife
	17	John Jakes mother in Law, Show make
	28	James Thamson, Marioner, living in melstreat, Pr his wife
Jun	3 *c*	Thomas m'Conell, showmaker, in Norstreat
July	8 *c*	mr William mittchel, MarChant, Living besids mr John m'Cartnays
	12 *w*	mr William ffarlie, at Lisburn, Living in Lesnetronk, Pr mr James m Clure, marClant
	15	David Pinkerton, beaker
	19 *c*	mr Gillbart m'Dowall, MarChent
	19 *w*	mr Wallter Cromel, Pr mr James m'Clure
	20	Chanceler M ncall, of Port of ffery, Pr mr James M Clure, marChant
	28	mr John Kinkaid, Pr mr James M Clure
	30	mr Allext Moor, Marchent, in Peter Hill, Pr mr Getty
Agest	15 *c*	Allext Henderson, Gleaser
	17 *gc*	John Johnston, beacker, in nor-streat
Agest	25 *c*	Jorge Johnston, barber, in Mill Streat
Sept	9 *c*	mr Hugh Linn, Living in Casel-streat
	20	olld Madam Dalaway, Pr mr Samull Smith, MarChent
	24 *c*	mr James Henderson, Living in warensteat
	26	mr John Taylor and his mother in Law
Octbr	7	Mrs bruse, Pr mr John Roose, MarChent, at the Stonbridg
	24 *c*	Thomas Lowrie, beacker
nor	5	Jorg williamson, Smith, in Church lean
	6	mrs Hutcheson, near beleclair, Pr mr John fforgeson, Potegar
	23 *c*	william Osborn
	28 *c*	mr Andrew Smith, marChent
Desm	1	Gillbart moor, Sinr, his mother in Lawe
	13 *c*	James Campbel, watterman
	18 *gc*	James Lawe
	27 *w*	mr Robt Johnston, in mellone
	29	mr Thomas Lyle, Pr mr mosentine
1728/9		
Janr	4	mr John M'Cartnay, marClent, Pr the Reud mr Samull Helleday
	6 *s*	Andrew barnet, Pr mr John Smith, marChent, broad Streat
	15	mr John Shaw, beleytwedy, Pr mr James m'Clure
	18	Capt M'Cologh, in Ronaldstoun, Pr mr James m'Clure, marClent
	20 *c*	mr John Sharpe, MarChent, in broadstreat
	27	Mr Walles Granmother, marChent in broadstreat
ffebr	5	widdo m'Canlie, Pr mrs m'Canlie, liveng in the plantesion
	9	margrat miller, in mr David Cra-fords, his seruant
	10	mr Samull M'Clenton, Pr his wife
	13	A strenge, Pr mr Jon Smeth, in broad streat
Mar	2	mr John Smith, Liung in Mr Pa-tricket Smiths, MarChent
	9 *m*	Ringen [*Ninian*] ffresel, in Long lean

Mar 20 w Georg Campsie, in norstreat
24 Gaien Hamelton, Pr mr Jon Colbert
Epr 1 c mr John Johnston, MarChent
2 w Doacter Smith, in town
8 c James Singelton, in mill ffeld lean
13 c William hamelton, Cooper, in Roose mereylean
23 c mr John Mairs, in Town
24 w william mathies, in Loonglean
30 m Thomas Lowrie, beaker
May 1 Iserall Coates, Liung in the ffalles, Pr obedia Groaues
3 Thomas ffeares, Sealler, his mother in Lawe
7 mr John m'Ceben, at Kerkdonel, Pr mr Adam m'Ceben, marChent in town
20 the Revd mr John Mallcom, in Dunmorey, Pr mr John walles in broad Streat
20 c Mrs Petecrow, in NorStreat
Jun 13 c Robert Ashmor, Hatter
13 c Alexr Daueson, Marioner
16 Daniel Handerson, tobacones, Pr mr Robert Henderson, Taner, in norstret
16 c mr Samull Mittchel, MarChent, in norStreat
July 8 c A sister of mr Samull Mitchell, in norStreat, MarChent
14 c william Henderson, taner, in norSt
20 Mr Adams, yearn Marchent, At the Ston bridg, Pr his wife
25 c mr William Sharply, Taner, in norstreat
Agest 4 c David Layens, Cafey Hous
5 c mr william Staford, Marinor
13 Agnes Leas, Pr Ronold, in Mr James blowes
14 Mrs Leas, Pr hir Son Ronold, in Mr James blowes
20 Andrew Tood, in the Countie of Down
22 mr James Woods, Living at the ffowr Lone Ends in mellone, Pr his Doghter Mrs m'Gee, in warenstreat, weddo
26 c John Dreanen, Roper, in NorStreat

Agest 29 Olld Madam Pottenger, Pr hir Son mr Joseph Pottenger
Sept 1 c mr ffranses Atcheson, Fall seler
4 c mr James Henderson, Living at the Shoger house
5 c mr John walles, MarChent, broad Streat
7 c mr William m Caulie, liung in the plant teshen, sealer
10 w Andrew wattson, Carman
11 c James nelson, Carman, tor Streat
14 c Samull brown, Peter hill
20 wido m'Calester, in the Long lean
22 Mr John Sharp, in broad streat, his onkels Doghter
22 c Andrew m'Comb
Octr 3 c mr William Mittchel, MarChent
8 c Dauid Craghton, Marinor, in Norstreat
11 John fram, weaver, Peter hill
11 c Rittchard Offerall, Petterhill
14 c John osborn, beaker, in melstreat
15 c Geiorg Carson, water man, at the plantteson
20 c John Slloan, beacker, in norstreat
Nor 3 c John m'Dowald, Carman, in norStreat
5 d wildow Parkhill, in Peter hill
10 gc John Gades, at north Geat
23 c John Taylor, tobackenst, in norstreat
25 c widdo boyd, in mr Allexr yowngs howse, teneneneman
Dems 1 c John m'morey, Taylor
2 c william moor, Chanclar, at the sllus bridg
7 Gain Rodgers, in Long lean, Pr his ffather william Rodgers
13 olld mrs Craford, Pr hir son Dauid Craford
16 mrs Sinkler, Pr mr Dainel mosentine
16 John osborn, beaker, Pr his wife
25 Hanna bell, Pr mr John Collman, Clark of the olld meting house
25 Olld william Rusel, olld Park, Pr his Son Georg Rusel

1729/30

Janr 13 c mr James Challmbrs in waren Streat
21 John brown, in Peter hill, Pr John Singelton, weauer

Janr 23 wido Maxwel, norStreat, Pr David Craghon, Marinon
30 c william Innes, whipmaker
ffebr 4 A stranger in the Contre, Pr Alexr orr, marChent
4 c Thomas Geleland
7 c Mr Sam Smith marChent
12 c Isaack AGnew, Copper
24 the Revd mr James bruse, Keleleah, Pr mr John Smeth, at the Peoack
24 c mr John Knoox Gold smeth
Mar 4 John Catterwood
4 c John M questen
16 c John umfres, Scoll master
24 Mr Matthew Ramsey, Clark of the neow meting house
28 Mrs Read, in Kellenchie, Pr mr James M Clure
30 c James Loaggan, Eall seler, in norstreat
Apr 8 c John m'Glahlen, brower
11 Nathan Smith, Pr John Hughs, in Carmoney
18 c mr James ballief, Marioner, Pr mr Hoadkis, nealer
19 c Moses Cunigham
24 c Georg Gemeson, beacker, at the Ston bridg
May 1 Thomas Agnew, Pr his Son in Law, mihel m'feall, butcher
13 wido m'Cormick, in the Long Lean
16 c mr Cobbam, Returnie
18 John Marten, Long lean
27 oll mrs Kittchie, Pr hir son Robt Dallzel, Carpenter
30 c Thomas ffife, Carpenter, in norstreat
July 4 c mr James bigger, marChent
18 Dauid Potter, Church lean
19 c mr John Gordon
20 c John Picken, in Long lean
Agest 17 c John mean, Shomaker
Sept 12 c James baillef, Marinor
22 Mrs Ashmor, Hatter, Pr hir Son Robert
Octr 4 brown Georg m'Cartney wido, Pr mr Patr Smith, MarChent
30 A brothers Child of Walter Sandelens
31 w Kittchard ffinnley, Town Sargen
Nor 10 Madan shaw, in Lisburn
14 c mr Daniel Mosentine
17 mr Georg Manken, at the millwater
21 Thomas Marten, in Rose marie Lean, Pr his ffather in Law Robert M'ffeall
30 w James monsie, in Long lean
Desm 1 mrs Rosse Hamelton, Living in mount Hamelton, Pr mr James m'Clure, MarChent in Town

[1731]

Janr 2 Allexr orr, for his Cosens ffunerall
3 w Mr Arther Tattford, Pr the Revd mr Neelous Tatford
7 the Revd mr Sinklear, Pr mr John fforgson, Potegar
ffebr 15 Olld widdo boyd, in the Plantesion, Pr mr William M'Canlies, maioner
27 mr William m'whorter, in Carmoney, Pr mr Joseph Jinnes, MarChent
28 c mr William M'ckelwreth, marChent
Mar 7 mr John Damster, Pr his wife
19 Doacter Cromie, Pr his brother in Law Mr John magenis, Liung besids Drummor
19 mrs fforgeson, in tampel Patreck parish, Pr mr Jon Smith, in broad Streat
27 mrs Manken, at the Millwater, Pr hir Son Thomas manken
28 mr oferall, in Peterhill, Pr his wife
30 c widd bell
Apr 9 mrs Hadenton, in Town, midwife, Pr mr Joseph Innes, MarChent
27 mr James Robeson, marChent, in Norstreat, Pr his wife
may 27 c John Eger, Smith, Rose mery lean
31 c Astrenger, in the Long lean
Jun 4 si mr Adam Adam m'Ceben, marChent
9 mr James wear, maironer, his mother in Law
10 James Scoat, in Drumbo
18 mrs Johnes, play howse
July 8 s mr Georg maCertney Esqr
13 c James Rodgers
15 John Donelson, in Church Lean, beacker

July 15 neas of Toallen, in the ffalles
22 c John m'Cert
24 c Thomas willson, barber, one the keay
Agest ye 3 Maigor blaire, Livng at Carn Castel, Pr mr James burges, marChent
12 William Geals, Showmaker
12 Robert ffisher, in the ffales
27 Astreanger
30 w Mr wear, one the Kee
31 Robert Scoat, taylor
Octr 17 s mr Robert Donaldson, in Peter hill
18 w Thomas Gilleland, buttcher
Nor 2 David Throw, miller, of the Corn mill, Pr his wife
3 d widdo Agnew, at Cewaghter [*Kilwaughter*] Pr mr James burges, marChent
6 John Gaddas, Coriner, Pr his wife
15 A frind of mr Joseph Innes, in the Contre
15 olld mrs Tavernor, in the ffalles, Pr Sam M'Cadam, in the Long Casa
15 c Sam Joy, meason, in norstreat
20 w Thomas Singlton, in the Long Lean
24 c mr ffranses Cromie, MarChent
29 wido ffife, Pr William m'Callogh, Taylor
Desm 6 Mr ffranses Cromie, Pr mr James bllow
6 Capt Hamelton, Living in Cushin-Dun, Pr mr James M'Clure, marchent in town

[1732]

Janr 6 c John ffife, Sope boyler, in Nor streat
7 Mr Patrick Kennedy, Marchent
9 c Thomas Gueleland, butcher
9 c Samull m'Calliue, Museshenar
10 c mr John Maiers, in town
22 m Lahlen M'neal, mairnor, in the planteshon
25 A sister in Law of Thomas Gilleland, botcher, in Town
ffebr 1 c mr John Alld, marchant, in Town in the back of the Grean
Mar 2 mrs black, at Drummor, Pr mr mosentine
Mar 16 w mr John Mairs, in town
16 mr Hugh Sharp, Pr mr John Sharp
Apr 2 mrs Joanes, in melone
7 mr James Hamelton, Chaneler, Pr mr James M'Clure, in town
7 c mr Hugh Linn
21 c will Cros
May 20 wido bell, at the Coaue hill
21 Astrangers Chill, Pr James Easdealld, botten maker, in Town
22 mrs bleair, living at CarnCasel, Pr mr James borges, marChent, in town
Jun 2 c James Lure
3 c mr Robt Ashmor, Hater
19 c John Jake, Showmaker
23 william Dicks mother in law
24 c James Rodgers, ship Carpenter
July 5 Alexr m'Dowalld
15 c mr John Ashmor, marClent
20 d David m'men, at the Coawe hill
Agest 3 c will Lason, Smith
7 Maigor upton, in tampelpatrek, Pr mr James m'Clure, marClent, in Town
8 s the Revd mr wolson, in beley Clair, Pr mr James burges, in town
15 w John m'Clune, mairnor, Pr his brother Robert m'Clune
22 s Pall Redd, in Tampelpatrek, Pr John Sampel in Norstreat
Sept 2 c Thomas whittsid, Ship Carpenter, one the kee
13 widdo Craford, one the kee, Pr John m'Ceben, Copper
Octr 1 c Thomas whittsid, one on the Kee, ship carpenter
15 c Hendrie fegen
16 w Robert m'ceall
21 necloas Sharp, Pr his sisters
23 w William osborn, butcher
nor ye 17 c mr Patr Smith, marChent
ye 16 mr Gabriel Andrews, MarChent, Pr his brother Hugh Andrews
ye 26 James boyds mother in Law, marinor, in scepers Lean
30 mr John Taylor, in broad streat, Pr his wife

Dems 7 w Andrew m'Clenchie, Dunmorey
10 w Timothy Shelds, beaker, in Rose mary lean
10 s John Taylor, Carman
14 John Kerns, snuf man, Pr his mother, wido Kerns
19 William Lowrie, buttcher, Liuing at the wattersid, Pr his wife
21 mrs Shaw, of beley Gelly, Pr mr James M Clure, MarChent
22 s the Reud mr Clugston, in Larn
24 c Antoney Thobron, sealler
25 mrs Potter, mother in Law to Robart Armstrong, marChent in town, whos mother in Law Liued in Kelenchie
27 wido swondeall, in HarColes Lean, Pr hir Doghter marey and Thomas Lowrie, beaker

[1733]

Janr 15 mr James Challmbrs, marioner
16 c John Gafoge, botcher
22 Robart Ranton, Pr mr Robart Donelson
27 c mr James yowng
31 c Georg Ross, ship Carpenter, in the backplantesion

ffebr 16 w James Layon
17 c mr Isaac Agnew, Copar
19 mr Gelbart Moor, MarChent, Pr his Doghter Elisabeth
20 Peter Alexande, in Peterhill
21 c Robt Stwart, in Drumbo, Pr Robert m kee, in the Paresh of Drumbo, in beley Coaen townland
24 c mr Isaack Agnew, Copper
24 widdo Guning, in Roess merie Lean, Pr mr ffranses Atesion, at the Punshbowl
25 mrs Creag, harclos Lean, Pr John Henderson, weauer
26 w John ffife, barber, Pr hir son John, Chanler

Mar 3 w Mr John Sharp, MarChant
5 mrs m'Cullogh at Shaes bridg, Pr mr Dauid Craford, in Town
16 William Scoat, in Drumbo, Pr neuin m'kee, in belecoan
17 c Georg Johnston, melstreat

Mar 18 william ffergeson, at the Clownie, Pr his son Georg ffergeson
20 w mathew m'nealley, Pr John Sempel, Peter hill
26 Harcoles m'Gomrie, Esqr, in beley Leson, Drumbo, Pr Capt Hamelton, Drumbeg
26 c mr Hugh yowng, marChent
27 wido Sttwart, Plantesion, Pr hir son in law, Antoney Thobron, marioner

Apr 3 w William ffergson, in the Clownie,
24 Pr hir Son Georg ffergson with Sqr mcartney Colector
22 c mr William Walles, at the bredg End
24 Hugh Morrow, in the ffalles
28 c John Orr, in Drumbo

May 9 c mr William Sinkler, in mellstreat
12 c mr James Challmbrs, marinor, in waren streat
13 olld John m'faden, Pr his son Hendrey m'faden, barber, in Church lean
19 mr William Henderson, for two children at Deferant times
20 c mr John Jack Show maker
20 c John forsieth, Taner, in Ropwack
24 c William Kenen, Ship Carppenter, in the Plantesio
27 c Georg Lashel, Cardmaker
31 Georg Swarbreck, liuing in the ffalls, Pr his wife

Jun 2 d James Smith, Coppar, in Roesmary lean
2 c mr Hugh Pringel, marChant
3 c John Dowald, bangbeger
3 c John fife, Sopboyler
4 c Robert forsieth, in the falles
4 c wido Arbockels, in Rosse marey Lean, Pr olld mrs Ardbockels
6 c Samull Mitcheall, in norstreat
6 c mr Paterek Smith, marChant
9 c mr Robart walles, marChant
10 c mr Isaak Agnew, Copper
10 mr Joseph Innes nephew
12 Hendrie m'Gomrie, Carman
12 c John boald, weauer, in Rossmerey Lean

Jun 12 c John m'Glahlen, hoxter, in norstreat
14 c Charles Garner Gardner, Marinor, at ye Slows bridg
15 c John Lawes, Hoxter, in norstreat
16 c James Sowrbot, on the kee
17 c James m'Calserar, in norstreat, Carman
18 c James nelson, in norstreat
19 c Charles Garner, Marinor, at the Slows bredg
21 c mr William Mittchall, one the hanouer kee, marChant
23 c Willm Lason, smith, in Church Lean
24 c William Hamelton, Copper, in harcoles lean
24 c Thomas Anderson, opeset [*opposite*] to mr Archbld m'neall, Doctor
24 c John Gafogen, botcher, in melstreat
25 c Georg Endsly, in norstreat, Glower
26 c William mathies, Carpenter, in the Long Lean
c Patr mackrorey, marinor
29 c samull brown, Peterhill
29 c mr James Moor, marinor
30 c mr James m'Clure, MarChant
July 1 c Robart m'Clelan, in skeprs lean, Marinor
1 neuen Parker, in ye Long casa, Pr John Sempel, in Peter hill
3 c Dauid Teatt, Leuing one the hanower kee
4 c John filemen, in Long Lean
6 gc Robert m'fealle, in Ross merey Lean
9 c James Percy, weauer, in Harcoles lean
10 c Thomas Wason, Carpenter, in Ross merey Lean
10 c Mr William M'Canlie, Marinor, in Plantesion
12 c mr Handley, heall maker, in watenstreatt
15 c William hanna, Taylor, in Church lean
15 c James boyd, in skepers Lean, marinor
15 c Adam Patty, Plantesion, marinor
July 15 c Widdo m'Cartney, Plantesion
16 John Wollson, on the kee, Pr his wife, Ene keper
18 c mr John Johnston, MarChent, in Town
18 c William Nutt, hatter, in Church Lean
19 c Georg Carsan, waterman, in Plantesion
19 c John Mean, Marinor, on ye olld kee, Pr his onkel, Alexr Tamson, waterman
19 c Robert Dallzel, Carpenter
19 c John wharton, Church Lean, Showmaker
20 c William Hanna, Taylor, in Church lean
21 c John M'Dowald, Carman, Peterhill
21 c Wido Swarbridg, in ye ffalls, Pr mr James Moor, in ye ffalls, Elder
22 c Patreack harbert, Carpenter, in ye Plantesion
24 Robert Gastowns Mother, who Lived at ye 4 Corners and was boried at Antrem, Pr hir Son Robert Gasken
27 c James M'Clune, butcher, in Town
28 olld William fferguson, at ye Clownie, Pr his son Georg with ye Colecter
31 c John Winentown, book binder
Agst ye 1 c John M'faden, hatter, in Church Leat
3 c Rittchard ffenely, Surgen
9 Elinor M'Crom, hoxter, Pr William Lason, Smith
10 mary M'Dowald, Pr hir brother
20 c John Teatt, Glower
Sept 6 c Samull brown, Peter hill
16 c Widdo Donelson, in ChurCh Lean
17 olld widdo Arbockels, Pr mr James Arbockels wife
24 mrs Mash, Pr hir son mr Hugh Pring, marChant
Octr 3 c William PateyCrow, Taylor
15 c Hugh barneat, who was boried in sant feield
20 Wido M'Cotchen, in Plontesion
23 2c the Reud mr Mihel bruse
30 Dinis ohegan

nor 6 mr William Sttenson, at bears bridg, Pr mr John Knox, Goldsmith, in Towin
11 m mr John Ross, marchant, at the stonbridg
17 c Patr Agnew, marinor
18 William Anderson, at the whitt hovse
25 c Andrew Harper, taner, in norstret
Desm 3 c mr Hugh Linn, melstret
7 w Dauid Loggan, in Rossmery Lean
9 c Hugh barnet, in Town
9 Alexr besbbe, at ye Long Casa, Pr his son John busbe
15 William Ashfield, in ye falls
23 Widdo M Dowald, at ye brurie
[1734]
Janr 3 w William Lason, in Church Leam
9 m William Kennen, Ship Carpenter, in Cow Lean, near the Plantesion
10 mrs Potter, Pr mr Robert Armstrong, marChent
17 mr Andrew Kelsay, in at the Roghforth, in Tampelpatreck Peresh
22 mr James Park, marChant, in Town, Pr his brother, Arthur Park
1733
4
ffebr 4 mr oahtrie m'Dowald, Pr mr John Holmbs and James burdges
9 c William brown, in beleygomarten
10 wido m'Cormeck, Pr mr Samull Willson, Prenter, at the Stton bredg
16 mr Hugh yowng, MarChant, at the ston bridge, Pr his brother mr Allexr yowng
19 William m'Clenchy, in the falles
21 oll widdo m'Clelan, in scepers lean, Pr mr John Chapman, marinor, in warenstreat
22 c mr James m'Clure, marChant
27 c Robert Thamson, Marinor, in Millstret
Mar 8 w James Singeltow, weaver, in Melfel Lean
14 c William Sttaford, Marioner, in Clugstons Entrie
Apr 5 mr Aunger Robeson, Eall seler, Pr his ffather, John Holmbs, at ye Adam & Eve
8 w Mr John Carr, at the olld Park
14 Arther Graye, shoger man with mr Pringel
18 Widd Robeson, Longlean, Pr hir son John Robeson, Copper
21 c Alexr Mogerland, butcher
26 James M'Gee, at ye fowr Lonends up melon, Pr his son Thomas
May 2 ye Revd mr [*William*] Taylor, in Carn Castel
2 c John Wharton, show maker in Church Lean
8 Mr David Craford, in Town, Pr Mr Archbald m'neall, Doctor
25 c Samull Rathue, waterman
Jun 5 d Widd m'Call, liuing in Dunmory
7 c John Kean, Living in melon
12 c James yownge
23 c Widd fferall, in Peterhil
30 c mr Archabld, at the fowr Corners
July 1 c Robert Lowrie, Carpenter
3 m Mr Hendrie m'Culogh, in Ronoldstown, Pr mr m'Clure
8 c mr Craford, in Tempelpatrek Peresh, Pr William brown in Peter Hill
12 c James M'Gefort, botenmaker, in norstreat
13 c John Picken, Carppenter, in the Longlean
16 c Robart Ashmor, Hatter
18 w Alexr M'Celie
22 c Andrew Sloan, Taylor, Church lean
23 c David m'neight, book binder
24 mrs boggs, Astrenger
29 m mr Alexr Sttaford
30 s John m'fferan, Taylor
Ags[t] 3 Doacter m'neall, Pr mr Archbald m'neall
7 mr whitifeald, shoger man, Pr mr benjam Gegg and Compnie
9 c mr John M'Geagh, in Peterhill
10 c mr william M Candlie, plantesion
19 James Teatt, at the fforth Riuer, to his wife
24 c John boald, weauer

Agst 30 *c* mr benjam Legg
30 *c* Alexr Mogerland, botcher
Sept 4 *c* John M Glahlen
10 Mr Moor in Caregfergos, pr Mrs Moor in Peter Hill
21 James M'millen, in Melon [*Malone*]
26 Thomas Seadge, pr mr William Ringland, Gowld Smith
26 *c* mr Joseph m'mun
29 *c* mr Georg Orr, Marinor
Oct 2 Wido Yeowart
13 *w* John ffife, Chanler in norstreat
14 *c* Charles Gardner, marinor, at the Slows bridg
22 Samull mittchall, in norstret
22 *w* mosses Keain, marinor, pr mr John umpher, Scoallmaster
Nov 30 mr John Donelson, at Glenarm, pr mr James m'Clure MarChant in Town
Desm 7 mr Kelsa, at the Rogh forth in Tampelpatrek peresh, pr mr John Howstan, Ealseler [*ale-seller*] in Town
12 mr Philop bears, near belenie ffay [*Ballynafeigh*]. Pr mr James Read, marChant in Town
13 *w* Allexr m'Cay, in Keper [*innkeeper*], in Norstreat
25 *c* mr Thomas Whittsid, Ship Carpentar
31 John m'elmen, at the Coaue hill, pr his ffather David m'elmnen

[1735]
Janr 14 *c* William Endslie, Glouer, in Rossemery Lean
16 *c* William Lasons, Smith, in Church Lean
ffebr 7 *b* mr Joseph Innes, in Castelreah
11 mr Gelbert mathies, in the ffales
14 *w* William Sttaford, marinor, pr his brother Allexr Sttaford
15 mr Ross, of Portyvow, pr mr James mcClure
16 Mrs bleair, in Town, pr mr John fforgeson, potegar [*apothecary*]
16 *g* mr James Wears, marinor, in ChurCh lean
21 *w* Lowes [*Lewis*] Shae, book binder
25 Alexr park

mar 2 *c* mr Hendrie wharton, Showmaker, in Curchlean [*Church Lane*]
4 *m* mr Alexr m'Keney, wine Copper with mr beggers Seler
14 *s* William Carson, breaklear, in Roossmery lean
29 *c* mr Joseph Potengar
Apr 4 *c* mr William Lason, Smith, in Church-Lean
12 *c* Willm browne, Linnen Laper, at the whit hows
14 mr James burdges ffather in Law, Liuing in bely Easton
19 Hugh Doagh, at Tempelpatrek
19 *c* William Heanen, in norStreat
26 mr James Whotel, in Lisburn, Pr mr James m'Clure, MarChant, in Town
May 5 *w* John Mean, in the plantesion
16 mrs Harper, in Gleanarm, Pr mr James m'Clure, in Town
Jun 2 *c* mr Musentine, mar Chent, in Town
5 *c* Robart dowrie, Carperter, in norstreat
8 wido warkly, in Melon
July 4 *w* mr Hugh Donnaldson, marChait, at the Ston bridg
7 *c* William Crue
mr Ramsa, Shogerhouse
16 *c* James Rodgers, ship Carpenter
Agts 2 *c* Haigh Kelley, weaver, harklous Lean
11 William fforgeson, in Casel Reagh
13 *w* William Trallfor, in the ffalles
19 *c* James Paterson, in the Planttesion
28 *w* David wotherspon, Drumbo
Sept 4 *c* Georg bell, weauer
12 Robert brown, millwater
22 *c* mr John Ashmor, Glower
Octr 23 mr William Smith, in the Lope, Pr mr Smith, broad sttreat
23 *c* Angas waker, seaman
nor 1 James M'Dowald, Carrman, in the Plantesion
26 *c* John Ligget, in Long, weaver, for on of his ightbrs [*neighbour's*] Children
Desm ye Reud mr bruse [*Rev. Michael Bruce, Holywood, died 1st Dec.*]

Desm 4 c Georg Endsly, Glouer
12 William m Cullogh, Taylor
16 c Andreew Townds
19 c John Clotworthie, far end of Church, brower, to mr Wallas
23 c Alexr Philleps, beaker
25 w John M Crakan, at Petershill

1735 6

Janr 3 w Alexander Mogerland, batcher
3 mrs Woods, at fowr lonends, Pr hir Doghter, mrs M Gee, in Skepers Lean
5 b mr Samull M Tear, in norstreat
14 m Mr James hameltoun Maxwel, at the Drumbridg
24 mr John Clugston, in Town, Pr sister mrs Elenar Clugston
28 mrs Elizabeth M'Certnay, Pr mr Isaac M Certnay, MarChant

ffebr 12 c Alexr Mairs, Taylor, in Clugstons Entrie
13 c Alexr Mogerland, butcher
20 m mr Shawe, in beleygely

March 4 olld wido nickel, Pr hir Doghter, Doroty willson, in Ross marey Lean
27 c William M'Clearey, beaker, in Rossmery lean
29 the Reud mr Scoat, at Tampelpatreck
29 w mr Dallzel, the Carpenter
30 Mr James Ardbokels, Pr his son mr James Ardbokels

Apr 17 mr John Robeson, Pr mr Hugh Pringel, MarChant
14 A Coson of mr Innes, in The Town
28 c William Kenenan, Ship Carpenter, in Plantesion

May 8 c mr John vmphres, Scollmaster
9 c Robt streain, in Petershill
12 A brother son of mr Joseph Innes

Jun 5 s mr Whitsat, in bangor, Pr mr James m Clure, marchant
20 c David Layons, at stton bridg
29 Capt Craford.........Dunegor, Pr mr James burdges, marchent

July 4 ....Pr mr Daniel Mosentin.........
13 mr John Gregg in Gleneua, Pr his his son William Gregg in......stret
14 w James.........in Rogh forth in Tempelpatrek Parish
25 Mr John Alld, Marchent, in broad sttreat, Pr his wife

Agst 18 Mr James Weor (?). Marioner, Living in Church Lean
26 John Gregg. Junr. in Gleneua, Pr his brother William Gregg, scolar, in norstreat

Sept 2 c Alexr Thampson, Malster, norstreat
4 Antoney Thoborn, Marinor, Pr his wife
8 Mrs Teatt, Kirk Donel, Pr mr James m'Clure
15 olld mr M Kie, in banger, Pr his Gran son Reud mr M Kie, minester in banger [*i.e., Rev. James Mackay, afterwards of First Belfast*]
22 c A brothers Child of mr Hugh Linn
24 mrs Ann brumly in Lurgan, Pr mr Hugh Pringel, MarChent
25 Thomas Spark, Carman, at Peter hill
28 c mr John Asmor
29 John m'Cearts Mother in Law, in Peter hill

Octr 11 w Thomas Wason, Carpenter, in Millstreat
14 c Abrothers child of John Carter, in Peterhill
19 c Henery Coner, at the Pownd, weauer

[Here the Register ends.]

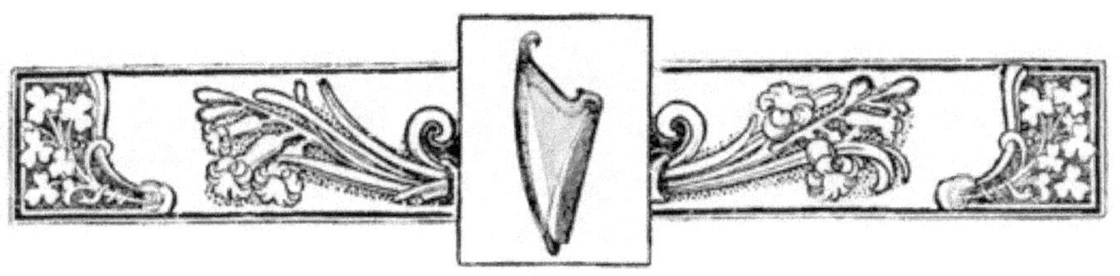

VARIOUS LISTS OF MEMBERS, &c.

EARLIEST LIST OF MEMBERS

Present at a Meeting of "heads of familys & principal members," on Wednesday, 3 Sept., 1760.

Mess. Jam[s] Adair
William Wallace, Sen[r]
Sam[l] Mattier, Sen[r]
Hugh Donnaldson
Doctor Haliday
Doctor Mattier
John Ross
Daniel Blow
John Fivey
John Mathers
James Park
William Wilson
Samuel Mattier, Jun.
John Hay
Captain Stewart
Thom[s] M'Ilwean
Charles Cuningham

At this date the Session consisted of—

Samuel Smith
Samuel Mattier
John Gordon
John Ross
Robert Wallace
James Magee
John Jackson

A standing committee to be elected annually, and act with the session, was for the first time appointed at this meeting, the persons chosen being—

Mr. James Adair, Chairman
Doctor Haliday
Hugh Donnaldson
Daniel Blow
Robert Gordon
Benjamin Legg
Thomas Sinclair
Captain Stewart
John Hay
Joseph Wallace
James Getty
John Mathers
John Galt Smith
Charles Cunningham, Secy.

EARLIEST COMPLETE LIST OF CONSTITUENTS.

Being the Stipend list of 1st Octr, 1775.

[The aisles &c are those of the Meeting House taken down in 1781. The Stipends range from 3d per month to 8s / 1½d per month; the total amount of Stipend due per month was £13 0 11½ (Irish currency). The list is in the handwriting of the Treasurer, John Galt Smith.]

NORTH ISLE.

Messrs. M Kedy & Elder
Mr. William Ramsey
Mr. James Kinley
Mr. Galon & Mr. Thompson
Mr. Samuel Mitchall
John Brown
Mr. Mussenden Auld
Mr. Samuel Wilson
Mr. Jess Taylor
Mr. James Dunn
Mr. William Gregg
Mr. James Grahams
Mr. John Gregg
Mr. John Campbell
Mr. Hugh Montgomery

SOUTH ISLE.

Mrs. Legg
Mrs. J. Panton
Mrs. Dougless
Mr. James Park
Mr. Davd Park
Mrs. Park
Miss Sharp
J. G. Smith
Mr. C. Roberts
Miss Hamilton
Mr. Hugh Allen
Mr. Fr: Hamilton
Mr. John Hamilton
Mr. T. Sinclair
Mrs. Hamilton
Mrs. Gordon
Mr. Robt Wallace
Mr. Jos Wallace
Mrs. Caldwell
Mr. Wm Wilson
Mr. James Getty
Mr. Her: Heyland
Mr. Is: Miller
Wid Smith
Mrs. Banks
Mrs. Drennan
Miss Bigger

EAST ISLE.

Docr Mattear
Miss Mattear's
Mr. Saml M'Tier
Mr. Jno Rainey
Docr Haliday
Mr. John Holmes
Mr. Hugh M'Master
Messrs. Scott & Armstrong
Mrs. Donnaldson
Mr. Fr: Hamilton
Messrs. Wm & Jno Brown
Mr. Apsley
Messrs. Orr & Stevenson
Mr. Thos M'Ilwean
Mr. Thos Lyle
Mr. Jno Hay Junr
Mr. Jams Hughes
Mrs. Harvey
Mr. Wm Stewart
Mr. Jno Hunter
Messrs. Ewing & Brown
Mr. Thos Greg

NORTH GALLERY.

Mr. John Mathers
Mr. David Henderson
Mr. Robt Smith
Mr. Thos Grahams
Mr. And: Neilson
Mr. James Cooper
Mr. James Magee
Mr. D. Manson
Jno Sykes
Jno Robinson
Jno Kennedy
Messrs. Linns
Margt Broom

SOUTH GALLERY.

Mr. Henry Shaw
Mr. John Dorman
Mr. Thos Irwin
Robt Harper
James Robinson
Wm Warnock
Marthaw Patterson
Mr. Robt M'Cleary
Mr. Robt Herdman
John Dunbar
Robt Hanna
Marth: Rice
Alexr Kirkpatrick
Walter Finley
Mark Ward
Mr. John M'Cormick
Mr. John Wilson
Mr. Thos M'Cabe
Mrs. Hathron & Sistr
Mrs. Blackwell
Mr. Alexr M'Cormick
Ann Brown
Mr. Jams Perrey

EAST GALLERY.

Mr. John Hay
Mr. Dan: Blow
Mr. C. Montgomery
John Stewart
Capt. Martin
Mr. Robt Smyth
Mr. Wm Brown
Mr. An: Crawford
Mr. Wm Osborn
Mr. Row. Osborn
Margt M'Bridge
Mr. Jno Ward

LIST OF SUBSCRIBERS (APRIL, 1781) TO THE BUILDING FUND OF THE PRESENT MEETING HOUSE.

I.

OLD MEMBERS OF THE CONGREGATION.

Rainey Maxwell Esq
Mr. John Rainey
Mr. Wm Rainey
Docr Alexr Haliday
Mr. John Holmes
Mr. Thos Sinclair
Mr. John Ewing
Mr. Wm Brown
Mr. John Brown
Mr. Thos Brown
Mr. Francis Hamilton
Mr. Her: Heyland
Mr. John Mathers
Mr. Charles Roberts
Docr John Mattear
Miss Mattears
Mr. Robt Stevenson
Mr. Alexr Orr
Mr. Wm Irwine
Mr. James Magee
The Wid: of Mr Henry M'Kedy
Mr. James Stevenson
Mr. Robert Gordon
Mr. Francis Hamilton, Donegall St
Mr. John Galt Smith
Mr. James Park
Mr. William Ramsey
Mr. James Grahams
Mr. John Hamilton
Mr. James Dunn & his son David
Mr. Thos Lyle
Mr. Cath: Callwell
Mr. John Campbell
Mr. Hugh Montgomery
Mr. Isaac Miller
Mr. Thos McCabe
Mr. Hugh Allen
Mr. Wm Gregg
Mr. Hugh M'Ilwean
Mr. Robt Hindman
Mr. Saml Mattear
Mrs. Mary Park
Mr. Robt Thomson
Mrs. Ann Drennan
Mr. Joseph Wallace
Mrs. Apsley
Messrs. Robt & Michael Linn
Mr. Thos Greg
Miss Leggs
Mr. John Cumming
Mr. Davd Henderson
Capt. Hugh Hathron
Mr. Robt Smith
Mrs. Jane Hamilton
Mr. Rowley Osburn
Mr. Robt M Cleary
Mr. Samuel Mitchell
Capt. John McKibbin
Mr. Saml Stewart
Capt. Edwd McCormick
Mr. Cunningham Greg
Capt. Steel
The Revd Docr Crombie
Mrs. Hamilton
Mr. John Hay
Mr. Davd Manson

The gross amount was £960 11s 1½d Irish Currency

II.

NEW MEMBERS OF THE CONGREGATION (1783).

Mr. John Cunningham
Mr. Saml Brown
Mr. Pat. Gaw
Mr. Thos Millikin
Miss Ker
Mr. James Ferguson
Mr. Stewart Beally
Mr. Thos Major
Mr. J: Luke
Mr. Robt Wilson
Capt. Hugh Henderson
Mr. Davd Watson
Mr. James Ferguson, Junr
Mr. Saml Hyde
Mr. John Murdock
Mr. Henry Bamber
Mr. Thos Culbert
Mrs. Houston
Mr. Hugh Cairins

The gross amount was £68 16s 4½d Irish Currency

III.

NON-MEMBERS.

The Earl of Donegall
The Earl of Bristoll with the following note,

"Lord Bristoll's compliments wait on Mr. Maxwell & is sorry that his absence from Belfast necessarily obliges him to trouble Mr. Maxwell with the above Draft, he woud have sent it sooner but waited for the welcome permission to Contribute to a Building which does equal honor to the taste of the Subscribers and the talent of the Architect."

James Adair Esq, London
Hugh Pringle Esq, Liverpool
James Brown Esq, London
Robt Stewart Esq, Newtown Ards
Alexr Stewart Esq, Ditto
Hugh Johnston Esq, London
Herculas Rowley Esq
Right Hon.ble John O'Neill
Thos Greg Esqre London
Mr. Daniel McCormick, New York
Edwd Jones Agnew Esq
George Portis Esq
Mr. John Magee, Dublin
Stewart Banks Esq
Daniel Mussenden Esq
Rowley Heyland Esq
Edward Brice Esq
Messrs Francis Turnley & Co
Mrs Armstrong
Thos Batison Esq
John Brown Esq
John Crawford Esq, Crawfordsburn
Revd Mr. Stope, Malone

Mr. James Patterson
Mr. Nath: Wilson
Mr. Thos Lyon
Mrs. Collyer
Mr. George Darley
Mr. John Alexander
Capt. Ch: M Kenzie
Capt. Robt Moor
Mr. Wm Anderson
Mr. John Bashford
Messrs Ansley & Lilly
Docr John Campbell White
Mr. James Clelland
Mr. Stewart Hadkis
Mr. Robt Carson
Mr. Alexr Arthur
Mr. Thos Hyde
Mr. Samuel Ashmore
Mr. John Montgomery
Mr. Wm Boyle
Mr. Charles Gaine
Mr. William Burgess
Mr. Henry Joy
Docr James Ferguson
Mr. Alexr Blackwell
Mr. James Suffern
Mr. Thos Hardin
Mr. John Smyth
Mr. Joseph Stevenson
Mr. Wm Wilson, Apothacary
Mr. Robt Getty
Mr. Francis Savage

Mr. James Murphy
Mr. Hugh Crawford
Mr. Robt Lylburn
Mr. John Robinson
Mr. Robt Knox
Messrs Moor & Emerson
Mr. James Mattear
Mr. Barker
Capt John M Cracken
Mr. Blizard
Mr. Auchenleck
Mr. Dunsmore
Mr. J: Bradshaw
Mr. A: Armstrong
Mr. John Caldwell
Mr. Henderson
Mr. John Scott
Mr. Elliots
Mr. Wm Brecon
Mr. M Crum
Mr. M Ilroth
Mr. Hugh Johnston
Mr. Hudson
Mr. Hamil
Mr. Richd Seeds
Mr. Archd Scotts
Mr. St. John Stewart
Mr. Hugh Hindman
Mr. S: Ferguson
Mr. Mattear, Castle Street
Mr. Allen Searson
Mr. James M Kane

Mr. James Trail Kennedy
Mr. Sutherland
Mrs. Blizard
Mr. Simm
Mr. Gilbert M Ilvean
Mr. Val: Joyce
Mr. Francis Taggart
Mr. Her: M'Comb
Capt Thos Cavan
Mr. John Montgomery
Mr. Ch: Salmon
Mr. Isaac Ramage
Mrs. Crawford, Bridge Street
Mr. John Neilson
Mrs. Henderson, Church Lane
Capt Lewis Thomas
Mr. Phelps
Mr. Wm Stevenson
Mr. James M'Grigor, Glasgow
Mr. Robt Joy
Mr. Robt Scott
Mr John Goddard
Mr. John Boyle
Mr. Charles Britts
Mr. Robt Wilson
Mr. James Montgomery
Wad: Cunningham, Esq
Capt James Bristow
Davd Conyngham Esq
Mr M Aully, Brickmaker
The gross amount was £714 3s. 8d. Irish currency

"The Ladys of Belfast" who subscribed for the New Pulpit, 1783.

Mrs. Collyer
Mrs. D: Cunyngham
Mrs. Holmes
Mrs. Saml Holmes
Mrs. Jno Hamilton
Mrs. Patrick
Mrs. Dobbs
Mrs. Caldwell
Mrs. Jno Brown
Mrs. Thos Brown
Mrs. Tomb
Miss Joy
Miss Dunbar

Mrs. Portis
Mrs. J. Park
Mrs. M. Park
Mrs. Allen
Mrs. Irwine
Mrs. M. A. Harrison
Mrs. Docr Mattear
Mrs. Haliday
Miss Greg
Miss Banks
Mrs. W. Cunningham
Mrs. Robt Thomson
Mrs. Robt Gordon
Mrs. Pottinger

Miss Lydia Smith
Mrs. J. G. Smith
Mrs. Donnaldson
Mrs. Hugh Allen
Mrs. Stewarts
Mrs. Lyle
Mrs. Ferguson
Mrs. Hamilton
Mrs. Magee
Miss Fivey
Miss Sharp
The gross amount was £39 4s. 10½d Irish currency

LIST OF MEMBERS, 1790.

FROM DR. BRUCE'S MANUSCRIPT.

Robert M'Cleary
Richd Getgood, *Rosemary Lane*
Wm Mulrea, *Church Lane*
John Robinson
Miss Allen, *Mill Gate*
Arthur Thompson
Miss M'Dowell, *High Street*
Robt Smith, *Bridge Street*
Robt Wilson, *Parade*
Stewart Beatty, *Hercules Lane*
Mrs. Graham, Jno C. Graham } *Bridge Street*
Hugh Montgomery, *Linenhall Street*
Samuel Brown, *High Street*
James Dunn, David Dunn } *Donegal Street*
Dr. Mattear, *High Street*
Miss Mattears, S. M'Tier } *Cunningham's Row*
James Magee, Wm Magee } *Bridge Street*
Mrs. Callwell, John Callwell, Robert Callwell } *Bridge Street*
Thos Milliken, *Donegal Street*
Jno Gregg, *Waring Street*
Capt H. Henderson, *Hanover Quay*
Robt Thompson, *Mile Water*
Mrs. Donaldson, *Bridge Street*
Miss Bigger, Miss J. Hamilton } *Hercules Lane*
Thos Lyle, *High Street*
James Ferguson, *Woodville*
Alexr Orr, *Linenhall Street*
Robert Stevenson, *Donegal Street*
John Campbell, *Ann Street*
Mrs. Park, *High Street*
James Stevenson, *Chichester Quay*
Rowland Osborne, R. Osborne, Jr, W. Osborne } *Church Lane*

Mrs. M'Kedy, *High Street*
Samuel Mitchell, *Ann Street*
Capt J. M'Kibbin, *Chichester Quay*
David Manson, *Donegal Street*
Thos Sinclair, *Mill Street*
W. Sinclair, *Do*
Will. Nichol, *Pottinger's Entry*
David Watson, *Bridge Street*
Dr. Haliday, *Castle Street*
Mrs. Drennan, *Donegal Street*
J. Ewing, *Belfast Bank*
Edwd M'Cormick, *Chichester Quay*
Jno Cumming, *Ann Street*
Jno Hunter, *Church Lane*
Miss Hays, Robt M'Cleary } *Bridge Street*
Jno Hamilton, *Belfast Bank*
Mrs. Crombie, *Donegal Street*
Rainey Maxwell, Jno Rainey, W. Rainey } *Greenville*
Thos Greg, Cun. Greg } *Gaw's Place*
Robt Gordon, *Parade*
D. Gordon, *Linenhall Street*
W. Brown, *Waring Street*
Jno Brown, *Linenhall Street*
Thos Brown, *Waring Street*
Jno Oakman
W. Oakman, *Waring Street*
Mrs. Allen, *Linenhall Street*
Jno Mathers, *Waring Street*
Chas Roberts, *Waring Street*
W. Irwin, *Ann Street*
Mrs. Hyde, *Parade*
Isaac Miller, *Bridge Street*
Miss Legg, *Bridge Street*
Capt. Steel, *Waring Street*
Robt Montgomery, *Arthur Street*
Hugh Kairns, *Parkmount*
Mrs. Jackson, *Waring Street*
Mrs. Joy, *Linenhall Street*
Mrs. Haven, *Hercules Lane*

Capt. Scott, *High Street*
Mrs. W. Blackwell, *Donegal Street*
Mrs. Rabb, *Rosemary Lane*
Robt Herdman, *Ann Street*
Jno Murdoch, *Bridge Street*
Robt Linn, *Skipper's Lane*
P. M'Master, *High Street*
Wm Ramsey, *High Street*
Mrs. Kenley, *High Street*
Jas Luke, *Donegal Street*
Jno Holmes, *Belfast Bank*
Jno G. Smith, *High Street*
Mrs. Park, Miss Sharp } *High Street*
Miss Eliz: Apsley, *Castle Street*
Mrs. Houston, Jno Houston } *Linenhall Street*
Geo. Bamber, Miss Bamber } *High Street*
Simon M'Creery, *North Street*
Jas Ferguson, *North Street*
Robt Hodgson, *North Street*
Robt Patterson, *Bridge Street*
Jas Holmes, *Donegal Street*
Mark Ward, *High Street*
Mrs. Mills, *Caddle's Entry*
Mrs. Wills, *Rosemary Lane*
Jas Mason, *New Brewery*
Wm Wilson, *Donegal Street*
Jas Hyndman, *High Street*
Robt Major
Jno Thompson
Jas Davidson
Al. M'Gregor
Geo. Knox
Jas Glancy Jan 12 1791
David Mattear, *Castle Street*
J. M'Donnell, *Bridge Street*
E. Cochran
Jas Brown
Mrs. Robinson
Jno Thomson, *Jenneymount*
J. Graham
Jas Patterson
Thos Graham

FIRST PRINTED LIST OF CONSTITUENTS, 1812.

[The pew numbers (G = Gallery) and addresses are added from Rev. W. Bruce's Manuscript, 1812.]

Belfast, 1st June, 1812.

ANNEXED you have the names of the MEMBERS of the FIRST DISSENTING CONGREGATION who pay Stipend. An Election of a Committee for one year, will take place in the Meeting-House, on SUNDAY the 7th inst. immediately after the Evening Service, when you are requested to come prepared with Lists.

The present Committee are marked thus *

31 Mrs. Allen, *Donegall Place*

5 Wm. Armstrong, *Donegall Street, afterw. at North St*

55 Allen Barklie, *Donegall Street*

27 Mrs. Batt, *Donegall Place*

31 Miss Bigger, *Castle Street, corner of Chapel Lane*

50 *Alexr. Black, *High Street*

37 Henderson Black, *Donegall Square East*

G 12 Mathew Black, *Bridge Street*

43 Mrs. Blackwell, *Donegall Street*

17 James Blair, *Merville*

G 8 Samuel Brown, *Donegall Street*

26 Mrs. Brown, *King Street*

69 James Burden, *Falls*

20 Miss Cairns, *York Street*

18 Robt. Callwell, *Chichester Street*

47 Ernest Cochran, *Wilson's Court*

13 Arthur Crawford, *Donegall Street*

35 John Cunningham, *Castle Street, afterw. at Chapel Lane*

G 10 James Davison, *North Street*

34 John Davison, *Donegall Street*

60 *Robert Delap, *Quay*

25 Mrs. Doolittle, *Anne Street, at Reid's.*

G 17 James Douglass, *Donegall Place*

G 7 Dr. Drennan, *Cabin Hill*

G 7 Miss Drennan

J. & R. Dunn

1 Mrs. Durham, *M. Row*

G 8 *John Ewing, *Macedon*

34 Miss Fleming

G 11 Thos. Ferguson, *Legg's Lane*

46 Thos. Garrett, *Donegall Street*

11 John Gillies

28 Robt. & A. Gordon

G 19 John Graham

G 5 Jas. Grainger, *Anne Street*

27 Cunningham Greg, *Donegall Place*

27 Miss Greg, *Donegall Place*

21 *John Gregg, *Castle Street*

G 4 Dr. Haliday, *Clifton*

23 John Hamilton, *Donegall Place*

G 6 Robt. Hamilton, *Wilson's Court*

49 Robert Herdman, *Butter Market*

36 John Heron, *Donegall Street*

40 Miss Hevin, *Arthur Street*

G 15 Robt. Hodgson, *High Street*

55 *John Holmes, *Donaghadee*

55 John Holmes, Jun.

57 *John H. Houston, *Greenville*

16 James Hyndman, *Donegall Street*

Mrs. A. Hyndman

38 *Henry Joy, *Donegall Square North*

G 2 Mrs. Kearns, *Anne Street*

52 Mrs. Kenley, *Castle Street*

24 Mrs. Law, *Donegall Street*

54 Mrs. Luke, *North Street*

62 Thos. Lyle, *High Street*

33 *William Magee, *Lodge*

15 Miss Mattear, *Castle Street*

15 Mrs. Mattear, *High Street*

70 John Martin, *14, Anne Street*

41 Miss Miles, *Rosemary Street*

71 Gawn Montgomery, *L. George Street*

51 Henry Montgomery, *Bridge Street*

12 *Hugh Montgomery, *Benvarden*

12 James Montgomery, *Bank Buildings*

71 James Montgomery, *High Street*
38 Robert Montgomery, *Sandymount*
G 14 Arthur Moreland, *Cornmarket, afterw. at Cromac*
2 William Mulrea, *Bridge Street, afterw. at High Street*
6 George M'Adam
7 *James M'Adam, *High Street*
6 John M'Adam, *High Street*
52 Miss M'Aulay, *Castle Street*
29 Hugh M'Calmont, *Abbey Lands*
G 12 Mrs. M'Cleery, *Smithfield*
32 Robert M'Cluney, *High Street*
G 13 Dr. M'Gee, *North Street*
30 Gilbert M'Ilveen, *Castlesburn*
67 Miss M'Kedy, *York Street*
24 David M'Tier, *Hazle Bank*
G 7 Mrs. M'Tier, *South Parade*
39 William Napier, *Back of the River*
G 9 William Nichol, *Skipper's Lane*
64 James Orr, *South Parade*
66 James Park, *Bally Macarret*
6 James Patterson
53 John Patterson, *High Street*
59 Miss Patterson, *Castle Street*
G 16 *Robert Patterson, *High Street*
8 William Radcliffe, *North Street*
52 James Ramsey, *Donegall Street*
Samuel Rankin
62 John Riddel, *High Street*
G 11 Miss Robinson, *High Street*
55 John Russel, *New Forge*
55 William Russel, *Edenderry*
72 Jordan Rutherford, *Church Street*
61 Mrs. Seed, *Donegall Square North*
G 1 John Sinclair, *Donegall Place*
G 1 Mrs. Sinclair, *Donegall Place*
G 1 Thomas Sinclair, *Donegall Place*
1 George Sloan, *Arthur Street*
G 3 John Sloan, *Donegall Place*
26 Edward Smith, *Auchinbrack*
56 John G Smith, *High Street*
56 Miss Smith, *South Parade*
10 Mrs. Smith, *John Street*
63 Samuel Smith, *Woodville*
73 James Stevely, *Waring Street*
G 10 David Stormont
5 Christ. Strong, *Anna's Cottage*
14 Campbell Sweeney, *South Parade*
4 Arthur Thompson, *Back of the River*
22 John Thomson, *Jennymount*
56 Dr. Thompson, *Castle Street*
68 Robert Telfair, *County*
68 Robert Telfair Jun., *Prince's Street*
William Telfair
65 William Tennent, *Hercules Street*
G 18 John Ward, *Arthur Street*
19 George Whitla, *Donegall Street*
19 William John Whitla, *Donegall Street*
45 Miss Wills, *High Street, Pottinger's Entry*
9 Mrs. Wilson, *Castle Street*
48 Mrs. Wilson, *Long Lane*

LIST OF CONSTITUENTS, Dec. 1, 1831,

At the beginning of the Ministry of Rev. J. Scott Porter.

[The list, with addresses, is from the Minute Book; the pew numbers are from the printed list of 1833.]

39 Hugh W. Armstrong, *College Square*
39 Mrs. Armstrong, *College Square*
20 George Bamber, *Mr. P. Quin's, High St.*
13 Allen Barklie, *Donegall Street*
27 Mrs. Batt, *Purdysburn*
50 Alexr. Black
Matthew Black, *Bridge Street*
43 Mrs. Blackwell, *Dromore*
49 Thos. Blain, *Chichester Street*
Cunningham Boyd, *Fort Breda*
John Boyd, *Fort Breda*
66 William Boyd, *Fort Breda*
68 William Boyd, Jr., *Arthur Street*
63 James Bristow, *Castle Street*
63 Joseph Bristow, *Castle Street*
63 William Bristow, *Donegall Square South*
G 14 Saml. Bruce, *Chichester Street*
Dr. Burden, *Alfred Street*
69 Miss Burden, *Alfred Street*
John Caird, *College Square*
18 Robert Callwell, *Wellington Place*
1 James Carruthers, *Newtonbreda*

72 Thos. Chirmside, *Bridge Street and College Square*
G 22 Chas. Creek, *North Street*
47 Barber Cunningham, *Rosemary Street*
14 Mrs. James Cunningham, *Chichester Street*
35 John Cunningham, *Queen Street*
35 Thos. Cunningham, *Mill Street*
9 John Currel, *Linen Hall and Murray Terrace*
G 13 James Davison, *Sandy Row*
60 Robert Delap, *James Street*
32 Mrs. C. Dickey, *Myrtlefield*
Mrs. Drennan, *Arthur Street*
Lenox Drennan, *Arthur Street*
5 Miss Dunn, *Donegall Street*
5 Miss Margaret Dunn, *Donegall Street*
48 Miss Ferguson, *Castle Place*
G 18 Mrs. Ferguson, *Chichester Street*
46 William Ferguson, *Ferguson's Entry, High Street*
G 19 F. D. Finlay, *Whig Office and King Street*
52 Thomas Garrett, *Cromac*
Miss Gelston, *Arthur Street*
G 8 Miss Grainger, *Anne Street*
G 9 Robert Hamilton, *Wilson's Court*
37 John Harpur, *Great George's Street*
51 John Hartley, *Gloucester Street*
31 Misses Haven, *Arthur Street*
36 John Heron, *Queen Street*
G 10 Rev. T. D. Hincks, *Royal Institution*
8 John Hodgson, *High Street*
8 Robert A. Hodgson, *High Street*
57 John Holmes Houston, *Orangefield*
16 Geo. C. Hyndman, *Castle Place*
58 Henry Joy, *Donegall Square North*
G 5 Mrs. Kearns, *Anne Street*
13 John Kennedy, *Tomb Street*
54 James Luke, *Chichester Street*
54 Samuel Luke, *York Street*
G 17 John Machan, *North Street*
6 Mrs. Malcom, *York Street*
70 John Martin, *Donegall Square East*
25 Mrs. Mason
7 James M'Adam, *High Street*
G 3 John M'Adam, *Donegall Street*
29 Hugh M'Calmont, *Abbey Lands*
32 Robert M'Cluney, *Chichester Street*
G 28 Alexr. M'Donnell, *Skipper Street*
G 28 Alexr. M'Donnell, Jr., *Skipper Street*
31 Mrs. M'Gee, *North Street*
31 Miss M'Gee, *North Street*
31 Miss M. A. M'Gee, *North Street*
67 Miss M'Kedy, *York Street*
67 Miss A. M'Kedy, *York Street*
67 Miss C. M'Kedy, *York Street*
67 Miss J. M'Kedy, *York Street*
67 Miss M. M'Kedy, *York Street*
24 David Matear, *Hazel Bank*
15 Miss Matear, *Donegall Square North*
15 Mrs. Matear, *Donegall Square North*
G 12 Alexander Mitchell, *Ballymacarret*
19 Francis Montgomery, *Queen's Street*
19 Misses Montgomery, *Queen's Street*
34 Rev. H. Montgomery, *Royal Institution*
13 James Montgomery, *Arthur Street*
12 James Montgomery, *High Street*
38 John Montgomery, *Beer's Bridge Cottage*
38 Mrs. Montgomery, *Beer's Bridge Cottage*
Mrs. Montgomery, *Donegall Square North*
30 Mrs. Montgomery, *Donegall Square South*
Mrs. Montgomery, *Union Place*
30 Robert Montgomery, *Donegall Square South*
Alexr. Moreland, *Anne Street*
Arthur Moreland, *Cromac*
G 21 Thomas Moreland, *Hercules Street*
G 6 P. L. Munster, *James Street*
55 Mrs. Napier, *Wellington Place*
59 Miss Patterson, *Castle Street*
G 23 Robert Patterson, *High Street*
G 23 William Patterson, *High Street*
62 John Riddel, *High Street*
62 Miss Riddel, *Mrs. Savage's, Chichester Street*
62 Miss M. Riddel, *High Street*
17 Mrs. Rowan, *Merville*
45 John Russel, 10 *Cromac Place*
33 John Russel, *New Forge*
28 William Russel, *Edenderry*
G 4 John Sinclaire, *Donegall Place*
10 Miss Sinclaire, *Alfred Street*
G 4 Thos. Sinclaire, *Wellington Place*
53 George Sloan, *Chichester Street*
John E. Sloan, *Queen Street*
26 Edward Smith, *Linen Hall and Donegall Street*
John Galt Smith, *High Street*
63 Miss Smith, *Donegall Square*

G 16 Joseph Smyth, *High Street*
73 James Staveley, *Waring Street*
48 James Staveley, Junr., *Waring Street*
Miss Stevenson, *Donegall Place*
G 13 David Stormont, *Sandy Row*
4 Mrs. Telfair, *Chichester Street*
William Tennent, *Hercules Place*
63 Saml. Thomson, M.D., *Castle Street*
F. D. Ward, *Coleraine*
41 John Ward, *College Square*
41 Marcus Ward, *Gloucester Street*
G 20 William White, *Bridge Street*
64 Francis Whitla, *Donegall Square North*
64 Vale. Whitla, *Donegall Square North*
G 27 Thomas Williamson, *Barrack Street*
G 21 John Wilson, *Union Place*

LIST OF CONSTITUENTS, 31st MARCH, 1877.

[At the time of the Call to Rev. A. Gordon.]

34 Allen, W. J. C.
27 Andrews, Mrs.
60 Armstrong, Mrs.
28 Arthur, Miss M.
G 8 Baird, Samuel
32 Baxter, Mrs.
32 Baxter, R.
32 Baxter, W.
65 Bell, Mrs.
65 Bell, Richard, Jr.
67 Benn, George
30 Blackley, Mrs.
29 Bowles, Charles
18 Bowring, Miss
14 Boyd, Mrs.
54 Boyd, R. (Representatives of)
71 Briggs, Henry
41 Bruce, Henry
2 Bruce, James
44 Bruce, Mrs.
41 Bruce, Miss
41 Bruce, Miss J. E.
74 Burden, Dr. H.
37 Campbell, John
75 Campbell, N. A.
50 Campbell, Miss
50 Campbell, William
11 Carlisle, John
33 Carr, James
1 Carruthers, Miss
1 Carruthers, Miss J.
G 21 Cavan, James
4 Charnock, Mrs.
10 Creighton, Mrs.
G 23 Cronne, James
35 Cunningham, J. (Representatives of)
G 15 Davison, John
39 Dickson, Mrs.
39 Dickson, R.
10 Dixon, Mrs.
G 10 Drennan, John, M.D.
G 10 Drennan, Lenox
37 Drummond, Mrs.
18 Dugan, J. J.
14 Dunn, John
14 Dunn, Miss
G 19 Ferguson, Miss
G 19 Ferguson, Miss J.
G 29 Forsythe, Mrs.
28 Gamble, Mrs.
51 Gault, John
G 5 Gawn, James
G 28 Gibson, Robert
G 28 Goldstein, Mrs.
4 Gordon, Alex., M.D.
10 Gordon, Thomas
G 7 Graham, James
G 16 Graham, Thomas
G 13 Graham, W.
G 9 Graham, W., junr.
G 17 Gray, James A.
43 Gray, Mrs.
43 Greer, Mrs.
66 Greer, W. H.
G 25 Haffern, William
G 16 Hall, Samuel
G 16 Hall, William
G 13 Hamill, James
15 Hamilton, W. T.
57 Harland, E. J.
15 Hill, A. C.
31 Hill, Rev. George
G 16 Hinchey, William
25 Home, Wm.
G 22 Johnston, Alexander
40 Kennedy, John
G 24 King, Mrs.
45 Kirker, Archibald
6 Kirkpatrick, Mrs.
G 5 Laird, Marshall
G 12 Lawson, John
12 Ledlie, Mrs. G.
15 Leslie, James
52 L'Estrange, Thomas
48 Little, Frederick
G 29 Lowry, Mrs.
G 9 Lyle, Hugh
7 MacAdam, R. S.
G 26 M'Aneaney, Miss
G 21 M'Caul, Joseph
24 M'Caw, Alex.
G 6 M'Caw, James F.
G 14 M'Clenaghan, James
58 M'Cloy, Joseph
G 13 M'Cracken, R.
G 15 M'Cumm, Robert
51 M'Ervel, E. J.
12 M'Ervel, James
12 M'Ervel, Thomas
59 M'Fadden, James
17 M'Fadden, Mrs.
17 M'Fadden, W. H.
31 M'Gee, Miss

G 18 M'Keag, Miss
G 13 M'Keen, John
G 28 M'Kinstry, Miss
G 26 M'Loughlin, Miss
G 16 M'Mullen, Elizabeth
21 M'Murray, Thomas
2 M'Ninch, James Watt
2 M'Ninch, Joseph
3 M'Ninch, Robert
2 M'Ninch, William
G 8 M'Quitty, Thomas
8 M'Tear, David
55 M'Tear, George
55 M'Tear, J. S.
55 M'Tear, Miss
55 M'Tear, Miss F. M.
63 M'Tear, Miss A. C.
63 M'Tear, Miss E.
G 30 Mairs, Thomas
20 Major, James
25 Malcolm, Mrs. A. G.
70 Malcolm, Bowman
70 Malcolm, Mrs.
31 Malcolm, W. H.
G 23 Martin, David
G 9 Mateer, John
30 Maxwell, Miss
74 May, Mrs.
73 Moore, James
66 Mulligan, Mrs.
68 Murray, Henry
72 Murray, Robert
18 Musgrave, J. R.
G 24 Neeson, Mrs.
15 Nelson, John
36 Notcutt, Miss
47 Oakman, Nicholas
36 Palmer, Benjamin
G 12 Palmer, James
G 12 Palmer, Miss Susan
26 Patterson, Mrs.
26 Patterson, D. C.
26 Patterson, E. F.
26 Patterson, R. L.
26 Patterson, W. H.
19 Porter, Andrew M., Q.C.
19 Porter, Hon. Wm.
G 22 Quee, Patrick
G 27 Rankin, Mrs.
G 11 Rice, Mrs. Jane
61 Riddel, Hill
61 Riddel, Samuel
62 Riddel, William
62 Riddel, Miss
62 Riddel, Miss I.
63 Riddel, Mrs. E.
5 Ritchie, Thomas
G 18 Robb, Alex.
G 11 Roberts, Walter
53 Robertson, William
8 Roche, Mrs.
G 23 Roddy, Hugh
38 Rogers, John
38 Rogers, Thomas
30 Rowland, Mrs.
58 Russell, J. W.
8 Scott, Miss
37 Sherrard, Misses
G 20 Sinclair, George
56 Smith, George K.
56 Smith, J. Galt
16 Smyth, Brice, M.B.
45 Smyth, Miss
45 Smyth, Miss A. J.
64 Smyth, Mrs. H. C.
49 Spackman, William
28 Steen, Henry
G 28 Stevenson, James
70 Stewart, Miss
G 20 Stewart, Misses
G 8 Stewart, Thomas
69 Taylor, A. O'D.
G 13 Templeton, Robert
13 Thomas, H. F.
20 Thompson, John
4 Thompson, Miss
4 Thompson, Robert
4 Thompson, Thomas
G 14 Todd, Miss M. C.
9 Ward, F. D.
1 Ward, John
41 Ward, Mrs.
G 18 Watson, Miss Anna
64 Whitla, Miss
G 21 Williamson, James
42 Williamson, Joseph

ADDITIONAL NOTES.

Patrick Adair (p. 54).

According to the MS. *Sketches of the History of Presbyterians in Ireland*, by William Campbell, D.D., 1803, Patrick Adair married Margaret, daughter of Rev. Robert Cunningham, of Holywood, and sister of Rev. James Cunningham, of Antrim. She must have been his first wife, as Campbell states that she was the mother of William Adair, afterwards minister of Antrim. Campbell is not always accurate; but inasmuch as he was himself minister of Antrim (1759–64), his statement is of some weight. If it be correct, Patrick Adair was thrice married.

Samuel Bryan (p. 54).

He was chaplain at least as early as 1664, for in 1666 he was paid £80 for two years' salary (*Benn*, i. 143). In 1667 he became minister of Cooke Street, Dublin. He died at Chester (*Armstrong's Appendix*, p. 86).

John M'Bride (p. 54).

He was called to Ayr in June 1691. He supplied the Blackfriars or College Church, Glasgow, from 12th March, 1705, returning to Belfast after 5th January, 1709.

ANNALS OF THE CONGREGATION.

1636. 11th August.—Conference in Belfast Church between Henry Leslie, Bishop of Down (assisted by Bramhall, Bishop of Derry), and five Presbyterian ministers, on the points at issue between the prelates and the nonconforming clergy.

1642. June.—Army eldership erected in Belfast. Subsequently, Rev. John Baird appointed to preach there every third Sabbath (*Adair's Narr.*, pp. 96, 100).

1644. July.—Supplication presented from "many in Belfast" for erecting a session, and Patrick Adair appointed to perform that duty (*Chr. Moderator*, 1826, p. 353).

,, Thomas Theaker, sovereign, states (18th July) that all the free commoners of Belfast, "except a very few," had taken the covenant, and that there was a session of about 20 elders and 4 deacons (*Benn*, i. 110).

1646. September.—Anthony Shaw ordained at Belfast (Scott's *Fasti*).

1649. Lieut.-Colonel Wallace, elder, appointed governor of Belfast (*Adair*, p. 168).

,, John Milton stigmatises the Presbyterians, who protested (15th Feb.) against the execution of Charles I., as "that unchristian synagogue of Belfast."

,, Anthony Shaw upbraids Montgomery (June) before his officers for betraying the cause of the covenant, by supplanting Wallace, in virtue of a commission from Charles II. (*Adair*, p. 169).

,, Shaw removes to Colmonell, Ayshire; he is said to have been succeeded by Read.

1650–60. During these years there is no trace of Presbyterian church government in Belfast; from 1650 to 1656 the church was turned into a fort. In September, 1657, Rev. William Dix, who in 1654 had been appointed by the Cromwellian Government to preach in Belfast, was forcibly pulled out of the pulpit by Rev. Henry Livingston, of Drumbo, acting under the authority of the Presbytery (*Benn*, i. 136, 139–141, 398).

1660. Rev. William Keyes settles in Belfast, the first of an unbroken line of ministers.

1668. Keyes began to preach at Carrickfergus every other Lord's Day, after the removal of Rev. Timothy Taylor (Independent) to Dublin.

,, In this year, says Adair, Presbyterians "began in divers places to build preaching houses, and there met publicly."

1671. December.—Carrickfergus congregation applied to the Antrim Meeting to settle Keyes exclusively with them.

1672. 19th February.—Keyes was ordered by the Antrim Meeting to go and live in Belfast, which he did, on a promised stipend of £60 a-year.

,, July.—Keyes was sent by the Antrim Meeting, at the request of Dublin Presbytery, to supply Bull Alley Congregation, Dublin, and remained there till December. [The date, "December, 1673," on p. 53, should be "December, 1672."]

1673. January.—William Muir, Michael Briggart, and John Briggart appeared at the Antrim

Meeting as commissioners from Belfast, to oppose the removal of Keyes to Dublin.

1673. April.—The Committee of all the Meetings (at this time there was no General Synod) confirmed the removal of Keyes to Dublin. Messrs. Anderson and Chalmers, commissioners from Belfast, appealed to the Antrim Meeting against this decision, but in vain. (*Extract from Minutes of Antrim Meeting.*)

„ 7th May.—Keyes expressed to the Antrim Meeting his unwillingness to remove to Dublin, and intimated the dissatisfaction of Lady Donegall in the matter of his transportation. The Meeting allowed him to stay a few days longer in Belfast, and directed Patrick Adair to communicate with Lady Donegall, through Samuel Bryan, her chaplain.

1674. 6th January.—The Antrim Meeting appointed Revs. Thomas Hall, of Larne, and Robert Cunningham, of Ballycarry, "to wait upon my Lord and Lady Donegall upon advertisement from the people of Belfast, and to represent to those noble persons the sad condition of that place by want of a settled minister, and deal with them for the people's liberty to choose whom they pleased, with the Meeting's consent, according to principles owned by us, which, if they refuse to grant, the brethren aforesaid are to leave the obstruction of the planting of that place at their door."

„ 3rd February.—Nothing seems to have been done, and the Belfast people are advised to make the first application, through Bryan.

„ 3rd March.—John Adam, merchant, appeared as commissioner from Belfast, and said the people had made application. Hall and Cunningham were appointed "to repair to Belfast, and then, after conference with the most judicious of the elders, to make address unto my Lord and Lady Donegall—(1) proposing to them the desire of the people of Belfast to have a minister settled among them; and that as the brethren are ready to concur with them for their supply upon their unanimous call, so they humbly hope their honours will be pleased in that affair to let that people have their liberty as other people have, as to their free choice, according to principles owned among us; (2) and if, after conference with the elders and mature consideration, it be found expedient to move anent the House of Worship, they shall humbly represent to them what weighty reasons make for the people having their liberty as other congregations have, without irritation, so far as possible." [This is the earliest known reference to a Presbyterian Meeting-house in Belfast; it seems to imply that such a building was in existence, but under the control of the Earl of Donegall.]

1674. 7th April.—Hall and Cunningham reported that they had fulfilled their commission, and that the Countess of Donegall "promised that she should be no hindrance of the settling of a godly minister in Belfast; but she advised the brethren to forbear making any address to my Lord at this time, but to leave it upon the people of Belfast to make application to his Lordship." [Probably, this last reference is to the question of the free use of the Meeting-house.]

„ 21st April.—Two commissioners (not named) from Belfast reported that "they have a favourable answer" from Lord Donegall; "and further, they represent unto the Meeting that the representatives of that congregation have fixed their eyes upon Mr. Patrick Adair, and that they were appointed by the said representatives to come to the meeting for advice." The Meeting deferred consideration of the matter, after laying before the commissioners "the difficulties that appear."

„ On 26th May, William Moore and Alexander Arthur appeared as commissioners from Belfast, and reported "that although they have not as yet a call in readiness for Mr. Adair, yet they have not laid that business aside."

„ 7th July.—"Several persons commissioned" brought a call from Belfast to Patrick Adair. The consideration was deferred till next meeting. Adair declared himself "unclear to be loosed from Cairncastle."

1674. 4th August.—The decision was referred to "the advice of the rest of the Meetings."

„ 1st September.—Rev. Robert Henry, of Carrickfergus, clerk of the Meeting, reports that Down Meeting was for, and Route Meeting against, the removal of Adair.

„ 13th October.—The clerk reports that Laggan and Tyrone Meetings are for the removal. The Antrim Meeting accordingly "did at length proceed to a vote, which is, that in consideration of the greater good of the Church in the North of Ireland, and the considerable unanimity of the rest of the meetings for said transportation, they judge Mr. P. Adair now called by the providence of God to serve in the ministry at Belfast." They placed the call in his hands, enjoining "him and his family with the first convenience to repair to Belfast." (*Extracts from Minutes of Antrim Meeting;* compare *Benn*, i. 400-1; *Christian Unitarian*, 1865, pp. 153-4.)

1689. 12th January.—Adair was appointed one of two "commissioners from the Presbyterian ministers of the North to wait on the Prince of Orange before he was proclaimed king, to congratulate him on his safe arrival, and encourage him in the great enterprise he had in view." (*Christian Moderator*, 1826, p. 354.)

1691. 30th September.—At Coleraine was held the earliest meeting of General Synod of which there are minutes (probably the second meeting). Adair was present, being the senior member of the Presbytery of Antrim; there was no elder from Belfast.

1693. James Stewart presented a silver communion cup "to the Meeting-house of Belfast."

1694. Early in the year Patrick Adair died, being nearly 70 years of age.

„ William Crawford, sovereign of Belfast, induced the two printers, Patrick Neill and his brother-in-law, James Blow, to settle in Belfast, and entered into partnership with them. All three were members of this congregation. (*Benn*, i. pp. 425 sq. 735; *Kirkpatrick*, p. 421.) Crawford had been elected burgess on 24th March, 1686; he was elected M.P. for Belfast in 1703 and 1707.

1694. 5th June.—Meeting of General Synod at Antrim. As commissioners from Belfast appeared William Crawford, sovereign, David Smith, burgess, with others, desiring "that the Synod would countenance their call for the transportation of Mr. John M'Bride from Clare to them." The Synod referred the whole business to the Presbytery of Down. (*Extracts from Min. General Synod.*)

„ 3rd October.—John M'Bride was installed at Belfast, by Rev. William Adair. (*Christian Moderator*, 1826, p. 309.)

1695. About this time a Meeting-house was built for M'Bride on a new site, in Rosemary Lane.

1697. 2nd June.—M'Bride was chosen moderator of the General Synod at Antrim by plurality of votes out of a list of six. At this Synod the Antrim Presbytery was dissolved, and Belfast was placed in the new Presbytery of Belfast. The Presbyteries of Down, Belfast, and Tyrone were formed into a Sub-synod, to meet twice a-year, on the first Tuesday of November and May. William Adair was allowed forty shillings out of the *regium donum* "for defraying what expenses he has been at to an amanuensis" in copying out "his father's collection, containing a history of this Church from the year 1625 to the year 1670." [This was Patrick Adair's *True Narrative*, first published by Dr. W. D. Killen, 1866.] "In case a bill from England be sent to this kingdom in favour of our legal liberty, that then Messrs. William Adair and John M'Bride attend the Parliament of Dublin, in case one sit, to agent our affairs." (*Ex. Min. Gen. Syn.*)

„ This year M'Bride published *Animadversions, &c.*, being a defence of toleration for Nonconformists without a sacramental test.

1698. Thomas Craford presented a silver communion cup to the Presbyterian congregation of Belfast.

„ 10th Oct.—M'Bride was examined at Dublin Castle on the subject of his synodical sermon, preached 1st June at Antrim, and published. A point raised was that he was described in the title-page as "minister of Belfast." He was dismissed without censure, and with an advice to "carry rectably towards the Established Church." (*Killen's Reid*, ii. 476 sq.)

1700. During the illness of Fairfoul, curate to Rev. James Echlin, vicar of Belfast, M'Bride and his elders made up a sum of £5, which was presented to Fairfoul by M'Bride. (*Kirkpatrick*, p. 442.)

1702. 3rd June.—The General Synod at Antrim revised the arrangement of Sub-synods, placing the Presbyteries of Down, Belfast, and Antrim in a new Sub-synod, "to be designed the Synod of Belfast." (*Ex. Min. Gen. Syn.*)

„ This year M'Bride published, anonymously, *A Vindication of Marriage, as solemnised by Presbyterians, &c.*

1703. 1st June.—At an *interloquitur* of the General Synod at Antrim, "Mr. John McBride was required his reason why he, with advice of Belfast Presbytery, advised this Synod to meet here at this time, the former Synod having appointed the second Tuesday of July; to which he answered, that the Parliament of England and the Government here having enjoined an oath which reaches us, and the time appointed for taking said oath being the first of August at farthest, and this Synod not to meet till July, to which time it referred their meeting, there had not been sufficient time for a due concerting so momentous a matter; therefore he, with Belfast Presbytery, judged it advisable that the Synod should meet now: which reasons, being now considered, were by this *interloquitur* sustained as relevant." This oath was the Abjuration Oath, which M'Bride and five other Irish Presbyterian ministers declined to take for two reasons: (1) it required them to swear that the Pretender was not the son of James II.; and (2) it bound them to support the Established Church. (*Ex. Min. Gen. Syn.; Kirkpatrick*, p. 528.)

„ 19th October.—A committee of the Irish House of Commons recommended that M'Bride and another be deprived of *regium donum* for refusing the oath; but this was not done. (*Killen's Reid*, ii. 500.)

1705. David Smith presented "to Belfast Meeting-house" a copy, bound in tortoiseshell and silver, of Patrick Neill's edition of the Psalms in metre, 1700. David Smith, who is mentioned above (1694), was elected a burgess of Belfast on 26th May, 1690; he was sovereign in 1698 and 1699. (*Kirkpatrick*, p. 421; *Benn*, i. 726.)

„ This year the General Synod passed a law requiring, for the future, subscription to the Westminster Confession.

„ The meeting for theological discussion, afterwards known as the Belfast Society, was founded by Rev. John Abernethy; among the original members was Rev. James Kirkpatrick.

„ At the end of the year, information was sworn against M'Bride as a non-abjuror, before Rev. John Winder, a magistrate residing at Carmoney. M'Bride retired to Scotland, preached for some time at Glasgow, and as Moderator of Glasgow Presbytery was the first to sign the Presbytery's address to the Queen (1708), expressing abhorrence of the designs of the Pretender. (*Killen's Reid*, ii. 520; *Kirkpatrick*, p. 538.)

1706. Early in the year a call from Belfast was given to Rev. James Kirkpatrick, of Templepatrick, as assistant and successor to M'Bride. The Synod at first refused its sanction, and granted supplies to Belfast.

„ 18th June.—M'Bride wrote from Stranraer that if there be 3,000 persons in Belfast congregation, there must be two meeting-houses and two distinct congregations.

„ 24th Sept.—Kirkpatrick was released from Templepatrick, and settled in Belfast. (*Disciple*, June 1882, p. 175.)

1707. A second Meeting-house and a Manse were set on foot.

1708. 2nd March.—The session of Belfast petitioned the Belfast Presbytery "that Mr. James Kirkpatrick might be ascertained to the new Meeting-house now built, and that Mr. M'Bride might be ascertained to the old Meeting-house and the Dwelling-house built for him." This was granted.

1708. 3rd March.—Messrs. Edward Brice, Isaac M'Cartney, and Robert Lennox, on the one part, and Messrs. William Crawford and Ferguson on the other, subscribed an agreement that the stipend, £160, "should be equally divided between the two ministers, and the dwelling-house now built should be reserved from [? for] Mr. M'Bride."

" 12th April.—The session presented a further petition to the Presbytery "for erecting a new congregation in Belfast, to meet and be under the particular pastoral charge of Mr. James Kirkpatrick." This was also granted. Both petitions were signed by Hugh Cunningham, clerk to the session of Belfast.

" 1st May.—M'Bride wrote to the Presbytery complaining of their dividing the congregation before the meeting of General Synod.

" 1st June.—The General Synod met at Antrim, when the following commissioners from the old congregation, Messrs. Andrew Maxwell, Henry Chads, and John Black, elders, Edward Brice, Esq., Dr. Peacock, Messrs. Isaac M'Cartney, Robert Lennox, Richard Ashmore, Samuel Smith, John M'Munn, Gilbert Moore, and some others presented an appeal against the action of the Presbytery, which was heard at great length, and many personal matters were brought in. The Synod administered a rebuke to the Presbytery for precipitancy; but ultimately carried out their arrangement, and ordered "that a kind letter be written to Mr. M'Bride, inviting and requiring him to come over as soon as he can." One John Johnson, barber in Belfast, who had been brought forward to prove that Kirkpatrick had been heard to speak disrespectfully of M'Bride, was ordered to be rebuked, but he "could not be found." (*Ex. Min. Gen. Syn.*)

" Samuel Smith, merchant, was sent to M'Bride, at Glasgow, to invite his return, and was successful in this mission.

" M'Bride, on his return, "appeared before the judges of assize at Carrickfergus, and was discharged without a trial." (*Killen's Reid*, iii. 2.)

1711. August.—Warrant issued by Westenra Waring, of Belfast, and Brent Spencer, of Trumra, for the apprehension of M'Bride and others as non-abjurors. M'Bride fled to Scotland, but returned next year.

" Probably in this year Rev. Thomas Milling became M'Bride's assistant. (*Chr. Mod.*, 1826, p. 309.) He is said to have held the office five years.

1712. At the spring assizes, M'Bride and others were presented by the Grand Jury of County Antrim as disloyal men. M'Bride again returned to Scotland at the beginning of May.

" 10th June.—Funeral Register begins.

" 27th Aug.—Three silver cups brought from Dublin. (*Funeral Register.*)

1713. May—M'Bride published, anonymously, at Glasgow, *A Sample of Jet-black Pr——tic Calumny, &c.*, in reply to *A Sample of True-blue Presbyterian Loyalty*, by Dr. Tisdal, vicar of Belfast.

" 8th June.—M'Bride again arrived in Belfast. (*Killen's Reid*, iii. 45.)

1714. 15th June.—The General Synod at Belfast considered in *interloquitur* the case of Samuel Smith, junior, and Joseph Kyle, both of Belfast, who had been excommunicated and prosecuted for being married by the Presbyterian form. They had been "told that if they will re-marry they are promised that their penance shall be easy." The Synod "are unanimously of opinion that they should not re-marry, and do advise that they never do it." (*Ex. Min. Gen. Syn.*)

1718. Rev. John Abernethy, of Antrim, was called to be assistant and successor to M'Bride, but the Synod did not sanction the removal.

" 21st July.—John M'Bride died, æt. 68. Of M'Bride's humour two stories are preserved. When taxed with his non-abjuration he said, "Once upon a time there was a bairn that would not be persuaded to bann the Deil, because he did not know but he might soon come into his clutches" (*Kirkpatrick*, p. 529). It is said that John Clugstone, Sovereign of Belfast (but he was not Sovereign till 1727), sat in the gallery of M'Bride's Meeting-house, and accidentally pulled out a pack of cards with his handkerchief, scattering them on the people below. "Hech, Sir," said M'Bride, "but your psalm book is ill-bund." (*Chr. Mod.*, 1826, p. 428.)

1718. 29 Dec.—"Cash lead out for sweping the Streats at Two sever Sacrements, 10d." (*Funeral Register.*)

1719. Rev. James Fleming of Lurgan was called to be successor to M'Bride, but the Synod did not sanction the removal.

,, 2nd Nov.—The Irish Toleration Act received the Royal assent.

1720. Early in the year the congregation gave a call to Rev. Samuel Haliday, at that time chaplain to Colonel Anstruther's regiment of foot.

,, The term "New Light" was first applied to the principles held by members of the *Belfast Society* in a polemical tract—*Some Friendly Reflections*, by Rev. John Malcolm, of Dunmurry. (*Killen's Reid*, iii. 119.)

,, 21st June.—The General Synod met in Belfast. Haliday appeared and complained of reports circulated about him, especially by Rev. Samuel Dunlop of Athlone. The matter was gone into at great length, and the Synod unanimously resolved: "That the Reverend Mr. Samuel Haliday has sufficiently cleared his innocency, and fully vindicated himself from the aspersions of Arianism and militating against all church government, to the great satisfaction of this Synod." Dunlop was rebuked. This Synod passed the *Pacific Act*, confirming subscription to the Confession, but also sanctioning the practice of Presbyteries which permitted those who scrupled at particular phrases to substitute approved language of their own. (*Ex. Min. Gen Syn.*)

,, 27th July.—Haliday drew up the confession of his faith in the following words:—"I sincerely believe the Scriptures of the Old and New Testament to be the only rule of revealed religion, a sufficient test of orthodoxy or soundness in the faith, and to settle all the terms of ministerial and Christian communion, to which nothing may be added by any synod, assembly, or council whatsoever: And I find all the essential articles of the Christian doctrine to be contained in the Westminster Confession of Faith; which articles I receive upon the sole authority of the Holy Scriptures." (*Killen's Reid*, iii. 130.)

1720. 28th July.—Haliday was installed by Belfast Presbytery on the strength of the above confession.

,, 7th Dec.—The *Belfast Society*, of which Haliday had become a member, issued a circular vindicating its principles.

1721. Jan.—The Sub-synod of Belfast found Haliday's installation irregular, and publicly rebuked the installers. Haliday was then in England.

,, At the next meeting of Presbytery after his return, he was called upon by some members to subscribe the Confession, but the meeting was adjourned till after the General Synod.

,, 20th June.—The General Synod met in Belfast. Among the documents produced was "a certificate from both congregations of Belfast, bearing testimony to the soundness of both their ministers' faiths, subscribed by a great number of hands of both congregations." The moderator was directed to ask Haliday whether he adhered to his assent to the Westminster Confession, given when licensed at Rotterdam. Haliday replied: "My refusal to declare my adherence to the assent I gave to the Westminster Confession of Faith when I was licensed, does not proceed from my disbelief of the important truths contained in it. . . . But my scruples are against the submitting to human tests of divine truths (especially in a great number of extra-essential points, without the knowledge and belief of which men may be entitled to the favour of God and the hopes of eternal life, and, according to the laws of the Gospel, to Christian and ministerial communion in the Church) when imposed as a necessary term of such communion." Ultimately the matter was dropped, *nem. con.* The Synod then, by a large majority, carried a resolution to "allow" such members as were willing to subscribe the Confession of Faith. Those who did not subscribe accordingly, were henceforth

known as NON-SUBSCRIBERS, a term already used, in a somewhat similar sense, at the Salters' Hall Conference in London, 1719, and occasionally found, at a much earlier date, as a synonym for Nonconformist. Petitions for the erection of a new congregation in Belfast were laid before the Synod by minorities of both the existing congregations. John Young, Wm. Simm, and others presented the petition from dissatisfied members of Haliday's flock. The Synod left it to the Presbytery to take action.

1721. August.—The Presbytery erected a third congregation in Belfast. The erection was confirmed by the Committee of Synod at Dungannon in October, and by the General Synod at Derry in June, 1722. Among the most active laymen in promoting the erection was Samuel Smith, who visited Scotland in September, 1722, to obtain pecuniary help, setting forth the need of a third Meeting-house in so populous a town.

1722. Feb.—Kirkpatrick and Haliday publish at Edinburgh a *Letter* (dated 8th October, 1722) *to a Friend at Glasgow, with relation to the New Meeting-house in Belfast.*—(*Killen's Reid*, iii. 161.)

1724. Feb.—Haliday published his *Reasons against the Imposition of Subscription.*

" Feb.—The first communion was held in the Third Meeting-house. Haliday and Kirkpatrick wrote to Rev. Charles Mastertown, the minister, expressing their wish that they and their congregations should be admitted to communicate. This was readily granted as regards the congregations, but the ministers were requested not to "attempt to disturb the solemn work" by attending.

" 16th June.—The General Synod met at Dungannon. At this Synod the Subscribers and Nonsubscribers, at the request of the former, held meetings apart, with a view to find some settlement of their differences.

1725. Feb.—Haliday published his *Letter to Gilbert Kennedy.*

" 15th June.—The General Synod met at Dungannon. By this Synod the Presbyteries were remodelled, and all the Nonsubscribers were transferred to a newly erected Presbytery of Antrim

1726. 21st June.—The General Synod met at Dungannon. On the 22nd June the Nonsubscribers presented their Six Propositions (drawn up in January) as Expedients for Peace: they were received as a declaration of war. After long debates, on Saturday, 25th June, the Antrim Presbytery was excluded from the Synod. The majority for the exclusion was large; yet of the ministers in attendance only 35 or 36 voted for it, 34 voted against, 2 voted *non liquet*, and 6 did not vote at all. Though excluded from the Synod, the Nonsubscribers were not shut out from ministerial or sacramental fellowship, nor deprived of the *regium donum.*

" 6th July.—Haliday and Kirkpatrick convened "the whole town" of Belfast, "to relate to them the great injuries done to the Nonsubscribers, which causeth a great ferment in the place."

" 12th July.—Dublin Presbytery unanimously resolved to hold communion with Antrim Presbytery.

" 21st July.—Munster Presbytery unanimously came to a similar resolution.

" A week-evening lecture was established in the First Congregation. Rev. Michael Bruce, of Holywood, whose income had been reduced by the secession of the subscribing portion of his congregation, was appointed lecturer, at a salary of £20.

" Dec.—Haliday published his *Letter to Francis Iredell.*

1727. 29th June.—Antrim Presbytery (Haliday, moderator) authorise the publication of *A Narrative of the Proceedings of Seven General Synods, &c.*, which was issued in August.

1735. Haliday published a funeral sermon for Rev. Michael Bruce, preached 7th Dec.

1736. Rev. Thos. Drennan installed as Haliday's assistant and successor.

" 19th Oct.—Last entry in Funeral Register.

1739. 5th March.—Haliday died, in the 54th year of his age. (*Belfast News-Letter, Tuesday, March 6, 1738, i.e., 1739, present style.* The following character-portrait of Haliday, drawn early in his career, is less flattering than his funeral eulogy. It is taken from a manuscript in Rev. T. Drennan's hand, containing sketches of the members of the Belfast Society:—"The second is a gentleman of genteel education and polite manners; a fine scholar and of a generous spirit. He is not capable of a mean or dishonest thing. His temper warm, and not enough patient of contradiction. He is fixed, and not to be shaken in the opinions he has received, and cannot appear to be what he is not. His genius abhors perplexity, and all his performances are easy, clear, and correct. His mind is rather great than equal, and his passions appear excusable rather than well commanded. He is formed for enjoying prosperity handsomely rather than bearing distress. In his anger quick, but not surly; tender in his friendship, but too apt to resent." (*Chr. Mod.*, 1826, p. 432.)

1746. Some time before this, Rev. Andrew Millar became assistant (unordained) to Drennan.

1749. Millar removed to Summerhill, Co. Meath, and was succeeded by Rev. Clotworthy Brown, from Ballynure.

1750. 19th June.—The General Synod at Dungannon invited the Antrim Presbytery to join in the scheme for a Widows' Fund, projected by William Bruce, a nonsubscribing layman of Dublin.

1751. 18th June.—The General Synod at Antrim was attended by commissioners from Antrim Presbytery, including Clotworthy Brown.

1755. 26th May.—Clotworthy Brown died. (*Belfast News-Letter, Tuesday*, 27th May, 1755.)

1756. Rev. James Mackay, from Clonmel, was installed as assistant and successor to Drennan.

1757. 22nd July.—Earliest extant entry in Baptismal Register.

1760. 3rd Sept.—Earliest extant Minute Book of the congregation begins. A standing Committee, to act with the Session, was for the first time appointed. A Chairman and Secretary were to be chosen annually. The seats in the Meeting-house were numbered, and seat-rents charged. At this date an income was still derived from "Cloak and Pall-money."

1762. 21st September.—A boys' day school is mentioned as maintained by the congregation. Reading, writing, and singing were taught, and boys, in number varying from 14 to 19, were clothed, the expenses being met by a charity sermon on a Sunday in August or September, at five o'clock, to admit of the attendance of members of other denominations. The boys formed a choir in the Meeting-house, under the tuition of the singing clerk.

1767. 31st August.—Lease of the site of Meeting-house and Manse granted by the Earl of Donegall.

1768. 14th Feb.—Rev. Thomas Drennan died.

,, 15th June.—Resolved that the Session (which since 1760 had been reduced to seven) consist of 24 members.

,, Rev. John Beatty, of Holywood, was made temporary assistant to Mackay, pending the choice of a colleague.

1769. 16th Dec.—Rev. James Crombie chosen as colleague to Mackay, at a stipend of £80 sterling, with the Manse or £10 in lieu of it.

1770. 20th Oct.—Crombie writes from Belfast to Elgin Presbytery, saying that he had accepted the call to Belfast. He was demitted from Lhanbryd on 4th Dec.

1771. 3rd March.—"Resolved, that all the waste seats in the Meeting-house have immediately locks put on them, and the kays of these seats be kept in the vestry—from thence to be given to any person who may incline to take a seat."

,, 2nd June.—Crawford, the schoolmaster, having removed to America, his wife was continued in his place. The school was maintained under Mrs. Crawford till the reception of children by the Old Charitable Society rendered it unnecessary.

1772. 5th Jan.—Deputation appointed to wait on Rev. James Saurin (Vicar of Belfast), and make him an offer of the Meeting-house to perform divine service in. This was in view of the removal of the old Parish Church, St. Patrick's (on the site of the present St. George's). The building was not taken down till 7th May, 1774, when for two years and a-half the Episcopalian congregation worshipped in one of the Presbyterian Meeting-houses.

1772. 2nd Aug.—The Committee declined to grant to any members leases of their seats.

1777. Feb.—Crombie's *Essay on Church Consecration* (anonymous) published in Dublin. (*Disciple*, April, 1883, p. 97.)

1778. 19th July.—Crombie's first sermon to Volunteers (afterwards published).

1779. 1st Aug.—Crombie's second Volunteer sermon (afterwards published).

1781. 22nd January.—Rev. James Mackay died. He was born in 1709.

„ 18th Feb.—Resolution taken to build a new Meeting-house.

„ 4th March.—Crombie's third Volunteer sermon, in which he advocates drilling on Sunday (afterwards published).

„ April.—Old Meeting-house taken down.

„ 12th May.—Building Committee decided on the elliptical shape for the new house.

„ 1st June.—Foundation-stone laid.

1783. 1st June.—Present Meeting-house opened for worship.

1785. 9th Sept.—Crombie (now D.D.) issued proposals for the establishment of the Belfast Academy. It was opened in February, 1786.

1789. 8th June (Monday).—John Wesley, in his 86th year, preached in the Meeting-house, and describes it as "the completest place of worship I have ever seen," and "beautiful in the highest degree." He would have preached again next day, but "the sexton sent me word it must not be, for the crowds had damaged the house, and some of them had broke off and carried away the silver which was on the bible in the pulpit."

1790. 1st March.—Crombie died, in his 60th year.

„ 11th March.—Call given to Rev. William Bruce, D.D. (52 signatures). He entered on his duties on 1st May.

„ 25th July.—Number of the Committee fixed at seven; fine of one shilling for non-attendance.

1792. 4th Nov.—Singing clerk empowered to select as singers not more than 10 of the children in the Old Charitable Society, the congregation providing them with shoes and stockings.

1794. 9th Nov.—Rev. W. Bristow (Vicar of Belfast) acted as one of the collectors at the charity sermon.

1798. 25th June.—Address from the congregation to the Lord Lieutenant (Cornwallis) declaring abhorrence of "the present atrocious insurrection."

1801. 3rd May.—Dr. Bruce authorised to make "a new selection of Psalms for the use of this congregation" (edition of 1,000 copies published same year), under the superintendence of Henry Joy and John Holmes Houston; price in calf, best paper, 3s. 9½d.; in boards, inferior paper, 2s. 8½d. "A very liberal proposal from Mr. Edward Bunting, of Belfast, respecting the purchase of an organ," was communicated.

1803. 27th Feb.—Proposal made to heat the Meeting-house with stoves, but curtains were ordered instead.

„ 1st May.—Reported that John Mathers had left the reversion of a profit rent of £11 18s. 2d. for the use of the poor of the congregation, and also £50, to be invested until the capital doubled, and then the interest applied to the improvement of the psalmody.

„ In this year Dr. Bruce obtained from Government a recognition of the right of the congregation to a share of *regium donum*, in case of the appointment of a colleague.

1806. 3rd Aug.—Proposal to alter the hours of worship (eleven and one), "partly in consequence of the erection of an organ in the Second Congregation, which it is conceived may disturb worship in this house." No change was made.

1811. 7th July.—On application by Rev Edward May (Vicar of Belfast) the use of the Meeting house was granted, at half-past twelve on Sundays, to the Episcopalian Congregation, during the repairs of the Parish Church.

1812. 19th Jan.—Call given to Rev. William Bruce, A.B., as colleague.

„ 3rd March.—Rev. William Bruce ordained.

„ 7th June.—First printed list of constituents issued.

1812. 19th July.—Resolution to enlarge the galleries adopted.

1814. 17th July.—Use of the Meeting-house again granted to Rev. E. May, during repairs of the Parish Church.

1816. 5th May.—First appointment of Music Committee, and introduction of part-singing.

„ 27th Oct.—Renewed proposal for a stove. After a year's consideration, additional curtains were put up.

1817. 1st June.—First appointment of a secretary to the congregation.

1818. 4th Jan.—Reported that Mrs. Mary Hodgens had bequeathed £50 to the congregation.

„ 6th June.—First report from the Committee to the annual meeting.

„ 1st August.—New edition (1,000 copies) of the Psalm-book issued. It was edited by Dr. Bruce, and revised by Rev. W. D. H. M'Ewen of the Second Congregation. The paper, in two qualities, was specially made by Messrs. Blow, Ward, and Greenfield. The prices of the bound volume were 3s. 9d. and 3s. 4d. The book continued in use till 28th November, 1886.

„ 1st Nov.—Reported that Miss M'Ilwrath had bequeathed £50 to the congregation

1821. 26th Aug—Resolved that "it is inexpedient" to put the pulpit in mourning in consequence of the decease of Queen Caroline. This was usually done on Royal deaths.

1824. This year Dr. Bruce published his *Sermons on the Study of the Bible and the Doctrines of Christianity*; preface dated 17th March.

„ 4th July.—Congregation agreed to the erection of a stove, but nothing done in the matter.

„ Rev. W. Bruce began evening lectures at six o'clock.

„ 5th Dec.—First mention of a Ladies' Clothing Society.

1827. 30th Dec.—Charity sermon for House of Industry preached by Rev. H. Montgomery; the Marquis of Donegall was one of the collectors; £210 13s. 11d. collected.

1830. 25th May.—First meeting of Remonstrant Synod held in the Meeting-house.

1831. 1st May.—Dr. Bruce resigned his active charge of the congregation, retaining the position of senior minister.

1831. 17th June.—Service of plate presented by the congregation to Dr. Bruce.

„ 11th Sept.—Call (89 signatures) to Rev. John Scott Porter as colleague to Rev. W. Bruce.

1832. 22nd Jan.—Rules as to order of proceedings in Committee agreed upon.

„ 2nd Feb.—Rev. J. S. Porter installed.

„ October.—Meeting-house closed for repairs and improvements.

1833. 10th March.—Meeting-house re-opened, after rebuilding of frontage, introduction of hot-water apparatus, &c., at a cost of £681 3s.

„ 23rd June.—Reported that premises in Skipper Street have been bequeathed to the First and Second Congregations by William Tennent.

1834. 14th, 15th, 16th, 17th April.—Public discussion in the Meeting-house on the Unitarian Controversy, between Rev. Daniel Bagot and Rev. J. S. Porter.

1835. 1st May.—Application of Sunday collections as poor's money discontinued.

„ 9th Aug.—Dr. Bruce resigned *regium donum* in favour of Rev. J. S Porter.

„ 8th Nov.—Resolved to light the house with gas. [Carried out early in the following year.]

1838. 28th January.—Sunday-school begun; first superintendent, George M'Adam.

„ 6th May.—Congregational Library opened; first librarian, William Hartley. Engraved portrait of Dr. Bruce presented to the congregation by John Hodgson.

„ 11th July.—First record of a Visitation of the congregation by the Presbytery of Antrim.

„ October.—Day school for girls opened.

1839. 29th January.—Evening school for boys opened.

1840. June.—School in Fountain Street opened.

1841. 24th Feb.—Resolution requesting Rev. J. S. Porter to publish his evening lectures on Unitarianism. [Several similar resolutions in subsequent years.]

„ 27th Feb.—Dr. Bruce died. He bequeathed to the congregation £50, and his executors (on 16th April) presented the oil-painting

of Rev. John M'Bride, and portraits of Revs. Dr. Kirkpatrick, Dr. Abernethy, Dr. Crombie, and William Bryson.

1842. 21st Aug.—Meeting-house re-opened after erection of monument to Rev. Dr. Bruce.

1844. 19th July.—Royal assent given to Dissenters' Chapels Act. In recognition of their services in assisting to obtain this Act, the congregation presented to the editor of the *Northern Whig* (Mr. Simms) a salver and tea-service, to the proprietor of the *Northern Whig* (Mr. Finlay) a salver and dinner-service, to Mr. W. J. C. Allen a salver, and to Rev. John Porter (Second Congregation) a purse of 25 guineas.

1845. 14th April.—Meeting-house registered for celebration of marriages, under 7 and 8 Vict., cap. 81.

1851. 9th September.—Mr. Robert Montgomery, Treasurer, died. He bequeathed a legacy of £50 to the congregation.

1852. 8th March.—Donation of £100 by the Misses M'Kedy to the congregation.

1853. 27th Feb.—Opening of organ, purchased from Mr. T. A. Barnes.

1854. 27th July.—Freehold of the congregational properties in Rosemary Street purchased.

1855. 28th Oct.—New organ erected by Messrs Gray & Davison.

1856. 18th Oct.—Communion linen presented by Mr. Michael Andrews.

1859 10th April.—Bequest of £50 by Miss Jane Whitla reported.

1861. 6th Oct.—Reported that the congregation had become entitled to legacies of £100 (for investment) under will of Elizabeth M'Kedy, dated 29th October, 1836; £50 each under wills of Catherine and Mary M'Kedy, dated 17th August, 1854.

„ 10th November.—Hours of Sunday services changed to 11-30 a.m.; and 7 p.m. for lectures in the winter season.

1862. 19th January.—Congregation withdrew from ecclesiastical connection with Antrim Presbytery.

„ 23rd Feb.—Congregation united with four other congregations to form Northern Presbytery of Antrim.

„ 5th October.—Meeting-house re-opened after erection of memorial windows behind the pulpit, in commemoration of the completion of fifty years of the ministry of Rev. W. Bruce. On removal of the pulpit canopy, the following memorandum was found:—"This Meeting-house was erected by the inhabitants of Belfast under the care and inspection of Mr. Roger Mulholland, who executed the same, both external and internal parts thereof, on the first day of January, in the year of our Lord 1783—eighty-three, and this piece executed by Patrick Smyth."

1862. 25th Dec.—Presentation of plate to Rev. W. Bruce.

1867. 21st April.—Rev. W. Bruce retired from active duty, after a ministry of 55 years.

„ 5th May.—Present order of worship adopted.

1868. 25th Oct.—Rev. William Bruce died.

„ 8th Dec.—Collection of books forming the "Ministerial Library" presented by Mrs. Bruce.

1871. 14th March.—Rev. J. S. Porter commuted his life interest in the *regium donum* for the benefit of the congregation.

1872. 6th Oct.—Bequest of £100 by Mr. John Galt Smith, to be invested for the Music Fund, reported to Committee.

1873. 12th April.—Portrait of Rev. J. Scott Porter presented to him by members of the congregation (replica placed in vestry).

„ 5th October.—Meeting-house re-opened after erection of new pews and four memorial windows—Andrews, Hincks, Martin, Smith.

„ 19th October.—Present order of communion service adopted.

1874. 19th April.—Six new flagons introduced at communion.

1877. 18th Feb.—Call (272 signatures) to Rev. A. Gordon as colleague with Rev. J. Scott Porter.

„ 5th June.—Installation of Rev. A. Gordon by Northern Presbytery of Antrim.

1878. 6th Jan.—Regular evening services begun.

„ 29th April.—First soirée in connection with Annual Meeting.

„ Oct.—Institute of Faith and Science begun.

1879. 6th April.—Bequest of £100 by William Campbell reported.

1879. 24th August.—Addresses presented by Rev. A. Gordon to the General Synod of the Unitarian Church of Hungary at Székély Kereszatúr, on occasion of the ter-centennial of the death of Bishop Francis Dávid.

1880. 29th Feb.—Collection in aid of the erection of the Channing Memorial Church at Newport, Rhode Island.

,, 22nd May.—Portrait of Mr. G. K. Smith presented to him by members of the congregation, in recognition of his services as Secretary for 41 years.

,, 5th July.—Rev. J. Scott Porter died.

1881. 9th Oct.—Meeting-house re-opened after erection of memorial tablets to Revs. W. Bruce and J. Scott Porter. Address of condolence offered by the congregation to Mrs. Garfield, widow of the late President of the United States of America.

,, 23rd Oct.—First Harvest Festival Service.

1882. 29th Sept.—Donation of £50 from Miss Curell, in memory of her sister Mary.

1883. 20th June.—Centennial Meeting in Ulster Hall.

1884. 25th Feb.—Bequest of £100 by Mr. W. J. C. Allen, for investment, reported.

,, 22nd Nov.—Portraits of James and David Dunn presented to the congregation by Mr. Thomas M'Tear.

1885. 6th June.—Portrait of Mr. John Hodgson presented to the congregation by Mr. James Magill.

1886. 14th Jan.—Formal opening of Central Hall, erected in commemoration of the Centennial of the Meeting-house.

,, 25th July.—Death of Mr. G. K. Smith, Secretary from 1st September, 1839. By will he left £200 to be invested for the Music Fund.

,, 5th Dec.—New hymn-book brought into use.

TREASURERS OF THE CONGREGATION.

[Originally called Grand Treasurer, as there was a separate Treasurer for the Poor's Money.]

* * * *

1712. Thomas Lyle.
1713. John Ewing.
1714. John Euless.
1715. William Mitchell.
1716. Uchtred M'Dougal.
1717. John M'Munn.

* * * *

bef. 1760. John Ross.
1761. John Galt Smith.
1781. Robert Gordon.

* * * *

bef. 1802. John Holmes.
1802. John Holmes Houston.
1817. William Tennent.
1827. Robert Callwell.
1836. Robert Montgomery.
1851. William John Campbell Allen.
1869. James Carr.
1874. Nicholas Oakman.
1876. William H. Patterson.
1881. J. W. Russell.
1886. John Rogers.

SEXTONS.

bef. 1712. Thomas Swendill.
1718. David Ferguson.
1720. Samuel Pentland.

* * * *

bef. 1763. Robert Harper.
1791. John Scott (Assistant till 1793).
1791. Henry Whitfield.
1812. William Wilson.
1833. Geo. Ferguson (Assistant till 1852).
1849. Mrs. Hainey.
1850. Mrs. M'Quoid.
1853. John M'Cord.
1866. Moses Martin.
1879. James Bell.
1885. William Jackson.
1887. Henry Burniston.

SINGING-CLERKS.

bef. 1715. Hugh Cunningham.

* * * *

bef. 1760. ——— Vincent.
1771. John Cochran.
1801. John M'Vity.
1805. Thomas Stafford.
1808–27. William Hughes.

SECRETARIES.

1760. CHARLES CUNNINGHAM.

* * * *

1771. ROBERT GORDON.

* * * *

1782. REV. JAMES CROMBIE.

[The above were Secretaries of the Committee; after Dr. Crombie's death no appointment of secretary was made, minutes being taken by various hands. The following were Secretaries of the Congregation.]

1817. JOHN WARD.
1827. WILLIAM PATTERSON.
1837. THOMAS CHERMSIDE.
1839. GEO. KENNEDY SMITH.
1886. JOHN SMITH M'TEAR.

ORGANISTS.

1853. JOHN MOORE.
1853. WELBORE STEWART BURNETT.
1864. BENJAMIN HOBSON CARROLL, Mus. Doc.

SUBSCRIBERS TO CENTRAL HALL, 1883.

Name		£	s.	d.
John Campbell, Lennoxvale,	£150			
In memory of the late Wm. Campbell,	100			
		£250	0	0
Sir E. J. Harland, Bart., J.P., Mayor of Belfast, ...		200	0	0
George K. Smith, ...		100	0	0
J. R. Musgrave, D.L., J.P., ...		100	0	0
John Rogers, ...		100	0	0
W. Riddel, J.P., and S. Riddel, ...		100	0	0
James Bruce, D.L., J.P., ...		100	0	0
R. G. Dunville, D.L., J.P., ...		100	0	0
F. D. Ward, J.P., M.R.I.A., ...		100	0	0
A. M. Kirker, ...		50	0	0
Misses Bruce, ...		50	0	0
Misses Campbell, ...		50	0	0
William Spackman, ...		20	0	0
Frederick Little, ...		20	0	0
James Carr, ...		20	0	0
W. H. Patterson, M.R.I.A., and R. Lloyd Patterson, J.P., F.L.S.,		20	0	0
Nicholas Oakman, ...		20	0	0
Mrs. Greer, and in memory of Mrs. Gray,		20	0	0
Representatives of Robert Boyd, ...		10	0	0
W. Sinclair Boyd, ...		10	0	0
W. T. Hamilton, ...		10	0	0
Thomas L'Estrange, ...		10	0	0
Bowman Malcolm, C.E., ...		10	0	0
Dr. Brice Smyth, ...		10	0	0
Mrs. Andrews, ...		10	0	0
George Andrews, ...		10	0	0
Mrs. Macrory, ...	£7 0 0			
Miss Macrory, ...	3 0 0	£10	0	0
Henry Bruce, ...		10	0	0
Robert Tennent, Rushpark, ...		10	0	0
Gawin Orr, M.D., Ballylesson, ...		10	0	0
Miss Benn, ...		10	0	0
Marshall Laird, ...		8	10	10
Mrs. Home and Mrs. A. G. Malcolm,		5	0	0
Mrs. Orr, ...		5	0	0
Mrs. L. Hutton, Dublin, ...		5	0	0
John Hunter, ...		5	0	0
William M'Ninch, ...		5	0	0
Mrs. Blackley, ...		5	0	0
Robert Murray, ...		5	0	0
Thomas Ritchie, ...		5	0	0
Mrs. Rowland, and in memory of Miss Maxwell, ...		5	0	0
E. J. M'Ervel, ...		5	0	0
James M'Ervel, ...		5	0	c
Thomas M'Ervel, ...		5	0	0
James P. Orr, ...		5	0	0
Mrs. M'Caw, ...		5	0	0
John J. Dugan, ...		5	0	0
J. S. M'Tear, and Misses M. & F. M. M'Tear, ...		5	0	0
Mrs. Gamble, ...	£2 10 0			
Miss Arthur, ...	2 10 0	5	0	0
H. F. Thomas, ...		5	0	0
J. W. Russell, ...		5	0	0
Mrs. Charnock, ...		5	0	0
W. H. Kennedy, ...		5	0	0

Name		£	s.	d.
Misses Smyth,		£5	0	0
W. J. Luke,		5	0	0
W. H. M'Fadden,		5	0	0
N. A. Campbell,		5	0	0
Mercer Rice,		5	0	0
Charles Bowles,		5	0	0
Marcus J. Ward,	£3 0 0	4	0	0
George G. Ward,	1 0 0			
Mrs. Armstrong,		3	0	0
Henry Murray,		3	0	0
Mrs. Ledlie,		3	0	0
Alex. M'Cann,		2	10	0
John Dickson,		2	2	0
John Johnston,		2	2	0
Mrs. Hartley,		£2	2	0
Mrs. Malcolm,		2	0	0
George M'Caw,		2	0	0
Miss Stewart,		2	0	0
Miss Carruthers,		2	0	0
Miss T. Carruthers,		2	0	0
Miss Graham,		1	1	0
James Moore,		1	1	0
Edmund B. Roche,		1	0	0
Henry Ferguson,		1	0	0
The Misses Ferguson,		1	0	0
Miss Williamson,		1	0	0
A. H. Manderson,		1	0	0

First Presbyterian Church, Belfast, A.D. 1887.

APPENDIX.

PRESENTATION TO MR. GEORGE K. SMITH.

ON Saturday afternoon, 22nd May, 1880, a numerous company assembled at Meadowbank, Whitehouse, for the purpose of presenting his portrait to Mr. George K. Smith, who, for the period of 41 years, had discharged, with marked efficiency and unwearying zeal, the duties of Secretary to the First Presbyterian Congregation. Invitations were issued to the following subscribers to the portrait, viz.:—Rev. J. Scott Porter, Rev. Alexander Gordon, M.A.; Messrs. W. J. C. Allen, J.P.; E. J. Harland, J.P., Chairman of Belfast Harbour Commissioners (now Sir E. J. Harland, Bart.); Wm. Riddel, J.P.; J. R. Musgrave, J.P.; J. F. M'Caw, Hon. William Porter, J. Galt Smith, J.P.; F. D. Ward, J.P.; John Rogers, John Campbell, William Robertson, C. Bowles, N. Oakman, James Cronne, A. O'D. Taylor, Brice Smyth, M.D.; James M'Fadden, Henry Bruce, J. W. Russell, J. S. Drennan, M.D.; R. L. Patterson, J.P.; W. H. Malcolm, J. Dugan, Lenox Drennan, Geo. Benn, Thomas L'Estrange, J. S. M'Tear; Mrs. H. C. Smith; Miss Whitla, Beneaden; Misses Campbell, Miss Bruce, Mrs. Patterson, Miss M'Gee, Mrs. Andrews. Also to the following:—Sir Thomas A. Jones, P.R.H.A.; Lady Jones, Miss Porter and Mr. Drummond Porter, the Misses Allen, Mrs. Gordon, Mrs. Harland, the Misses Riddel, Mrs. L'Estrange, Mrs. Ward, Mrs. Rogers, Mrs. John Campbell, Mrs. Robertson, Mrs. Bowles, Mrs. Taylor, Mrs. Brice Smyth, Mr. and Mrs. Adam Duffin, Miss Drennan, Mrs. Malcolm, Miss Benn, Mrs. Cunningham, Miss Bottomley, Mr. James Glenny, the Misses M'Tear, Miss L. Bankhead, Miss Byrne, Mr. (now Dr.) and Mrs. Carroll, Mr. S. T. Smith, Dr and Mrs. Manley and Miss Manley, Mr. Manley, Mr. and Mrs. J. S. Salvage.

On the motion of Mr. J. R. MUSGRAVE, J.P., High Sheriff of the County of Donegal, seconded by Mr. JAMES F. M'CAW, the chair was taken by Mr. W. J. C. Allen, J.P.

The CHAIRMAN said—Ladies and Gentlemen, I have to thank you for the honour you have done me in placing me in the chair on this, I will say, very auspicious occasion: but I believe I shall consult your comfort and my own ease much better by proceeding at once to the business of the day than by any observations that I may be likely to lay before you. At the same time, you will permit me to say that it is a peculiarly gratifying thing to me to be here on this occasion. (Hear, hear.) The gentleman whom we here meet to honour is one of the oldest friends that I have in Belfast. We have known each other since we were boys at school, and we have been associated with one another, not merely as members of the First Congregation and of its committee, but also in a business capacity, and I must say that, during the whole progress of our intercourse, notwithstanding that, as a matter of course, we may have had some differences of opinion, those differences have never in the slightest degree diminished the respect we entertained for one another. (Applause.) Before reading the address, I may mention that we have received a number of notes expressing regret on the part of the writers that they are not able to be here to-day. Amongst those who have forwarded communications are Mr. E. J. Harland, J.P.—who, I may say, took the greatest interest in all the proceedings connected with the presentation, and who is unable to be present here to-day, as he is in Mullingar—Dr. Drennan, Messrs. Alexander O'D. Taylor, R. Lloyd Patterson (President of the Belfast Chamber of Commerce), and Henry Bruce. I have also to express on the part of my respected colleague, Mr. Carr, his regret that an engagement, which he had formed before he was aware of this meeting, prevents him from being present. With your permission I shall now proceed to read the address to Mr. Smith. It is as follows:—

TO GEORGE K. SMITH, ESQ.

DEAR SIR,—During the long period of forty-one years you have discharged the duties of Secretary to the First Presbyterian Congregation with great efficiency and unabated zeal. We know that this has been to you a labour of love.

Your hereditary connection with our worshipping society, extending beyond two centuries, has identified you with its history to an extent far exceeding that which can be claimed by any of its other existing members; and our present place of worship is especially endeared to you by the fact that your grandfather was the treasurer of the congregation when it was rebuilt, and an active and careful superintendent of the work. No wonder, then, that the welfare of the society and the maintenance of the fabric of our beautiful church should be objects of the deepest interest to you.

That you have spared neither time nor trouble, nor, when occasion called for it, your purse, in order to maintain the congregation in its place as one of the first of our churches, those of us who have been associated with you during your protracted tenure of office can abundantly testify; and we are happy to assure you that those who in more recent years have attached themselves to the congregation duly appreciate your exertions on its behalf. As a slight, and certainly very inadequate, expression of our gratitude to you, we have to request your acceptance of this portrait. When you look on it, it may recall to your recollection many interesting events connected with the church in which you have taken an active part, and may remind you of old friends with whom you have frequently taken sweet counsel. And when the day shall come—but may it be far distant—when you can no longer contemplate it, may it serve to future generations as a memento of the esteem entertained by his fellow-worshippers for the services rendered to the First Congregation by George Kennedy Smith.

(Signed on behalf of the subscribers)

E. J. HARLAND, *Chairman.*
W. J. C. ALLEN, *Treasurer.*
JOHN ROGERS, *Secretary.*

The address, embodied in a beautifully-bound volume, engrossed and illuminated most artistically by Messrs. Marcus Ward & Co., was then handed to Mr. Smith, and the portrait presented to him amid loud applause. The latter is a half-length in oil, by the president of the Royal Hibernian Academy, Sir Thomas A. Jones, and represents Mr. Smith seated at a table, his left hand raising his eyeglass, while with the right he caresses a favourite dog.

Mr. SMITH, who was deeply affected, then read the following reply:—

Heartily do I thank you, my pastors and fellow-worshippers, for the kind expressions contained in your address, and for the gift of this work of art. The presentation is the more endeared to me as the suggestion of a voice now speaking from a bed of infirmity, the voice of one who was my preceptor in youth, and with whom, as my beloved pastor, I have had uninterrupted sweet counsel throughout my official career.

It was a happy omen of my life that, at the age of twenty-seven, I was selected as the secretary of a congregation in which I had so many pleasing family ties, a religious society then comprising 110 seatholders, of whom now, alas! six only survive. It was my great happiness to find myself associated in my youth with such distinguished ministers as my esteemed relative, the late Rev. William Bruce, and the life-long friend already referred to, the Rev. J. Scott Porter; and with a committee whose names I delight in recalling, viz.:—John Holmes Houston, Dr. S. Smith Thomson, Valentine Whitla, William Boyd (Fortbreda), J. Thomson Tennent, Alexander M'Donnell, Thos. Chermside, W. J. C. Allen, George M'Tear, John Riddel, John Curell, Dr. Marshall, Dr. Burden, John Galt Smith, Francis Whitla, P. L. Munster, John Cunningham, Robt. Montgomery (treasurer); William Hartley, John Hodgson, and Robert Patterson. To work with these was, as it has always been with their successors, truly "a labour of love." Our worthy chairman on this occasion is now the only survivor of that committee, and, in thus referring to him, it is my wish to testify to the great interest he has always taken in the affairs of the congregation, of which he was treasurer for upwards of ten years.

That the spirit of kindness and friendship which was manifested originally towards me should have continued for such a long series of years is a fact of which I am proud, and that my services should be recognised as having been discharged with unabated zeal during forty-one years is to me most gratifying, more particularly as it appears that the congregation was never in a more healthy condition than at present, the constituency now numbering 191 stipend-paying members, exclusive of their families.

Naturally your address recalls to my mind many events connected with the history of our church during my term of office. A few years after my appointment an attempt was made, by proceedings in Chancery, to wrest from my Unitarian brethren the churches we had held from time immemorial. Parliament, however, secured our rights by passing the Dissenters' Chapels Act. Thank God, the spirit that then prevailed has to a great extent subsided. May the day not be distant when all denominations will set aside the sectarian strifes of Churches, as so many stumbling-blocks in the progress of genuine Christianity.

To render our properties unassailable in all respects, the First and Second Congregations procured in 1851, from the Commissioners for the Sale of Encumbered Estates in Ireland, the fee and inheritance of the congregational properties in Rosemary Street and Skipper Street, Belfast, thus acquiring the same absolute estate therein as had been previously vested in the Marquis of Donegall, free of rent. By these purchases the congregational grounds have become much enhanced in value, and their value will be still greater when the projected improvements are carried out in the adjoining streets.

Notwithstanding an expenditure of upwards of one thousand pounds within the last seven years, in repairing and improving our beautiful house of worship, the returns to be presented at our approaching annual general meeting show funded property to the credit of the congregation amounting to considerably above that sum.

In referring to our house of worship, I cannot forget the points of interest which it exhibits in the various mural tablets and memorial windows erected within my time to many whose virtues and services we revere, including the Rev. Dr. Bruce, Rev. Dr. Hincks, Rev. William Bruce, J. H. Houston, William Tennent, S. S. Thomson, M.D.; John Martin, John Riddel, Samuel Martin, Alithea Maria Ferguson, Michael Andrews, Robert Patterson, and John Galt Smith. Many other honoured names might be added as associated with the old Meeting House of Belfast during this century. Memorials of an earlier date are to be found in the portraits which adorn the walls of our vestry. Here may be seen, among the rest, the features of the heroic M'Bride, the gentle Drennan, and the erudite Crombie, founder of the Belfast Academy, all ministers of our church.

The latest important event affecting the interests of our worshipping society is the appointment of the Rev. Alex. Gordon, M.A., to the junior pastorate of the congregation. Like my other two ministers to whom I have alluded, co-operation with Mr. Gordon is a real pleasure. Sincerely do I hope, and with confidence do I rely, that his exertions for the welfare of the congregation will redound to the good of our common cause.

And now, my dear friends, after these allusions to a few of the more prominent events connected with my congregational career, give me leave to say that this will always be to me a memorable day. To have my portrait painted by such a distinguished artist as Sir Thomas Alfred Jones, P.R.H.A., and placed by your generosity among the collection of family portraits you see around, affords me a delight as great as I have ever experienced. It has been said that "a room hung with pictures is a room hung with thoughts," and so will the walls of this room be to me, both as reflecting your own extreme kindness, and as exhibiting the lineaments of honoured ancestors, several of whom were members of "The Old Meeting House," and all identified with the public institutions of Belfast.

The Chairman asked permission to express to Sir Thos. Jones the great satisfaction they entertained for the mode in which he had executed this commission. (Applause.) They had from time to time had specimens of his handiwork, and, though last not least, they had the one in that room. (Applause.)

Sir Thomas A. Jones, President of the Royal Hibernian Academy, who was warmly received, said it had given him the greatest pleasure to paint that portrait, and he hoped that when, in after years, Mr. Smith looked upon it, he would remember not only the friends who presented it, but also the friend who painted it. (Applause.)

The company adjourned to luncheon, after which vocal and instrumental music and other items brought to a termination an exceedingly pleasant evening under the hospitable roof of Meadowbank.

CENTENNIAL CELEBRATION, 20th June, 1883.

Early in 1882, at the Annual Meeting of the Congregation, the attention of its members was directed to the approaching anniversary of the completion of its beautiful Meeting-house, and various schemes for the celebration of the Centennial were suggested. The subject was brought up in the Committee's Report to the Annual Meeting in the spring of 1883, and a Special Centennial Committee was appointed. An assemblage of friends on a large scale was proposed by the Centennial Committee, and the largest hall in Belfast was taken.

The committee decided to invite officially all the ministers on the roll of the Nonsubscribing Association, and through them to extend a general invitation to their congregations; to solicit a deputation from the British and Foreign Unitarian Association; and to leave the members of the congregation free to ask their own friends. A thousand tickets were printed, but, as the responses and applications poured in, it became necessary to provide for a much larger number.

The day for the celebration, Wednesday, 20th June, was chosen on account of the fact that the Association of Irish

Nonsubscribing Presbyterians would then be in session in Belfast. For a Unitarian demonstration it was peculiarly appropriate, as it happened to be the birthday of Theophilus Lindsey (founder of Essex Street Chapel, the first erected for Unitarian worship in the British Isles), who was born 20th June, 1723.

The intention was, not simply to congregate an audience for the purpose of listening to speeches, but to afford a full opportunity for social converse and pleasant intercourse, the renewal of old friendships and the opening of new ones. Some of our veterans in the cause, who are now rarely met at public gatherings, greeted each other in the crowd of younger friends, and bright faces of children were not wanting in the scene. Two or three hundred visitors from other denominations were present, welcomed by all, and made to feel thoroughly at home.

A large and varied collection of objects of interest was exhibited on tables and in cases disposed about the Ulster Hall. Coins, medals, Irish antiquities, Japanese curiosities, a collection of old laces, valuable books and manuscripts, microscopes and stereoscopes, were placed on view. There was a special collection of engravings, autographs, and documents illustrating the past career of the Church, including the Solemn League and Covenant, bearing the original signatures obtained at Holywood in 1644; and another illustrative of the general history of Unitarianism, beginning with a curious Dutch engraving of Arius. In the centre of the hall were displayed two magnificent services of plate, presented to the late Dr. Bruce, on leaving the Academy, and on retiring from the active duties of the ministry. Around the walls was hung a very extensive and remarkable series of portraits of former ministers and members of the church, lent by private families and public bodies, the oldest painting being that famous one of Rev. John M'Bride, still bearing the marks of the sword-thrust which testifies to the exasperation of the Sovereign of Belfast, when he found that the minister he hoped to take into custody had fled, and his picture alone remained, to smile at the baffled representative of authority. Attached to the columns supporting the galleries were 17 bannerets, bearing the names of all the ministers of the church since its foundation. Floral decorations were conspicuous throughout the building. Objects of vertu were placed in every available corner. Indeed, as an art exhibition alone, the loan collection may be pronounced unique.

On the opening of the hall at six o'clock, and during the serving of tea, performances on the grand organ were given by Mr. B. Hobson Carroll, Mus. Bac. (now Mus. Doc.), organist of the church; and at intervals during the evening a programme of music was rendered by a special choir. Shortly after eight o'clock, a procession was formed, headed by officers and deacons of the church, and including the deputation and the clergymen present; and the chair, placed on a dais at the side of the hall, was taken by the pastor of the congregation.

The formal part of the meeting was opened by the singing of the hymn "Jesus shall reign," and by prayer offered by the Moderator of the Northern Presbytery of Antrim, Rev. C. J. M'Alester. Letters of sympathy from various quarters were referred to, including a very kind letter from Lord Waveney, a descendant of the family of Rev. Patrick Adair, and a letter from the Attorney-General for Ireland (now Master of the Rolls), the eldest son of the late Rev. John Scott Porter. The Secretary, George Kennedy Smith, was then called upon to read a historical statement, which gave, in brief, an outline of the congregational history, and concluding as follows:—"The occasion will be further commemorated by the production of a volume of *Historic Memorials*, dealing in full detail with our not inglorious nor uninstructive past. Two other projects, relating to the future of our usefulness and our aspiration, are also in view. A new hymn-book, to inspire our devotions; and a hall for our congregational meetings, with accommodation for Sunday Schools, Committees, and Library, are dreams which we hope will soon come true. May an impetus be given from this meeting to every righteous purpose of our hearts; that days to come may more than equal the glories of days bygone; and that, confiding in the One God, true to the One Master, animated by the One Spirit, we may increase in the life of faith and hope and love."

The CHAIRMAN then offered, in the name of the congregation, a hearty welcome to those friends who represented the Association of Irish Nonsubscribing Presbyterians, the British and Foreign Unitarian Association, and other bodies.

WILLIAM SINCLAIR BOYD, Esq., in seconding the welcome, said that this, he believed, was the largest assemblage ever held in Belfast in connection with the Unitarian community. Of those present, a very large proportion were members of other Unitarian congregations around them. A formal vote need not be passed to welcome them. Their influence had been felt outside the pale of their own Church, and never was felt more than at the present day. They found a marked tendency amongst the laity in the other Churches to turn their backs upon the very acts which were the causes of the Unitarians separating from communion with them. Moreover, they were pleased to find a decrease—a marked decrease—in the asperity of pulpit allusions to their church and to their doctrines. Referring to the members of other Christian Churches who were present that night, in the hall and on the platform, Mr. Boyd greeted them as among the most welcome of their visitors.

The Rev. WILLIAM NAPIER, hon. secretary of the Nonsubscribing Association, in a brief and graceful response, referred to the great and liberty-loving men who formed the Association, and thanked the First Congregation for the hearty welcome which had been accorded to the members of the Association that evening. The Nonsubscribing Association, as he understood it, was founded by men who had conceived the idea that the Church might be built on the principle of cherishing the unity of the Spirit in the bond of peace, whilst allowing each member to do what in his conscience he thought was right; and that principle they had consistently carried out since the day of its foundation.

Sir JAMES CLARKE LAWRENCE, Bart., M.P., who spoke next, was very warmly received. He began by saying:—Everyone knows what an Irish welcome is. It means not merely words uttered by the tongue, but sentiments springing from the heart; and, therefore, when I heard the words of welcome uttered by the President to-night, I knew full well that it was a real welcome, that it was meant, and that you desire to express that which you really and heartily feel. Reference has been made to the intimate association of myself with an honoured name, known not merely to this Association, but recognised throughout this country amongst Presbyterians of the liberal school; and recognised not only by them, but, I must say, by other inhabitants of the town of Belfast; for I never yet entered this town without hearing from other quarters the highest expressions of praise of the Rev. John Scott Porter. I have sometimes said to my Irish friends that I feel myself half an Irishman; for, having passed so many of my years in connection with friends from Ireland, and having had two tutors who were Irishmen, I think if anything could make me an Irishman, that should almost effect the object. Here I am before you as the representative of the British and Foreign Unitarian Association, and it is well, in these times, that men should know what that term means. There is not a town in Ireland, there is not a city or town in England, where there are no thousands who literally do not know what pure and simple Christianity means; and the aim of the Unitarian Association has been to say to such men: "Be not discouraged; take not Christianity as represented by ancient synods or ecclesiastical organisations, but go to Christ himself, learn what he tells you, and follow what he tells you to do." The aim of the Unitarian Association was, and is, to tell all such people that there is a Christianity not merely akin to, but identical with, that which Christ himself taught in Judea more than 1800 years ago; that his voice may be yet heard, his example yet followed. Without professing belief in any cramping systems of doctrine, men may be true Christians, if they only exercise loyalty to him as the only true exponent of what really is their duty to him as their Lord and Master, and to God as their Father. Such is the simple Gospel that Unitarians have to preach. They may live, and I hope will live, on the best of terms with men who hold views different from their own; and the only rivalry they desire to see, is as to who shall come nearest the Master, who shall tell again, in clearest language, what was uttered in Judea, and who shall say in accents none will fail to understand, "I follow Christ in every action of my life. There is no act of my business which is not of his example. There is no position in life in which his example is not kept before me." Do you think people will turn away from this doctrine; that thousands who now hold aloof from all religious opinion will stand off if you proclaim this doctrine? This religion, of course, is not the religion only of a Church, is not the religion of a Synod merely, but must pervade every workshop, and enter into every mercantile transaction. I can assure you, that if that is the Gospel you proclaim in Belfast, this congregation and this assembly will yet take a position, the first amidst all religious organisations. You will bear aloft a standard which admits of no rival, which boldly proclaims discipleship to Christ, and the Christianity which Christ taught. Are you, the representatives of the free Christianity of Belfast, prepared for this work? If so, triumph is before you, in such a way as the most sanguine has never expected.

DAVID MARTINEAU, Esq., who was also warmly welcomed, said—I rejoice exceedingly to be present at this meeting of Unitarians in Belfast. It cheers my heart to see this hall filled by those whom I believe to be earnest men and women. Two sentiments have brought us together—a feeling of going forward with the multitude, and a feeling that the assistance of friends is required to help forward this great and important movement. Those of you who are members of the First Congregation in Belfast, will feel that you are affected by both these sentiments, when drawn together at this centenary of the building of your chapel—an occasion of such importance that you may make it a fresh starting-point in the history of your congregation. Your fathers held aloft the banner of freedom, and you in this hall will lift the flag which your forefathers have handed on from times of greater danger than the present.

REV. DR. ALFRED PORTER PUTNAM, on being most cordially received by the meeting, referred to his previous visit to Belfast, twenty-one years ago. "On that occasion I heard the Rev. John Scott Porter preach a most excellent sermon, in which he presented Jesus Christ as the Lord and Master. It made a most deep and abiding impression on my mind and heart, and that expression is just as distinct and deep now as it was at that time. As we went from the church, Mr. Porter introduced me to his predecessor, the Rev. William Bruce, and then he took me out to dine with that noble man, Michael Andrews, of Ardoyne. I have Mr. Andrews' photograph, but even without it I should never have forgotten how he looked. All three are gone, but their memories abide, and will abide." In some further remarks, Dr. Putnam congratulated all present upon what he had seen and heard that day, of their glorious past, and upon what he believed to be their still more glorious future, winding up with a hearty "God bless you all!"

REV. DR. BRYCE said his appearance on that platform, as a stern old-fashioned Calvinist, would, he was sure, surprise some people. There were many things said that evening which, to use a Scotch term, he could not "homologate." But he could homologate what the chairman had said about the honest spirit, which he recognised as being kindred with his own; and he could homologate what Sir James had said about adhering to the words of Christ, though, perhaps, he might interpret some of those words very differently from the way in which Unitarians interpreted them. He thought that, as regards the practical part of religion, there was considerable unanimity between them. The chairman had pointed out the connection in which he had stood to some members of that congregation. Dr. Crombie was the founder of the Belfast Academy, over which he (the speaker) had the honour of presiding for rather more than fifty years. Dr. Crombie took the first step taken in Ireland to establish and extend a course of University training in Ireland. The Rev. John Scott Porter and the speaker were always on the most friendly and intimate terms, although they differed widely in their theological opinions. About 1874 he joined very heartily with Mr. Porter in an effort to maintain the National system of education in Ireland. On that occasion ministers of all Protestant denominations united together in the matter. He would appeal to his English and Scotch friends to take warning as to how that question stood at present, for the non-sectarian character of that institution was again threatened in a most formidable way.

After the welcome had been thus given and responded to, a vote of thanks to the contributors to the Loan Collection was proposed. This was done with exceedingly good taste in a capital speech by F. D. Ward, Esq., M.R.I.A., J.P., who was ably seconded by John Rogers, Esq., in a brief address, in which he referred to the great hopes of future effort excited by the meeting.

The speeches being concluded, the chairman vacated his post, and a general conversazione and promenade took place. Shortly before eleven o'clock the singing of the National Anthem brought the proceedings of a memorable evening to a close.

Among the number of those present were the following ministers:—Revs. F. M. Blair, R. J. Bryce, LL.D. (United Presbyterian); James Callwell, R. Campbell, R. Cleland, Jas. Cooper, English Crooks, J. A. Crozier, B.A.; T. Dunkerley, B.A.; Moore Getty, A. Gordon, D. Gordon, John Hall, James Kedwards, J. A. Kelly, A. Lancaster, C. J. M'Alester, D. Matts, J. M'Caw, H. A. M'Gowan, W. O. M'Gowan, J. Miskimmin, Hugh Moore, M.A.; W. Napier, J. A. Newell, R. J. Orr, M.A.; John Porter, A. P. Putnam, D.D.; T. H. M. Scott, M.A.; J. E. Stronge, F. Thomas, and D. Thompson. Among the laity present may be named Messrs. John S. Brown, J.P.; Dr. Samuel Browne, J.P.; Dr. W. Gordon, J.P.; Edward Greer, J.P.; John Jellie, J.P.; J. R. Musgrave, J.P.; F. D. Ward, J.P.; Hugh Hyndman, LL.D.; Dr. Ball, Dr. R. B. Davidson, Dr. H. E. Manley, Dr. Brice Smyth, W. Gray, M.R.I.A.; W. H. Patterson, M.R.I.A.; Robert Young, C.E.; John Smyth, sen., Lenaderg; John Smyth, M.A.; C. H. Brett, John Campbell, Herbert Darbishire, E. A. Fuhr, A. M. Munster, Henry Musgrave, W. Riddel, &c., &c. The list of contributors to the Loan Collection is as follows:—Mrs. Andrews, Miss Benn, Mrs. H. Boyd, Mrs. C. H. Brett, Mrs. E. J. Bristow, Mr. John Brown, Miss Bruce, Dr. Burden, Miss Carruthers, Mr. E. T. Church, Rev. A. Gordon, Miss Grattan, Mrs. John Hamilton, Mrs. W. Hartley, Mr. John Hunter, Dr. Hugh Hyndman, Mr. A. Jaffe, Mr. John Jaffe (President of the Chamber of Commerce), Miss MacAdam, Mrs. James Malcolm, Mr. M'Calmont (Abbeylands), Mr. E. J. M'Errel, Miss M'Tear, Miss F. M. M'Tear, Mr. J. S. M'Tear, Mr. Thomas M'Tear, Mr. A. M. Munster, Mr. J. R. Musgrave, Museum (Directors of), Mr. W. H. Patterson, Mr. R. L. Patterson, Mr. J. J. Phillips, Mr. W. T. Polley, Queen's College (President of), Mr. G. Raphael, Mr. Robert Reid, Mr. Riddel, Mr. R. Smeeth, Mr. G. K. Smith, Mrs. W. Smith, Miss Smyth, Mr. W. Swanston, Mr. A. T. Stannus, Mr. R. Tennent (Rushpark), Mr. H. F. Thomas, Mr. Thompson (Macedon), Ulster Bank (Directors of), Mr. J. Vinycomb, Mr. R. J. Walsh, Mr. F. D. Ward, Mr. G. G. Ward, Mr. J. H. Ward, Mr. M. J. Ward, Mr. J. F. Wilson.

www.ingramcontent.com/pod-product-compliance
Lightning Source LLC
Chambersburg PA
CBHW030608270326
41927CB00007B/1096

9783337429522